CASES IN

PERSONNEL MANAGEMENT

AND

SUPERVISION

ADMINISTRATION SERIES

Edited by Eugene E. Jennings
MICHIGAN STATE UNIVERSITY

Cases in Personnel

Management

and

Supervision

By **RICHARD P. CALHOON**
The University of North Carolina

NEW YORK

APPLETON-CENTURY-CROFTS
Division of Meredith Publishing Company

PRINTED IN THE UNITED STATES OF AMERICA
E16340

PREFACE

IT IS SELDOM DISPUTED that problems of personnel, individually and collectively, are the greatest single concern to management. Three recent studies show that most of the difficulties confronting executives center around people. In the world of work, *four interrelated factors of difference* are at the root of these difficulties in working with people: (1) differences in individuals; (2) differences in groups; (3) differences in organizations; (4) differences in situations. These four conspire to render the study of personnel the most challenging and rewarding of all phases of management.

The case method presents a way of attacking all four of these interrelated factors. Through this medium, it is possible to examine the specific, unique situations involving people confronted in a work setting and also to relate personnel principles, practices, and techniques to these situations. And in every case, obviously, there are considerations of individual and group behavior.

Because each case is different, it requires consideration of all phases confronted in decision-making—identification of issues, analysis, exploration of alternatives, and decision-reaching. The hope and expectation are that these cases will help the student of personnel management to weave knowledge of behavior, of maangement principles, and of personnel techniques into specific situations and to reach decisions which will hold the best promise of working out as anticipated.

The point of view running throughout the book is that personnel management is a major responsibility of executives at all levels of the organization, whether in production, sales, general management, or in the staff function of personnel. The vast preponderance of cases concern supervisory-subordinate relations, since, at any level, these constitute the principal management problems. Other cases concern policy, organization, the personnel function, labor relations, and the staff role of personal administrators.

This case book consists of thirty-six cases, organized into six major sections which cover the principal responsibilities, problems, and functions in personnel management. The cases are useful for upper-level undergraduate courses, graduate courses, or industrial training courses and have, in fact, been tested with all of such groups. The book can either supplement a text and readings or else constitute the backbone for a case course. The vast majority of these cases have been analyzed in class more than once and have proven to be "operable." The cases themselves exemplify the nagging, difficult, day-to-day problems and complex personnel situations that confront any representative of management, whether staff or line. The situations are real, but names and places have of course been disguised.

The author thanks the many business executives and graduate students who have contributed cases to this collection; to the Dean of the School of Business Administration, University of North Carolina, Maurice W. Lee, and to the Business Foundation of the University of North Carolina he expresses appreciation for case work support.

R.P.C.

The University of North Carolina

CONTENTS

Section III. TRAINING AND DEVELOPMENT

Section IV. SUPERVISION

Section V. ADMINISTRATION OF LABOR COSTS

CONTENTS

Section VI. THE MANAGEMENT OF LABOR RELATIONS

Introduction

IN THIS BOOK of *Cases in Personnel Management and Supervision*, the main focus is on complex situations of selecting, developing, utilizing and maintaining the personnel of an organization. Drawn from actual circumstances but given fictitious names, these cases cover a wide variety of industries, including steel, electrical products, botanical drugs, department stores, hospitals, textiles, chemicals, restaurants, railroads, airlines, a university, and even a commercial garden. All levels of management, both line and staff, are involved as are many different types of employees —men and women, young and old, college graduate and noncollege graduate, management at all levels, white collar clerical and blue collar, union and nonunion.

Cases are grouped into six (6) major areas that are important in the management of personnel:

1. Managerial concepts relating to personnel—field of personnel management; management functions; organization; policies and procedures.
2. Selection—bases for original selection and selection for promotion.
3. Training and development—orientation and training; development of employees and managers.
4. Supervision of personnel—communications; managing subordinates; administration of discipline and grievances; controlling internal mobility; measurements of performance; administering change.
5. Administration of labor costs—wages; salaries; incentives; benefits and services.
6. The management of labor relations—group dynamics; supervising special groups; unions and management; collective bargaining.

Although this book classifies cases by major areas, intricate problems in the management of personnel often include a number of different areas. In some instances, too, cases could fit just as well in some other major area. Because of this, it is difficult, if not impossible, to designate an area to which a case belongs exclusively. For example, a case with strong organizational features may have equally strong aspects of supervision and policy. A case centering largely around wages also can have implications of management principle or of collective bargaining. And every case concerns people with their interactions in business so that each one has numerous behavioral features.

1

Despite this overlap of involvement, a classification of cases serves the useful purpose of pointing out areas for major emphasis. Allied readings can be studied relevant to these areas which can aid in and reinforce case analysis. Focusing on a particular phase of personnel management need not reduce the scope of classroom case analysis, despite fears to the contrary.

Objectives of Cases in the Management of Personnel

The main purpose of these cases is to sharpen powers of analysis and decision-making in the management of personnel. The vast majority of cases involve one or more decisions to be made by some member (s) of management. Substantive knowledge of the personnel management field is important for adequate analysis, as is knowledge of managerial concepts and of behavior. It is assumed that students will attack these cases either with a strong background of knowledge in the field or else will have the help of substantial readings. Conceptual knowledge combined with improved situational analysis should increase the competence of students in matters pertaining to personnel.

Decision-Making in Case Analysis

Every action or move in personnel management involves a decision or a series of decisions. Whether the action concerns a penalty, a commendation, counseling with an employee, a promotion, encouraging a learner, or enlisting an associate's help, decisions precede and accompany the method of approach or interaction. Needless to say, errors in decisions cause a major portion of the difficulties in managing personnel.

Sound decisions are the cornerstone of sound personnel management, but all too little attention has been paid to the *process* by which sound decisions are reached. Since those who study these cases will be reaching decisions, they will need to know the foundations of decision-making and factors to consider in analyzing cases. The following, accordingly, is a brief discussion of the decision-making process.

Behind each decision is an element of risk because there are few perfect, elegant, or algorithmic decisions in the management of personnel. One has to weigh the consequences of a particular act and the probabilities of outcome relative to different alternatives. Anticipating consequences involves forecasting as accurately as possible with the analyst having a number of tools at his disposal in forecasting—the patterns of past behavior; knowledge of people's needs and wants; a picture of trends or trajectory as a guide to forecasting the immediate future.

Values are another basic consideration in decision-making—what are the desirabilities of a particular alternative or outcome? The worthwhileness of an act depends in great measure on what is important to the organization, to the supervisor involved, and to the employee or employees concerned. Values are intertwined with prejudices and feelings, all of which affect decisions. Moral and ethical values as to what is thought to be right and what is fair or what *ought* to be done also influence personnel decisions. Students who analyze cases need to develop sensitivity to their own values as well as to the values of others and to recognize that these values affect decisions.

In addition to such basic aspects of decisions, the decision process itself is worth examining since a sound process is a means of arriving at sound decisions. A first stage is to define the problem or basic issues. Although it is sometimes necessary in the management of personnel to treat symptoms (as for instance in penalizing for careless work) it is much more desirable to ascertain the causes of problems, the factors that brought about a problem situation. Factors of cause can also help in defining a problem. A further step in definition is to isolate crucial or critical factors that are basic or that seem to constitute keys to problem solution. Definition, in substance, aids in making important features of a problem clear. Starting out with the question, "what is the problem?" can serve to center attention on specific concrete features. It is virtually impossible to make an adequate analysis until the problem has been placed in focus. The student then, in studying *Cases in Personnel Management* needs to consider the definition of issues or problems as a first step in case analysis.

Analysis follows definition of a problem. This is the process of breaking down a problem into rational, easily understood divisions which can then be examined separately. What are the major aspects in the situation worthy of study? Unfortunately, case discussions can begin and end with analysis, leaving the student with a feeling of no accomplishment. Merely listing the various factors in a situation is only a beginning, not an end in itself.

Alternatives for solution or decision should grow out of analysis. Since a decision can be only as good as the best alternative considered, it behooves case analysts to spend considerable time developing alternatives that hold good promise for solution. A standard, unalterable rule is that effective decisions evolve from a *number of alternatives*. Asking "else" and "other" questions helps in formulating additional alternatives. Various possibilities for solution need to be attacked from different directions in order to avoid the common tendency of happening on one possible solution and then fastening onto it as *the* answer.

Every analysis should yield material for at least one hypothesis—a possible answer. In early stages of case analysis a hypothesis may be only a narrowing of choices of action and a testing of each prospect. An important point in case analysis is this review and testing of hypotheses, several of which may be operable. Then the question is one of ascertaining the best answer possible with the information at hand. The final solution may not be the most desirable one from management's point of view. It may be the answer that has the greatest number of satisfactory features, the least amount of risk, the greatest prospect for working out with minimal disturbance. Students need to learn that most decisions represent compromise, some adjusting of points of views, of interests, and of needs.

In weighing alternatives for solution, criteria include a calculation of risk in relation to expected gain, the degree or amount of disequilibrium expected, effort required, scope to be embraced, and resources available. In the management of personnel, alternatives generally include repercussions on the persons directly involved and on others; additional aspects of human relations, costs, efficiency, goals or needs of the organization and of individuals, and responsibility for the situation created.

Another feature of decision-making in cases as well as in the actual management of personnel concerns the sequence of moves. A solution rarely involves a single act. A series of moves may be necessary, in succession. Decisions may be reached at different stages and strategy altered as one proceeds. Additional information, with the passage of time, may require changes in hypotheses and shifts in emphasis. This, too, the student of case analysis needs to realize as he works with problems in the management of personnel.

DOMINANT FACTORS RECURRING IN CASE ANALYSIS

In cases involving people in business, it is worth noting that a number of causes for situations recur—again and again. They are practically universals, being so important that one or more appear in virtually every case. The reason for their mention here is not for purposes of limiting analysis to these particular aspects but rather to indicate their critical nature in an understanding of the management of personnel. These are not in any order of frequency but are roughly in the order of their importance in causing problems. They occur largely in terms of "failure to consider" or "weaknesses":

Communications—failure to inform or to consult; not allowing to participate; way of talking or writing; inability or failure to counsel.
Supervision—laxity or rigidity; innovations of supervisors or resistance to change; methods used in supervision; leadership.
Behavioral characteristics—Personality; adaptive devices; emotions; motivation; capabilities.
Selection and development—Poor selection for employment or for promotion; bad orientation; failure to help adequately in development.
Organization—Weaknesses in structure; uncertainties as to authority, responsibility, or job assignments; failure to delegate; by-passing.

The Student in Case Analysis

Case analysis has rigorous features to which both the student and the instructor are subjected. The student must explore a situation *in depth* before reaching a decision. Indeed, he protects himself by such probing since superficial answers or solutions are frequently wrong. His objective in analysis is to search for *cause* rather than for blame. This is one of the major benefits derivable from the case analysis in that it removes situational analysis from the realm of a "witch hunt."

He must exercise independent judgment and adhere to convictions even while he is increasing in his tolerance for other persons' points of view. One of the common experiences during courses using the case method is an increase in respect by students for the thought and opinions of others. When this respect, though, is accompanied by resigned acceptance of a majority-expressed point of view with which one does not agree, then tolerance becomes servile conformity. Conflict has noteworthy benefits in case analysis as long as argument does not occur for argument's sake. Differences of opinion are a means by which students learn in case discussion. Accordingly, any class hour in which there is no difference in point of view is likely to represent superficial thinking and lack of effort. A concomitant of this is the right of other class members to examine critically any reasoning, an obligation to seek the "why" of a thought with which they are not in accord or which they do not understand. A further benefit of case study is from students learning the art of disagreeing without being disagreeable. In fact many interactive features of case study are rewarding: the points of view of different members; variations in individuals' ways of attacking problems; the process of reaching a consensus; roles assumed by different class members.

Another rigorous aspect of case work is the responsibility of students to direct their thinking positively toward features that will lead to ultimate solution. Learning to curtail discussion of the interesting but trivial or irrelevant, to make statements without rambling discourse, and to adhere to a particular phase of the case under discussion takes self-discipline.

At the same time, case analysis depends upon participation for success. In practically every group some few talk more easily and may even have more of value to offer in discussion, but students develop more when they do their own thinking, too, and present their own ideas to the group. Moreover, a group as a whole benefits from breadth of discussion, from exposure to different ideas. Even a case analysis running as little as a class hour should find close to 75 per cent of a class of fifty or less students having at least something to say relevant to the case.

Numerous benefits accrue to the thoughtful student as a result of case study, in addition to those mentioned. His thinking should not only be deeper, it should also be sharper in discriminating between alternatives.

With time, his thinking should increase in validity, leading him more unerringly toward sound decisions. His "feel" for the management of personnel should increase also through contact with actual cases and through discussions.

THE INSTRUCTOR IN CASE ANALYSIS

The only respect in which case study should be easy on the instructor is in the exercise of his vocal chords. If he finds himself talking more than a small portion of the time, then he is teaching, not conducting case discussion. Except for less strain in speaking, case work is a more demanding method of instruction than is lecturing. The instructor is responsible for obtaining widespread participation, for seeing that analysis progresses, and for making certain that adequate consideration is given to reaching decisions or conclusions. Even though he may be completely permissive in his reception of student ideas, he has the task of interpretation through reflecting, of resolving disagreements, of attempting to determine consensus, and of summarizing at different stages.

How directive or nondirective he is depends on what he is seeking to accomplish and on the particular tools of discussion leadership he has at his command. There are degrees of directivity and nondirectivity, most case-discussion leaders falling somewhere short of extreme directiveness or complete nondirectiveness. The directive case leader controls dicussion. He asks questions about the case and, in the field of personnel management asks other questions suggested by material in the case. Directivity has advantages of assuring emphasis on various subjects in personnel administration as seen fit by the instructor. Efficient use of time in relation to specific case objectives is likely to result, too. The disadvantages are in the direction of sacrificing initiative and independent thinking on the part of the group. Moreover, it is difficult to shift from the directive to the nondirective. Once a group has settled down to a passive role of awaiting questions from the instructor, it is not easily moved over to active development of discussion.

Those who follow a mixed directive-nondirective approach generally find it easier to start out with the nondirective, moving perhaps to an interspersing of occasional questions on various features of the case. Such instructors bring out principles or concepts of personnel administration and question ill-considered or unclear statements. The danger here is one of going too far in the direction of comments and general questions, perhaps then consuming an inordinate amount of class time.

Another degree closer to nondirectivity is one of placing the burden on the class for analysis and using nondirective techniques of reflecting or mirroring by restating what a student has said. Using the Socratic approach of rephrasing questions by a student and asking them of the class keeps the discussion group-centered rather than instructor-centered. The instructor still maintains control of discussion by seeing that the case is processed in a logical and orderly fashion rather than skipping from one feature to another. Even here, short of full-scalle nondirectivity, the instructor can bring out principles, concepts, and generalizations as the occasion arises.

The purist in nondirective case discussion serves more to keep discussion going along lines indicated by the group. This approach requires a rather mature group and may be in its early stages frustrating to group members. As a group takes shape, however, it is possible for them to police themselves and to develop their own approaches to cases. Group initiative can avoid a stereotyped approach to cases and the instructor, even in his nondirective role, can help in such avoidance by asking the group if there are other ways of looking at a particular case. Pure nondirectivity may require more time for case analysis early in the semester. The leader can retain some prerogatives, though; as a very minimum, recognizing those who are to speak, thus controlling the spread of discussion.

What approach to use depends not only on the instructor but, as inferred, to a considerable extent on the sophistication and background of personnel administration in the group. When cases are used to supplement lectures or are interspersed with lectures, there may be more of an effort to relate cases to principles and practices. When cases are used as the main method of instruction, the approach used should relate to objectives of the course.

SECTION I

Managerial Concepts

THESE FIRST SIX CASES focus mainly on the many *management* features in personnel administration, more specifically with those concerning policy, organization, and relations between staff and line. These are constantly recurring problems in the best-managed concerns and hence constitute an appropriate first section.

With good reason, a great deal of emphasis has been accorded recently to the subject traditionally called "organization." Many difficulties in personnel management center around structure, relationships within the structure, and efforts to change these relationships. A number of these cases, accordingly, have organization as a major focus.

And behind all questions of structure and relations loom an organization's philosophies, principles, and policies. These affect managerial actions and interactions within any organization. Whether principles and policies are sound and acceptable affects their functioning; the way they are administered clearly and definitely determines their effectiveness. Running through all cases in this section, therefore, are questions of policy.

As stated in the introduction, any of these cases may have a *primary* focus (debatable as this may be, in a number of instances), but they all have other foci and numerous implications. In studying these particular cases, the analyst should be alert to related factors that bear upon a situation. In the management area, many features of communication, supervision, and relationships will certainly assume prominence as will, always, various behavioral implications.

1

Ardmore Manufacturing Company

THE ARDMORE MANUFACTURING COMPANY had developed through its research department a manufacturing process that was unique. The product made was a standard item, but the method of manufacture was sufficiently different in application that certain features were patentable. Other phases of the process were standard, the equipment used being in common use in the industry. When the process reached its final stage of development it was decided by the management of Ardmore to make a production-scale installation. To facilitate this installation the company bought a factory in a small town. The factory was already in production on the products so that the only novel feature was setting up the necessary new equipment. It was decided to retrain the present staff and employees to run the new equipment.

To assist in getting the production unit in operation, a group from the research unit which had developed the process was sent to the newly-acquired factory. The success of the pilot unit was so complete, with all "bugs" eliminated, that no particular difficulty was anticipated in getting the production unit started, and a rather tight schedule had been laid out for getting the equipment installed and the production started.

The job of getting this production started turned out to be not so simple as was anticipated. Many difficulties that had not arisen in operating the pilot unit appeared to plague the production unit. This schedule, that would have been difficult to maintain if all had gone well, became impossible, and pressure mounted on the group assigned to getting the equipment started. Prior to this time the production personnel had not taken any active part in the conversion, but as the repeated efforts of the research group met little or no success, they began to call on the production foremen for advice and assistance.

At this point Jack Carter, who was the foreman of the department where the production flow started, proved extremely useful. Carter was a man of limited education but one who had worked around the mill for some thirty years, starting in his early teens, and who had a good mechanical mind. By merely observing the attempts of the research group and the results they were able to obtain, Carter was able to form some sound judgments of where the troubles lay and what could be done to correct the difficulties. However, since the group had not indicated in any way that they were looking for any advice or assistance, Carter had kept his information to himself. It was only after the head of the group, in talking with the plant manager, indicated that they were not making much progress and would welcome any suggestions and after the manager had talked to all the foremen and asked for their suggestions that Carter finally came forward with his ideas.

Even then Carter offered only one suggestion, and not until it had been tried and found successful did he reveal his next idea. Thus, in several stages Carter revealed the whole of his ideas and introduced the spark that restored confidence in the group and enabled them to go ahead with the project. The plant manager was elated that one of his men had been so instrumental in getting the production unit in operation and reported the assistance that Carter had given in detail to the company officials at the main office. The head of the research group also expressed his gratitude both personally to Carter and to the company officials but with somewhat less enthusiasm than had the plant manager.

Carter was thanked by company officials when they came to the plant to observe the unit in operation and invariably they would go off telling each other or the plant manager that "Jack is one of the best in the business. Why, this thing would never have gotten off the ground if it had not been for Jack." Carter became the authority on this system of operations, and his opinion on all innovations or changes in production was sought and considered before any moves were made. His word carried more weight than the research department in matters concerning the section of the new process under his supervision.

Ralph Benson, the personnel manager, took a dim view of these proceedings. He and Carter did not get along well. Benson had not been on the job very long because the previous owners had no personnel department as such. The foreman was the only person to whom an employee would take his problems or grievances. Those few employees who presumed to go over a foreman's head and go to the plant manager were invariably sent back to the foreman with their problem. The employees then had a second problem, that of explaining to the foreman why they went to the plant manager.

When the Ardmore organization took over, Benson was installed as personnel manager, and the parent company's personnel policies were explained and put into operation. In general, the policies were well regarded by the employees. The main objection came from the foremen who objected particularly to one policy which permitted the employees to take their problems and grievances directly to the personnel manager. Of the four foremen, Carter was the most outspoken against this policy. He said: "that new fellow doesn't know anything about our departments. The help will go out and tell him a pack of lies and he won't know enough to know that they are not telling the truth."

Benson had found out that the few employees from Carter's department who came to his office, some with personal problems, were questioned thoroughly by Carter in his office as to what they had told Benson. Carter further let it be known that no one was to go to the personnel office without his permission. Since any request for permission was always followed with a full set of questions as to why the employee wanted to go to the personnel office, requests for permission and visits to the personnel office soon ceased entirely. When Benson spoke to the plant manager about this problem, the plant manager, Thomas Plarmer, assured Benson that he would straighten Carter out, but nothing was ever done to change the situation.

All of the supervisors had difficulty applying discipline because of the many family ties throughout the plant. In many cases a foreman had members of his own family working in his department. Practically all of the foremen had members of another foreman's family working for them. The enforcement of discipline for absenteeism was especially difficult, for in most cases the employee was reported by a member of the family or neighbor as being "out sick." On some such instances the employee would be seen by others around town in an inebriated condition or showing the signs of a severe "hangover." Since the plant was located in a rural area of a dry county, the employees who drank bought the local brand of bootleg whiskey. The results of drinking added considerably to the absenteeism problem at the plant, particularly on Monday and on payday, Friday.

Carter's attempts at discipline in such cases were restricted to a large extent by the offending employees' family connections and by his needs to meet production schedules. Discipline could take the form of nothing at all, a dressing down, a few days' layoff, or termination, depending upon the relative importance of those two factors.

This mode of discipline was the major source of grievances among Carter's employees, and the employees who received the more severe treatment were the ones who appealed to the personnel manager for modification of their discipline so as to be comparable to that meted out to others. Invariably the discipline instead of being modified was increased by Carter, if the employee had not already been terminated. Some employees after an appearance at the personnel office were refused further employment by Carter. More often than not, they were transferred by Benson to other departments. This Carter disapproved of but did not make an issue of. Actually, transfer was resorted to only in cases where Benson thought the employee's side of the grievance was strong enough to bring the matter to the plant manager. The plant manager would not insist that Carter take the employee back but would attempt to pacify both Benson and the employee by asking Benson to place the employee in another department. Benson soon learned the folly of trying to fight any of the borderline cases. In a few such cases the plant manager had pointed out to Benson that Carter was right and that Benson should not question Carter's decision. Benson, after one year as personnel director, was offered a similar position at one of the company's other plants and eagerly accepted the transfer.

Benson's replacement, Earl McLeod, was employed by Plarmer, the plant manager. Relations between the plant foremen and the personnel department did not improve to any great extent with the new personnel man. In fact, the foremen became even more independent in their personnel relations and for all intents and purposes they ignored McLeod. Because McLeod was not very familiar with company policies, policies were followed only when it was convenient for the foremen to do so. After a few months, he learned more about the various policies and began to realize how many were not being followed by the foremen. In his talks with Plarmer concerning these matters, he quickly learned from the responses he received that he had better let matters ride. He believed that if he should become involved with one of the foremen over such a matter, the plant manager would back up the foreman. McLeod continued to carry out routine matters of the personnel department but did not enter into problems of labor relations. He referred all such cases to the plant manager as he, Plarmer, had stipulated.

McLeod, being a native of the town, was familiar with the drinking habits of some of the employees and was also familiar with the fact that Carter, while not a regular weekend drinker, would every three or four months go off on a drinking spree that would last for a week to ten days. These sessions would more often than not follow some employee party or function or some foreman's stag party. Carter was particularly touchy after returning from such absences, and any of his employees who had the misfortune of crossing his path during the days immediately following his return to work would be severely dealt with. If anything went wrong during his absence his assistant foreman, Leroy Cook, would be brought to task. Aside from Carter's handling of employees, he was otherwise a good foreman. His production, quality of work, departmental costs, and housekeeping records were the best in the mill.

Tom Brennan, the assistant plant manager, did not become involved in the problems that arose between the foremen and the personnel department. He was not assigned to any fields with full authority and assumed none. He brought all problems for decision to the plant manager. Most of his duties kept him at his desk, and his relations with the foreman were for the most part superficial. Being a friendly person, his relations with the foreman, the personnel department, and the employees were good.

No one at the plant was surprised that Brennan was appointed plant manager when Plarmer was transferred to one of the company's other plants. Rumors immediately spread that George Banks, one of the other foremen, would become the new assistant plant manager. Banks and Carter were close friends and neighbors, and since Carter had no ambition to be plant manager he had expressed his approval of Banks. Banks had also received some encouragement from Plarmer along these lines and fully expected the promotion. Brennan strongly suspected that the company would not confirm Banks's promotion and stalled temporarily, telling everyone that he did not need an assistant and would carry on without one. He even mentioned this to company officials, and for two months the plant operated without an assistant manager.

The company finally realized that this arrangement was not satisfactory and transferred an assistant manager from one of their other plants. Ed Price, the new assistant, had visited the plant briefly in the past and was familiar with the plant layout as well as the manufacturing processes. He had also met all of the foremen.

One day in his first month at the plant, during the period when he had been advised to take his time and get acquainted, Price missed Carter while visiting in Carter's department and was told by the assistant foreman that Carter was out sick and would probably be out for a week or so. The assistant foreman, Niles Thrace, said he was not sure just what Carter's trouble was. Later, when Price was talking to Brennan, Brennan was just as vague about Carter's illness but assured Price that he would be back next week.

QUESTIONS

1. How should a company inaugurate a new personnel manager, particularly when there has never been one in the past?
2. What do you think of the company's policy on grievances after installation of Benson as personnel manager?
3. Is there anything Benson could have done about Carter making it difficult for employees to see him?
4. What sort of policy could be instituted as a protection to the company against absences due to drinking?
5. What can be done, if anything, about the problem of nepotism in this factory?
6. Why do you think Plarmer took the position he did in differences between the foremen and personnel manager Benson?

7. How do you evaluate McLeod as a personnel manager?

8. What should be the role of an assistant plant manager?

9. What would you anticipate to be the reactions of the foremen in the case where an outsider, Ed Price, was selected as assistant manager?

10. Why did Thrace and Brennan act as they did about Carter's "illness"?

2

Flint Memorial Hospital

FLINT MEMORIAL is a large, proprietary hospital. It is located in a grow-ing, progressive city. Originally built about twenty years ago, it is now in the midst of a large expansion program. Soon the original 250-bed capac-ity will have been enlarged to accommodate about 800 beds. The hospital has enjoyed increasingly good public relations recently because of good patient service and a fine School of Nursing.

Many changes have taken place in the Administrative staff during the past two years. A new, well-qualified hospital administrator was employed. About the time he arrived, several members of the staff left. Miss Jones, the director of nursing, was employed to replace the former director. This position involved both nursing service and nursing education. An experi-enced nursing administrator, Miss Jones held a M.S. degree in nursing from a well-known university.

The morale of the nursing staff and faculty had been affected adversely by years of inadequate leadership. Henry Collins, the new administrator, was anxious to do something about this morale problem. When he told Miss Jones that she had been employed to meet the growing needs of the hospital and that he expected changes to be made, Miss Jones replied that she intended to make haste slowly. Each agreed that too much change might be even more detrimental to morale during this period of adjust-ment. Collins delegated responsibility readily. Conditions seemed to im-prove gradually.

Miss Jones surveyed her staff and concluded that it was above average. The members of the staff with whom she had held discussions seemed friendly and willing to cooperate. The supervisors and faculty members seemed to accept her readily. In reviewing the personnel policies that affected her employees she realized that no policy changes had been made in years; she was anxious to begin making some necessary revisions. Soon she began holding meetings with the staff to find areas of weakness and of strength.

New problems arose daily, now in nursing service, now in nursing edu-cation. Miss Jones and the faculty reviewed the rules and regulations for the student nurses and revised these in the light of present-day democratic principles. Revision was time-consuming and left little time to work on the problems of the staff of nursing service; this was the most pressing need of the moment.

John Terrell, the personnel manager, had been employed about four months after Miss Jones, to head a newly established Personnel Department. Miss Jones worked cooperatively with the Personnel Department, transferring records, putting in job requisitions, and exchanging information. The associate director of Nursing Service and Miss Jones' secretary were less willing to delegate responsibility to the new Personnel Department, but after some persuasion they began to realize that this would lighten their work load.

Mr. Terrell had previously been employed as an administrative assistant in a small hospital. Because he was apparently insecure at first, Miss Jones tried to cooperate and support him in his efforts. She had several years' experience in hospital personnel management and made available to him the literature and information she had.

Several times Joe Brown, an assistant administrator, remarked about Terrell's practice of reporting every trivial incident to Mr. Collins; Miss Jones felt Terrell might just be following directions.

Mr. Terrell and Miss Jones had discussed several times the need to revise and implement the personnel policies. After six months on the job, Terrell told Miss Jones he was revising the policies and would like her to read them over before he presented them to his committee on personnel policies. She indicated that she was very interested and wished to see them even though reorganization and the daily stress of the many disciplines and personalities in the hospital organization kept her busy.

One Tuesday morning Mr. Terrell called Miss Jones to ask when he could see her to discuss the new personnel policies. Consulting her desk calendar she suggested Friday morning.

MR. TERRELL: But that's too late! My meeting is Thursday afternoon at 5 p.m.

MISS JONES: In that case bring them down and I'll go over them at home—I certainly want to see them.

Mr. Terrell's secretary brought the suggested policies to Miss Jones' office later that morning. Tuesday evening and Wednesday evening she read the new policy changes; she fumed inwardly. She could see the results of her efforts toward morale and cooperation evaporating. She wrote notes and recommended changes on the margin; she suggested additional policies. On Thursday morning Miss Jones called on Mr. Terrell in his office.

MISS JONES: Terrell, you can't take things away from people and expect a satisfied staff. One of your policies reduces some of the supervisors' vacation period by a week. I have 450 employees in my department. I can see nothing but hostility arising from many of these changes. Here are *my* suggestions—in writing!

MR. TERRELL: I'll look over them before the meeting this afternoon.

MISS JONES: I've been around hospitals too long to be sensitive, and as I've said, most of the employees in this institution are under Nursing. I intend to be at your meeting this afternoon, invited or not.

Miss Jones then angrily left Terrell's office.

That afternoon she attended the Personnel Policy Committee meeting. Copies of the suggested policies were passed out. Miss Jones asked for the copy on which she had noted her suggestions. Mr. Terrell, looking pained, said he had made her suggested changes. On glancing through her copy, she realized he had. Miss Jones was appeased.

Matters went along smoothly for a while after that; the combination of new-old policies was approved. One of the new personnel policies stated: "Those employees who have been employed over five years and are no longer receiving periodic increment salary raises will have their records reviewed on the anniversary of employment date; merit raises will be given consistent with performance appraisal by the supervisor."

Bob Jordan, one of the assistants to the Controller, called Miss Jones about a month after the policy had gone into effect and asked if he could see her for a minute.

MR. JORDAN: This guy Terrell is getting into everyone's hair. I thought you might be interested in these.

Mr. Jordan had two authorization slips for merit raises for two of Miss Jones' supervisors. She had signed these herself, and they had been counter-signed by Joe Brown, the assistant administrator. Mr. Terrell had cancelled the authorization.

Miss Jones took the authorization slips and went to Joe Brown's office. After he read them, the two of them appeared at Mr. Collins' office and requested a short conference.

QUESTIONS

1. What is happening here?
2. Whose responsibility is it that this situation exists?
3. Could Miss Jones have helped Mr. Terrell
4. Should this matter of merit raises have been taken up with Terrell—or had it gone too far?

5. How should Miss Jones approach Mr. Collins?
6. How should Mr. Collins handle the interview with Miss Jones and Joe Brown?
7. What should Mr. Collins do in his subsequent interview with Mr. Terrell?

ORGANIZATION CHART

Flint Memorial Hospital

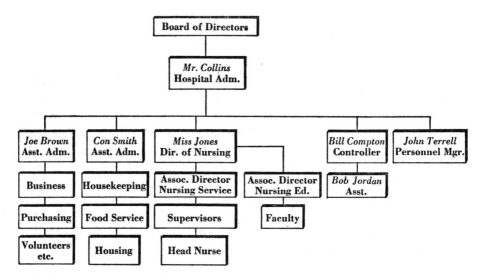

3

Brooks Manufacturing Company

THE BROOKS MANUFACTURING COMPANY produces light-weight tents of all types for camping. The manufacturing process is basically a cutting and sewing operation.

The Brooks Company is located in a small town of 5,000 in New York and employs approximately one hundred and fifty people of whom only twelve are men. The Company was begun during World War II and was engaged in producing parachutes for the Army. To utilize the personnel and equipment, Lyman Barker, president and majority stockholder, suggested that the Company produce tents and other canvas camping equipment. Since parachute production was primarily a sewing operation, the change-over was easily effected. After World War II, the Company expanded only slightly but has greatly increased production largely with present facilities. The owners do not desire to become a large producer but wish to produce quality equipment and maintain production at the present level. The Company is not organized.

Most of the sewers are married women and several of them are in their forties and fifties. Almost all of the women are "loyal" workers. The Brooks Company pays the highest wages of any company in the area engaged in similar activities. In fact, when the $1.25 per hour minimum rate became effective, 95 percent of the workers were making considerably more than $10.00 per day. The workers not making the "code" ($10.00 per day) were to be given three to four months to make it. Action (termination of employment or more training) was not to be taken until after this time. Other companies in the industry allowed only six weeks for their workers to make $10.00 per day before taking action.

All of the women remark about the friendliness that exists in the Company—everyone calls one another by the first name, including floor ladies and top management. The only person who is not called by his first name by any of the employees is Lyman Barker, the president. A worker remarked: "Mr. Barker is real friendly. He comes through the plant and chats with us. He never says a harsh word. In another small sewing plant, the

Thursday. Madge also reminded Thelma that the absences that previous Friday and Monday were unexcused.

A situation arose the week prior to Easter in which a special order was to be completed and shipped on Wednesday before Easter. The cloth necessary for the order had been delayed, and Mr. Barker and Barney realized that if the cloth were not received by the Monday before Easter it would be necessary to work Easter Monday to complete the order. This order, as all orders, had a specific delivery date. On Monday, March 26, six days before Easter, the cloth had not arrived. Mr. Barker and Barney called a group meeting and explained the situation. Both men asked the workers to be present for work on Easter Monday and explained that any absences would be unexcused. No notice had been posted on the bulletin board reporting whether Easter Monday would be a holiday. The Company does not pay time and one-half for work on days normally considered to be holidays.

On the Tuesday before Easter, Mr. Barker and Barney again had one of their "get-togethers" with the employees and requested everyone to report for work on Easter Monday. They impressed upon the workers the necessity of getting the order out to avoid a cancelled order and to keep the account. They also related that this was the order of a "good account" and if it were lost the work might not be as regular in the future.

On Friday, Barney went to each department and asked each worker: "Can we, as far as you know now, depend upon you to be here on Easter Monday?"

On Easter Monday, a "skeleton crew" reported for work—there were approximately one-third of the total workers present.

In the Finishing Department, there are twenty-one workers, and on Easter Monday ten reported to work. This department usually completes 300 tents. On Easter Monday, this department completed 136 tents.

It rained on Easter Monday, and Madge, the floor lady, remarked to two workers, "I hope the girls are enjoying their day off." Pearl, one of the workers to whom Madge was talking said, "Yeah, and watch them start screaming when someone has to be off." Carrie, the other worker in the conversation, added, "Yeah, watch the frying pan get hot when it is time to be off. To this, Madge, the floor lady, remarked, "Just watch me cool it off real fast."

QUESTIONS

1. What is your evaluation of the personnel policies of the Brooks Manufacturing Company?

2. What do you think of the Company's philosophy—"If you work with the Company, we will take care of you when you are in need"?

3. What is your reaction to the use of the public-address system to announce that a certain operator should pick up her repairs?

4. What is your reaction to Barney's "get-togthers"? Do you anticipate any trouble in the future about starting time?

5. Is it good, bad, or indifferent that all the workers in a department keep up with whose time it is to be "laid-off" when lay-offs are necessary due to delays in production?

6. Should the floor lady be the determiner of whether absences are to be excused or unexcused?

7. Could anything have been done to cause employees to work on Easter Monday? Should Easter Monday work have been attempted? Why do you suppose only a "skeleton crew" reported for work Easter Monday?

8. Do you anticipate any consequences on the part of management, workers, or between workers as a result of the Easter Monday incident?

4

Lurkin Manufacturing Company

IN JANUARY, 1959, the Lurkin Manufacturing Company completed its most profitable year. Riding on the crest of the postwar boom, sales had increased annually since 1945, but during 1958 they had more than doubled. Edgar White who had only eighteen months earlier accepted the position as President was pleased with these results, but he was disturbed by a personnel problem in his sales organization which was steadily becoming more critical.

The Lurkin Manufacturing Company had been established in 1932 by Mr. John Lurkin in Centralia, Illinois. Its major product at that time was a custom-made, two-wheel trailer purchased primarily by construction firms for use as a temporary office on building sites. By 1936, the firm was producing a standard model and had added a small, open-bed trailer. Even during the depression the business prospered, and in 1937 Mr. Lurkin had incorporated to obtain expansion funds. When the war broke out in 1941, the firm was able to continue operations because of the need for trailers by construction firms performing essential defense construction. By 1945, the company had expanded considerably and had six district sales offices throughout the five-state area of Illinois, Indiana, Iowa, Missouri, and a portion of Ohio; and its sales volume was approximately $800,000 a year.

Until the postwar period, the Lurkin company had few competitors, especially within its five-state area. In the 1930's, the use of trailers was limited to hauling or construction, and with the depression, both uses were greatly curtailed. When the war started in 1941 and trailer sales were increasing, few new competitors were able to enter the field because of the material shortage.

At the close of the war, in 1945, demand for trailers by construction firms was only one factor involved in increased sales. Trailers had become popular as a means of alleviating the housing shortage, and the Lurkin Company was in an excellent position to expand into the new field. The phenomenal trailer market soon attracted more competitors to the field who, together with existing national trailer manufacturers, began to encroach into the Lurkin Company's five-state area. In spite of increasing competition, though, Lurkin's sales volume reached $2 million in 1958.

During this postwar period, Lurkin had made few organizational changes in spite of rapidly increasing sales. By 1957, he was 68 years old and no longer completely active in the firm. At this time the firm was organized as shown in Exhibit 1, and this was the organization Edgar White, the new president, had inherited in June, 1957.

The Board of Directors had considered White to be extremely well qualified to assume the president's role. He was forty-eight years old, able, conscientious, experienced, and had earned a reputation as a "hard-driver." He had been brought into the organization from another firm by the Board upon the recommendation of the retiring Mr. Lurkin. Lurkin had convinced them that there was no logical replacement available from within the company. White had twenty years of experience in all phases of steel manufacturing operations, the last ten years serving as vice-president for sales of a large steel company. Lurkin had become acquainted with White during the war when they had numerous dealings in the sale and purchase of sheet metal.

When Lurkin was contemplating retirement, he immediately thought of White as his replacement. He had to spend some time in convincing White of his better opportunity in this comparatively small but growing company in which he could obtain considerable equity. When White later appeared before the Board and told them his ideas for directing the firm, its members were greatly impressed, especially with his confidence in the future of the trailer business and his firm conviction that the economy would continue to expand.

White's first act upon joining the organization in June, 1957 was to familiarize himself with its organization chart. The total employment of the company at that time was 450 workers. In its home office and plant in Centralia, Illinois, there were 400 workers; and the field staff of 50 was made up mainly of sales personnel. At the time Lurkin relinquished full-time participation in the firm's direction in 1956, he had established the position of executive vice-president and general manager and promoted Ted Exeter, the sales director, to the position. Exeter continued as acting sales director in addition to his new duties and in this capacity retained direct control over a field staff of six district managers with their sales and clerical staffs. Exeter was one of the original members of the firm, having been a member of the sales organization since 1934.

The production manager and the secretary-treasurer constituted remaining top executives. William Towns, the production manager, joined the firm when it was first established. He was fifty years of age and was considered to be an extremely efficient craftsman in the trailer construction field. Lurkin gave him credit for much of the firm's success because of his ingenious ideas for improvements. The secretary-treasurer was John Troy who had held the position since 1941 when the original occupant left for military service. In view of Troy's youth and inexperience, Lurkin himself had supervised all financial operations after Troy became secretary-treasurer and was still in charge when he retired.

In January, 1958, after observing the firm's operations for six months, White submitted a reorganization plan (Exhibit 2) to the Board of Directors and obtained approval of its implementation. His major changes were in the sales organization which he believed was inadequate to plan and carry out the aggressive sales program he believed was essential. Unlike most managers of this period, he felt that the postwar boom would continue indefinitely, and that his firm should expand as rapidly and as boldly as possible during the period while competitors were curtailing their expansion to fortify themselves for the postwar recession they had believed inevitable.

The new organization reflected White's intentions of actively directing all phases of the firm's operations. This was indicated primarily by his elimination of the position of executive vice-president and general manager. He realized this meant the demotion of Exeter, but felt it was essential even though Exeter, who was sixty-three years of age, was expected to retire within five years. However, in recognition of his long service and near retirement his pay was not reduced. In moving Exeter to the newly created position of controller, he also relieved him of his additional duties as acting sales director. As the controller, he was responsible for the former secretary-treasurer's functions, but he was also expected to initiate several cost- and operating-control measures which White desired to install.

Because of his experience in the field, White planned personally to exercise close operational supervision over all sales activities. He strongly believed that the firm's long-run success would depend on the effectiveness of the sales organization during this important expansion period. For this reason, he provided for the addition of a field director, advertising manager, and sales promotion manager to the sales director's staff. The field director was to have direct control over the field sales staff which included the six district managers and their sales staffs.

After the Board approved the reorganization, White began the task of hiring the required executives. Although he was unable to find a qualified sales director, advertising manager, or sales promotion manager from within the firm, he did find a field director. His original intention had been to hire the sales director initially and to permit him to select his own staff. But in view of his belief that the field sales staff was in urgent need of attention, he decided not to wait. Hardy George, the new field director, had been working as a salesman in one of the district offices. He was an excellent prospect for the position and had compiled an exceptional sales record with the firm in the three years since his discharge from the Marines. Besides this excellent sales record, he sold himself to White with his advanced sales promotion ideas on several occasions when he had approached White while visiting the home office. George was only twenty-four years of age, but White believed that his fine intellect and excellent appearance made up for his youth and limited experience. White was so impressed with George that he even considered him for the sales director's job, but decided to wait until he had considered prospects from outside the organization before he finally made up his mind.

White was unable to hire the advertising manager or sales promotion manager from among his present sales staff, but experienced little trouble locating experienced replacements from external sources. He selected William Spell for the advertising manager's position, and Winston Putten as the sales promotion manager. Both possessed excellent records and had considerable experience in their specialized fields.

A month later, after interviewing and rejecting numerous applicants, White hired George Meade to take over the sales director's position. Meade was then thirty-three years of age and had 14 years of sales experience, the last 5 years of which were as assistant sales manager for a large hardware manufacturing firm. Meade had been working under a sales manager personally known to White who had recommended him highly as an excellent prospect. He was mature, intelligent, and presented an extremely confident and distinguished appearance.

One year later, in January, 1959, the Lurkin Company completed its most successful year, but relationships between the key executives in the new sales organization had deteriorated to such an extent that the firm's continued success was doubtful. This situation came to a head when a senior district manager who was discharged a week earlier complained to several members of the Board of Directors with whom he was personally acquainted. The Board called a meeting to investigate the matter.

The Board Chairman began the meeting by calling on Charles Early, the discharged district manager, to state his complaints and allegations. The following is an account of his remarks:

> As some of you gentlemen know, I have been employed by the Lurkin Company since Mr. Lurkin himself hired me as a salesman for the southern Illinois area in June of 1937. I remained a salesman in the Illinois area until June, 1944, when I was chosen by Lurkin to open the new district sales office in Iowa, and was appointed the district manager. My relations with Mr. Lurkin and later with Mr. Exeter were always excellent and the sales in my district increased each year, particularly since the war's end. The fact that I am no longer with the firm after so many years of successful service I feel is extremely unjust and I believe you will agree with me when you know the facts surrounding my discharge and are aware of the completely demoralized state of the field staff.

A few months after Mr. White became president, Mr. George was appointed as the field director with control over all field staff operations. Naturally, I was a little disappointed when Mr. George, who had been one of my subordinates, was chosen for this new position. However, I accepted the fact without ill-will for I knew Mr. George had compiled a fine sales record in his two years with the firm. When he left my office for his new assignment, our relationship was mutually cordial, and I wished him success on the new job.

However, during the next six months we had several disagreements on some of the new control procedures he proposed. The worst of these controls was a series of report requirements he installed which I believed were nonsensical and time-consuming. No explanation was ever furnished as to the specific purpose for each of these reports. When I asked Mr. George their purpose or to explain how they should be filled out, he became belligerent and either ignored me or made hazy explanations. When I queried other district managers on the matter, they indicated similar experiences.

In addition to these harassing report controls, Mr. George also began to impose restrictions on the freedom of action of distict managers to the point that it was almost impossible to initiate any action without first requesting his permission at the home office. Direct contact between district offices and the various departments in the home office was forbidden; and all telephone and written communications, including routine matters, had to be routed through him personally regardless of delays on essential sales matters when he was absent. His interest in controls and formality seemed to have become an obsession with him, taking precedence over the primary job of selling trailers.

Besides these matters, Mr. George began to force the discharge of salesmen in district offices whose records were not up to his arbitrarily established standards. He applied these standards uniformly in each salesman's territory regardless of potential sales. Of course, I will admit that during the war years we picked up some employees we would not have hired ordinarily, because of the shortage of qualified personnel. However, Mr. George directed these removals in such an abrupt, heartless manner that it was and still is having a serious effect on the morale of sales personnel throughout the field staff of the organization. I am sure the other district managers will confirm this statement.

During the first four or five months after Mr. George's appointment, I accepted his changes without too much argument for I was aware that Mr. White and Mr. Meade were attempting to implement the firm's new sales program. That is, it was never quite clear to me whether Mr. George was taking these actions on his own or as a part of our overall sales plan. During my infrequent visits to the home office when I visited with Mr. Meade, he was most cooperative and informative. The general sales program he was attempting to carry out was sound in all respects and was already improving sales. When I brought up Mr. George's conduct, he became reticent and only said I should be patient with changes while the new program was being implemented.

However, on January 3rd of this month, Mr. George made another of his frequent visits to my office and, in an extremely arrogant manner, began to pace my office and shout because of what he vaguely termed as the lack of sales progress. From this subject he almost immediately launched on a violent criticism of the way his forms and reports were being prepared. I told him his conduct was completely out of line, regardless of the purpose of his visit or his position, and that if he persisted I would have to appeal to the home office. He said nothing more and stormed out of the office.

Last week, there was a meeting of all district managers here at the home office. At this time, I discovered that all of them shared my opinion of his high-handed tactics. In a private, all-night meeting we even considered preparing a petition and submitting it to the president, asking for Mr. George's removal. However, one of the group refused to sign the petition even though he agreed with the removal, so the idea was dropped because of the lack of unanimity.

I felt I could no longer work under these conditions and on this occasion went to see the sales director and president regarding the situation. After explaining these matters I have just related, I told them I was willing to sit down with Mr. George and attempt to reconcile our differences, but that I could not go on as things were now. They told me that they would look into the matter, and I returned to my district.

The very next day, Mr. George came storming into my office, raving about my having spoken to the president regarding his conduct, and discharged me on the spot. He also fired my secretary who happened to be sitting in the room with me at the time. It was then that I felt compelled to contact the Board and, though I do not speak with their permission, I feel I am expressing a common view held by all district managers that the morale of their staffs is extremely poor and is getting worse because of Mr. George.

Meade had been designated by the president to look into and to report to the Board on the circumstances surrounding Early's discharge. When Early had concluded and left the room, Meade was called in. The following is his statement to the Board:

I do not know how much background information Mr. Early has furnished you, but I believe it best to begin at the time Mr. George and I were hired. As you will recall, Mr. White had just reorganized the Sales Department and had established the positions of sales director, advertising manager, sales promotion manager, and field director, the functions of which had previously been performed by Mr. Exeter as acting sales director. At that time, I was informed by Mr. White that I, as sales director, would have full responsibility for these activities as well as the six district managers and their staffs. My duties would include the setting of sales policies, production quotas, sales budgets, and the handling of the personnel function for the sales organization.

At the same time, I was informed that the field director's job was that of maintaining liaison between the district managers and the home office and in implementing the overall sales plans of the organization under my direction. Mr. George's office was to be located in the home office in Centralia; however, it was expected that he would travel frequently to the various district offices.

In retrospect it is obvious that Mr. George has never fully accepted the fact or has never clearly understood that he, as the field director, reports to the sales director and not directly to the president. Whether his confusion resulted from ignorance of the new organization chart or because he initially worked directly with the president before I was hired, I do not know. However, I do know that his full acceptance of his position subordinate to the sales director never came to pass until last week when, after he had discharged Mr. Early, he was called in by the president and me for a complete review of this incident and his activities in general. As the result of these discussions and his premature action in firing Mr. Early, Mr. George has been suspended from his position as Field Director pending the completion of these Board hearings.

When I first reported for work as sales director, Mr. White informed me of his opinion of the poor state of the sales organization. He believed it was made up of considerable deadwood and, in addition, was in need of "shock treatment" to shake it out of its lethargy. After I had been with the firm a short while I was in complete agreement with him and was pleased to learn that Mr. George had already started action toward this end. Having started this action under Mr. White's direction before I arrived, he continued to consult him for the next four or five months on these matters until the revitalization was completed which was about three months ago.

In addition to the need to improve the field sales staff, Mr. White directed me to establish a completely new sales program as soon as possible emphasizing advertising and sales promotion. Naturally, I was engrossed in the preparation of these plans with Mr. Spell and Mr. Putten during the early part of my assignment and, therefore, had only limited contact with Mr. George who was often in the field. However, I knew I had a brilliant young man on my hands with tremendous potential as my assistant provided he was able to control his tremendous desire for power and his tactlessness. It had become increasingly apparent that he was extremely ambitious and had no concern for the position of those with whom he dealt. His habit of constantly submitting ideas directly to the president without my approval was an unceasing source of irritation; and, at the same time, complaints from district managers were becoming daily occurrences. He had even started to interfere with the activities of the advertising and sales promotion managers and was causing dissension among their personnel. Although I would normally have discharged such a man, I still held the hope that I could tone him down and get the use of his brilliant mind.

Also, I was fully aware that the excellent job he had done in removing ineffective sales personnel had caused some of these complaints. In addition, I knew that many of the complaints were the result of his efforts to install much-needed effective control procedures over field operations. Although I have not had the opportunity to review these procedures, I do know procedures were sorely needed.

At the time this incident with Mr. Early occurred last week, in spite of serious misgivings concerning his activities, I was still hoping I would be able to turn Mr. George's exceptional initiative and creativeness toward further constructive efforts.

In fairness to Mr. George, I feel I should mention other mitigating circumstances concerning his conduct which became known only during the past week. It has come to light that almost from the date Mr. George was appointed field director, Mr. Early has been writing letters to other district managers suggesting they join him in resisting Mr. George's efforts. In fact, Mr. Early was the one who instigated and conducted the all-night session of district managers, urging them to sign a petition for Mr. George's removal. It is apparent that Mr. Early was extremely disappointed when a subordinate was selected for this job which he himself coveted. Mr. White had considered him for the position in view of his experience and seniority with the firm, but had rejected him because he believed he lacked sufficient initiative and energy for the job.

It should also be mentioned that Mr. George had applied his strong-arm methods in forcing the removal of ineffective personnel only after district managers had failed to take this action themselves. Mr. White had told them that the action was necessary, shortly after he became President, but the Managers had been dragging their feet until Mr. George's appointment.

A final factor I wish to mention is the part played in this matter by Mr. Exeter who retired last month at his own request. As some of you gentlemen are aware, Mr. Exeter performed long and faithful service with this organization but was disappointed when he was not selected as president when Mr. Lurkin stepped down. He was further disappointed when Mr. White saw fit to abolish the vice-president and general manager's position and to place him in the newly created position of controller, even though his pay was not reduced. It has since come to light that his resentment in losing prestige, especially his control over the sales department and Field staff, was a cause of great concern to him and that in his resentment he often prodded and urged the young Mr. George into inopportune actions which he might not otherwise have taken.

QUESTIONS

1. *Selection*
   a. Was it advisable to pass over the district managers in selecting the field director? What would your answer be if the Field Director were older and more experienced?
   b. Discuss the advisability of selecting the new president, sales director, advertising manager, and sales promotion manager from outside the organization?
   c. Under the circumstances, should the president have delayed hiring the field director until the sales director had been hired?
   d. Do you think Mr. Early should be rehired? Would you replace Mr. George?

2. *Orientation*
   a. Discuss the importance of the proper orientation of new employees to their duties as reflected by this case?
   b. Should a firm print and distribute its organization chart as an aid to orienting new personnel?

    c. Do you think the president was at fault for the confusion on the part of the field director as to his authority and responsibility? Was it the sales director's fault? Is there an indication that the president was undecided concerning whether Mr. Meade or Mr. George should actually be the sales director?

3. *Leadership*
    a. If you had been the sales director would you have authorized the field director to consult directly with the president to this extent? How would you have handled this matter with the president? With the field director?
    b. Did the sales director exercise proper control over the activities of the field director?
    c. In view of the persistent complaints from the district managers, do you feel the sales director was negligent in not investigating the matter sooner?

4. If you had been president, would you have eliminated the position of vice-president and general manager in view of the near retirement of Mr. Exeter?

5. Do you think such sudden action in replacing ineffective personnel on a large scale is ever justified if it adversely affects overall morale?

6. Do you think the Board was justified in calling this board meeting or should the matter have been handled entirely with the President?

EXHIBIT 1

Lurkin Manufacturing Company

Organization *Before* Reorganization

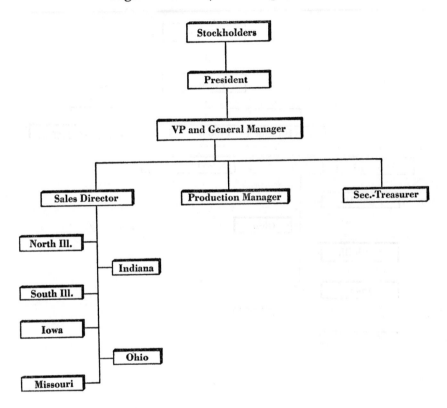

EXHIBIT 2

Lurkin Manufacturing Company

Organization *After* Reorganization

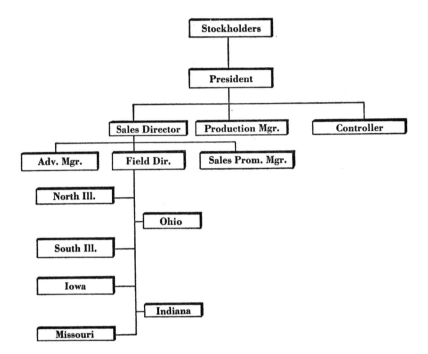

5

The Provident Company

IN 1943, THE QUALITY SERVICE STORES, INC. were sold to Family Service, Inc. J. H. Jones, who was vice-president of Quality Service Stores, immediately interested a sufficient number of men with capital in forming a new company to be known as The Provident Company. Several of the old managers of Quality Service and the secretary of Jones, Miss Bertha Smith, elected to go with Jones in the formation of his new company. Miss Smith became the "right-hand man" of Jones. The company started from scratch, and many responsibilities were placed in Bertha Smith's hands. She performed secretary, bookkeeper, personnel, and filing functions.

By 1946, The Provident Company had fourteen branches and, of necessity, had created a bookkeeping department headed by a C.P.A., plus various other departments necessary to the operation of a business of this size. Miss Smith found it increasingly difficult to relinquish her hold on the various jobs that had once been her responsibility. By 1951, the company had expanded still further and was operating some twenty-two branches. Internal friction between Miss Smith and newer members of the rapidly increasing organization began to be apparent. However, disagreements were more of an irritant to those involved than a handicap to the company in its growth.

Miss Smith was a competent person and, because of her original position with the company, felt free to invade the privacy of Jones' office even when he was in conference. This freedom extended itself to the offices of other key members of the now large organization, and irritation mounted. Her freedom of action and criticism placed the department heads in an awkward and sometimes embarrassing position.

Jones felt that it was necessary to "assign" Miss Smith duties that would relieve her of the responsibilities of his secretarial work and so, in effect, "promoted her upstairs"—with an increase in pay and away from his proximity. Her new job became that of purchasing and inventory control for the still-expanding company which now had about thirty-five branches. Jones thought this job would take all of her time and would prevent her interfering in the affairs of others.

To a certain extent this relieved Jones' own personal dilemma but, in effect, created more of a problem for the key people within his organization including his son who had been made vice-president of The Provident Company. Miss Smith found it extremely difficult to accept any instructions or authority other than by directive from Jones. Other key employees found it difficult to give her instructions because of her attitude and her "position" within the company.

There was no doubt concerning her ability since she developed into a first-class purchasing agent, and the inventory control was efficiently handled by her department. Her loyalty could not be questioned, and her intense interest in the welfare of the company made her a valuable employee. However, this same intense interest on her part continued to create personnel problems because she assumed a cloak of responsibility that extended far beyond the actual responsibility of her department. She insisted on determining to her satisfaction that each new order was actually needed by the particular department even when they were requesting new forms, new equipment, or new merchandise. Her consistent attitude was that "Mr. Jones and I did not need this and I do not see why we need it now." In many cases she was right, but in just as many she was wrong. However, the personnel problem with other key employees became much worse.

About 1958, The Provident Company decided to diversify its business and took on a kindred line of sales that required the hiring of personnel completely outside of its own existing force. Their requirements in regard to supplies were immediate and demanded their special knowledge. They found it impossible to procure what they wanted through the purchasing department headed by Miss Smith. She lacked the knowledge to fulfill their specialized requirements. To prove their need would require that she learn their business. She wanted "proof" of their needs. The new manager of this department threatened to resign unless Jones gave him the authority to order independently of Miss Smith. This authority was given. In effect, Jones created two purchasing departments. The purchasing affairs of the company soon were getting out of hand since there was some similarity and duplication of orders. Other departments soon began to order "on their own hook" rather than face the barrage of questions usually put forth by Miss Smith.

The matter finally came to a head, and it was necessary to call a meeting of the key department heads to determine what to do about Miss Smith and her purchasing department. In this meeting it was decided that she was to accept orders from the four key department heads without question and that her responsibility was only that of buying at the best price obtainable for the company. This was outlined to her in detail. With some loss of face, Miss Smith reluctantly and somewhat defiantly accepted the decision. However, her acceptance was only partial and her criticisms of the purchase orders and even of the management of various key people became biting. It even became bitter in some cases. Her attitude created quite a reputation for her—both from within the organization and from without.

On reaching his sixtieth birthday in 1964, Jones was promoted to the chairman of the board and his son Harvey, was promoted to president of the company at the age of 39. At this time Miss Smith had reached the age of 51. The new president recognized immediately that some degree of reorganization would be necessary. He felt that Miss Smith probably considered him her junior in years of service and experience. She helped start the business—he came in later. At the time she started in the business, he was still in college. He knew the morale problem involving personnel because, since actively coming with the company twelve years previously, he had made the business virtually his only interest and hobby.

His own reorganization plans that involved several problems put the matter of Miss Smith at the head of the list to be immediately determined.

QUESTIONS

1. Where was the glaring error first made in connection with Miss Smith?
2. Should she be retained in her present position?
3. If not retained in her present position, should she be retained in the company?
4. How should the new president decisively and finally handle this problem of what he called the "mother-hen" complex?
5. Is there any way the company can help an employee with Miss Smith's difficulties?
6. Why was Miss Smith not restricted in her purchasing responsibilities much sooner than she was?
7. What can a company do to prevent situations such as that involving Miss Smith from arising?

6

The Internal Revenue Service

THE INTERNAL REVENUE SERVICE, a division of the U. S. Treasury Department, maintains a district office in each of the fifty states. Each of these offices is headed by a district director who is responsible for all federal tax regulations applying to business enterprises and individual taxpayers within his respective state. An average of about 400 persons are employed in each of the district offices.

In 1959, the district director for the state, Ormond Somerville, retired. He was succeeded in office by a prominent attorney, Jerome Lanning. Lanning had worked with the government on several important tax cases, rendering valuable assistance in each instance. He had become familiar with the internal revenue service in its operations and with the district office in particular.

A short time after Lanning assumed his responsibilities as district director, a problem developed in the Returns and Receipts Branch of the Randler office. The Returns and Receipts Branch played a key role in the processing of tax returns since it was responsible for the initial classification and numbering of returns as they were received in the mailroom, as well as for preparing all checks for immediate deposit at the Federal Reserve Bank. During the months between February and August, almost $900,000,000 was received in the district office. It was imperative that this money—90 percent of it in checks—be deposited with the Federal Reserve as soon as possible. When this was not done, the government had no alternative but to seek short-term loans from commercial lenders to meet the bills for its purchases of goods and services. Although this type of financing was available to the government, the Treasury Department, naturally, did not like having to borrow money when it had money lying idle in district offices.

These explanatory facts are closely related to the problem that had arisen in the Randler district office. It became apparent that the Returns and Receipts Branch in Lanning's office was not making a sufficient volume of daily check deposits with the Federal Reserve. As a consequence, from time to time a considerable amount of money was held up in the district office which the government might otherwise have used in paying its bills.

In June, 1961, Lanning concluded that this condition could no longer continue unchallenged, and yet he had been unable to get at the root of the problem. On the basis of investigation, backed by past experience, he concluded that the trouble centered around a breakdown in operations and procedures in the Returns and Receipts Branch. And whatever the cause, he knew that it was essential to increase the number of daily check deposits being made at the Federal Reserve Bank.

For the purpose of ascertaining cause and recommending remedies, Lanning appointed a special task force to study the Returns and Receipts Branch. Three temporary (summer) employees, Charles Robinson, Tommy Donald, and James Howard constituted this special Task Force. Two of these men were the sons of personal friends of Lanning; all three were college seniors who had excellent records in the personnel files of the district office.

The special task force was given a private office to work in, as well as access to the services of a secretary and almost two weeks in which to complete its report. The Task Force decided that it would begin by making a study of operations and procedures in the Returns and Receipts Branch to see if there were any way in which the physical processing of checks and returns might be improved. Next, it was decided that a private, "in confidence" interview should be held with each of the thirteen female employees working in returns and receipts in order to ferret out any criticism of the branch which might bear on the problem or obtain any constructive suggestions for improving its operations.

From the first day that the task force began to function, there was grumbling among some employees of the Returns and Receipts Branch. A few of the women seemed to resent strongly the fact that "three college kids" had been given the job of finding out what was wrong with their department. Moreover, the chairman of the task force, James Howard, had actually been working as a temporary employee in the branch prior to his appointment as committee chairman. "Before he was just another summer temporary," one woman said, "and now he is in charge of a special committee to find out what is wrong with the way the entire branch is doing its job."

In spite of this irritation which a few employees felt towards the task force, they kept their thoughts largely to themselves or within the group. At first they gave willing support to the force's efforts to learn about their methods of work. Thus, as a result of almost one week of study, the special committee established some "data" it felt were related to the problem of frequent delay in depositing checks at the Federal Reserve. A few of the notes included in this preliminary data were:

1. The Returns and Receipts Branch is composed entirely of female employees. There are 12 women under the direction of one supervisor, Miss Emily Hassinger. All of the women have been with the Civil Service for at least 7 years or more and know that their continued employment is virtually assured.

2. Miss Hassinger is not a "strong" supervisor; nor is she generally respected by her subordinates. It seems that she was a very good friend of the former district director, Bascomb Somerville, who made her a supervisor a few months before he retired. Some employees in the Returns and Receipts Branch implied doubt on their own part as to her capability for, or right to have, the job which she now holds.

3. One employee, Nancy Elmore, who was known to be the hardest and most efficient worker—as well as the most outspoken—in the Returns and Receipts Branch, alleged that there was very little coordination or direction of activities in the branch. She said that before Miss Hassinger became supervisor operations ran very smoothly in the branch and everyone knew exactly which "block" of returns she ought to begin work on at the start of the day. "But now," she said, "everyone is pretty much on their own as to what gets done around here."

4. Talks with branch employees further revealed discontent over the amount of time Miss Hassinger spent preparing her weekly reports for the Regional Service Center. The reporting system had been initiated almost three years before as a means for comparing the performance of one district office with another, as well as forecasting the number of man-hours that would be required by each department for the following year. The system required that each employee keep an accurate count of how many times he performed a given task or operation and at the end of each day record his total on a specially provided work sheet. Almost every operation, from stamping numbers on envelopes to auditing corporation tax returns, had to be counted and handed in. From these figures was derived a "standard output" of so many items per hour, e.g., the standard for stamping envelopes might be 1200 an hour. In any event, it was the supervisor's job to compile all the individual worksheets from the branch office into a master worksheet to be sent to the Regional Service Center. The whole process was very time-consuming and involved many computations. The feeling expressed by some employees in the Returns and Receipts Branch, however, was that Miss Hassinger spent "almost all" her time compiling reports, which prevented her from performing her other duties and responsibilities with regard to the entire branch.

5. Another complaint in the Returns and Receipts Branch concerned the management of permanent employees who were sent to the branch, on a temporary basis, to help with a heavy backlog of work. Whenever such help was deemed available for the branch, a request was simply sent out to other departments in the district office without attempting to

secure specific employees who might have worked in the branch before. This being the case, it was frequently necessary to train such temporary help before any benefit could be derived from it. This problem, as well as the numerous errors resulting from inexperience, might have been avoided if some attempt were made to keep the same employees coming to the Receipts Branch who had worked there before.

6. James Howard, chairman of the special task force, had noticed, while working as a temporary in the Returns and Receipts Branch, that there was no set time for employees to begin either their lunch hours or their 15 minute breaks each morning and afternoon. As a result, several of the women were observed to take breaks lasting almost 30 minutes and lunch periods that were extended beyond the allotted time.

These, then, are samples of the type of information that was collected by the special task force as its study proceeded. In the private interviews held with employees of the Returns and Receipts Branch, it was soon revealed that considerable hostility existed between certain women in the branch. Furthermore, two or three employees were especially critical of Miss Hassinger. Their remarks implied that they felt she was not at all qualified for her job and that Somerville had only given it to her because of their close friendship and the fact that he would retire just a few months after her promotion.

Aside from whatever faults or qualities she possessed, Miss Hassinger was clearly upset by the study which the special task force was conducting. She believed it was a sure indication that someone "higher up" did not think she was doing a good job. Her apprehension increased steadily. She knew that she was not at all liked by some employees in the branch and knew that they would probably be very critical of her in their private, "in confidence" interviews with the task force. This belief was reinforced by the fact that the force was composed of young temporary employees who did not have any "standing," or occupy important positions, in the Randler office. Therefore, Miss Hassinger reasoned, employees would probably exercise more freedom with their remarks than they would if talking to someone who was in a position that commanded more respect. Indeed, the more she thought, the more worried she became. She knew that the task force was planning to write a final report to give to Mr. Lanning. Due to the age and inexperience of the force, she concluded that there was "no telling" what they might say in their report, or to what extent they would repeat the things said about her by other employees.

On Friday, Miss Hassinger did not leave the office at the regular closing time. She said that she needed to work late in order to finish a report that she was preparing for the Regional Service Center. After everyone had left the building, however, she entered the office where the special task force had been working. All of their working papers, calculations, conjectures, notes on employee remarks, etc. were lying on the table.

The next morning, at around 8:30, Mr. Lanning received a phone call from Nancy Elmore. She was sobbing so heavily that he could hardly understand her as she tried to tell him of the "horrible . . . awful . . . things" Miss Hassinger had said to her last night on the phone.

"She threatened me, called me names, and said she would never speak to me again because of the lies I had told about her to the task force," Miss Elmore cried. "She also said she was going to call one or two other people before the night was over," Nancy added.

QUESTIONS

1. How do you feel about Mr. Lanning's project of a special task force?
2. What do you think about his selecting three college students for the force?
3. How do you react to the task force conducting private, "in confidence," interviews?
4. Are there any problems relating to women working in large groups under female supervision?
5. Was the task force itself responsible for Miss Hassinger's "snooping"?
6. What action should Lanning take about Miss Elmore's telephone call?
7. What changes should Lanning make as a consequence of task force findings reported in this case?

Selection

THESE SIX CASES concern selection, a vital function in personnel management since decisions in this area determine the ultimate quality of any work force. *Standards* for selection are important in determining the level of competence of employees. The *selection process* should be designed to ascertain qualities that are necessary for effective employees and qualities that will cause eventual troubles. Selection is far from the entire answer to an efficient, smooth-running work force since training and supervision are important factors in molding a good staff of employees. These cases, accordingly, include situations in which management must deal with behavioral characteristics that become evident after selection.

The broad subject of "staffing" or "selection" includes bases for decision-making, questions of selection from within or outside an organization, and steps taken to determine the qualifications of applicants. All of these phases of selection are found among cases in this section.

7

Mum Gardens of Georgia

IN EARLY 1952, J. J. MACK, an employee of Flower Gardens of Florida, St. Augustine, became general manager of a farm the Florida firm had acquired in North Georgia for the sole purpose of raising chrysanthemum blossoms for the commercial flower markets of the eastern portion of the United States. Under Mack's tutelage, Mum Gardens of Georgia, the firm name eventually selected by the parent organization, had grown and prospered. For the 1965 growing season, it was contemplated that twenty-six acres would be planted in chrysanthemums—the largest acreage Mum Gardens had cultivated since its origin in 1952.

While some chrysanthemums are grown under glass throughout the year at Mum Gardens, the bulk of blossoms are grown on open acreage between early spring and mid-December. Subject to weather variables, actual flower shipments from field plantings are scheduled from the first week in June through the first week in December. The chrysanthemum business is basically seasonal, and labor requirements vary considerably throughout the year. The firm currently employs 38 personnel on a year 'round basis, 4 of whom are in a management category, and 34 in what the management refers to as a multiskill classification (Fig. 1, page 2).

In discussing the requirements for permanent employment at Mum Gardens, Mack pointed out that these employees, over the course of a year, were called upon to perform a variety of tasks, and unless the employee possessed considerable versatility, he could not long be utilized —there were no specialists, *per se,* working at Mum Gardens. Mack cited, as an example of the versatility required, those positions presently filled by the eight female employees. During the summer and fall blossom season, these women are engaged full time in wrapping, packing, and shipping operations. With the end of the bulk flower shipping season in early December, and after annual vacations, these employees concentrate their efforts on the propagation of plants for the following growing season. Propagation work requires both skill and patience. The women take cuttings (or slips) by variety from parent plants and set them in a special mix of loam, sand, and peat moss where the new plants are nurtured with what amounts to motherly care until they are transplanted to the open fields in the spring. Propagation requires careful selection and scheduling. Of the approximately 1000 commercially grown varieties of chrysanthemums, Mum Gardens specializes in only 55 varieties of various colors. Cuttings must be selected and scheduled so that mature flowers produced will meet commercial market demands. In pointing out the potential selection and scheduling dangers, Mack stated: "If we got our breeds mixed and came up with a crop of bronze or gold mums in June, we couldn't give them away, let alone sell them. June is the traditional wedding month and the market is demanding nothing but white mums. On the other hand, in September the demand is for bronze and gold, and the market for white mums is negligible." When one considers that 1,800,000 separate plants are scheduled to be grown in 1965 the magnitude of the selection and scheduling dangers become quite apparent.

For permanent male employees, the requirement for versatility is even more demanding. The acreage under cultivation is completely cross-hatched with three separate utility systems—an electric lighting system, a water irrigation system, and a butane gas system used to heat the fields in case of unseasonably cold weather. In connection with these utilities, employees are called upon to make installations and repairs without outside professional help. Furthermore, during the off-season there is the usual plethora of maintenance functions which require each employee at some time to be a glazier, carpenter, painter, canvas repairman, and on occasion, demolition expert. (Mack pointed out, however, that he was a graduate of mechanical engineering at Georgia Institute of Technology, and his engineering knowledge had probably saved the company considerable in outside fees. He had designed the utility systems, greenhouses, utility sheds, packing house, refrigerator storage, etc. and enjoyed thoroughly this particular facet of company operations.) In addition, permanent employees, during the peak season, frequently serve as first-line supervisors of groups of temporary employees.

Despite the demands made upon permanent employees, the firm has, since its inception, built a close-knit and loyal permanent labor force. The average period of employment with the firm is somewhat over eight years. Additional permanent employees, when needed, are usually selected from the large group of temporary employees hired during the peak season. Wages paid permanent employees are considered average for the industry and locale. The firm has no retirement or pension plan for either management or workers. Annual vacations, averaging two weeks with pay, are provided. There is an annual bonus plan for management personnel contingent upon profitable operations.

During the summer months, activity reaches a peak and labor requirements increase to 145-150 personnel. Of the approximately 110 summer-seasonal employees, about 35 are women utilized in picking and sorting operations and the remainder are men classified as general laborers. The principal prerequisite for summer employment at Mum Gardens is a strong back and the ability to work long hours out-of-doors in all kinds of weather.

Temporary summer employees are drawn from the towns and countryside in the vicinity of Mum Gardens and are usually employed from June through September. Many of these temporary employees have been with Mum Gardens for a number of summer seasons, although this is more true of the women than it is of the men. A large proportion of the male employees in recent years has been school boys who are large enough to perform hard manual labor. In recent years, Mum Gardens has found it difficult to obtain all the summer-seasonal help that they require for efficient operations; consequently, the geographic area from which employees are drawn is expanding each season. In addition to strong backs, employees must possess a reasonable degree of intelligence and be able to follow instructions.

Mack concluded that there were three hurdles the company has to cross annually in its quest for temporary employees—the pay, the temporary duration of the work, and the nature of the work. Average gross pay of temporary employees is $47.50 per week. Mack thought that the rate paid by the company is probably a little better than that offered by farmers, saw mills, etc., with whom Mum Gardens competes in the local labor market. Mum Gardens, however, has for some time been caught in a static market-price situation not faced by most businesses. "In 1952," Mack stated, "the standard 14-ounce bunch of chrysanthemums was wholesaling for $1.25. Twelve seasons later, in 1964, the same 14-ounce bunch of chrysanthemums was still selling for the same $1.25." In the interim since 1952, however, all costs and expenses—most of all labor—have risen considerably. By increasing the efficiency of operations and by expanding its markets, Mum Gadens has been able to meet rising costs; however, as Mr. Mack ventured, ". . . you can only wring so much efficiency out of an operation of this kind and most of that efficiency has already been wrung."

Chrysanthemums by nature are fickle, and raising them for commercial sale requires 16-18 weeks of hard work from original cutting to saleable blossom. Chrysanthemums have two unique properties which, in large measure, account for added work that does not apply to most flower-producing activities. One of these peculiarities is that in order for the chrysanthemum to bud and bloom, it must have ten and a half consecutive hours of darkness. This accounts for chrysanthemums being normal late autumn bloomers. But, since the best market for blossoms is in midsummer when the hours of darkness are the briefest, the added hours of darkness necessary to induce blooming must be artificially provided. To hoodwink the plants, the fields are hand-covered with heavy, black, satin-like drop cloths, which reduce the light reaching the plants to less than one-half foot candle. However, the daily covering and uncovering of acres of chrysanthemum plants in all kinds of weather, to provide the necessary ten and a half hours of darkness, is one of the more disagreeable manual chores required of temporary employees. At the other extremity of the growing season in late autumn there is ample darkness provided by nature; but, in this situation, since too many plants would normally blossom at once, floodlights are utilized over some sections to create artificial daylight and alter the blossoming period. By this time in the growing season, the need for additional manpower is pretty well over —it only takes one man a second or two to throw the light switch on or off.

On the other hand, chrysanthemums, unlike most other flowers, will blossom only on the plant. They cannot be prepicked as buds and induced to bloom en route to market. When the plants do bloom, the blossoms must be picked promptly, processed and shipped with minimum delay. Again, the plants having been regulated to a considerable degree, once they do bloom they make unusual demands on the labor force for immediate attention in all kinds of weather.

In seeking its seasonal labor force, Mum Gardens has never formally recruited. Some potential employees just show up at the farm and request employment; some are repeaters from prior years. For the most part, information that Mum Gardens is hiring or needs additional employees is usually carried by word of mouth from acquaintance to acquaintance. Occasionally permanent employees are enlisted to contact prior year, part-time employees and ascertain if they will return to Mum Gardens for another season.

In view of increasing competition for the seasonal laborer, Mum Gardens, in recent years, has added a couple of inducements designed to place the firm in a better bargaining position. Two of the company's van-type trucks, normally utilized during the day to move packaged flowers to the air-freight terminal at Atlanta, have been equipped with removable seats and follow scheduled routes in the morning and evening, picking up and returning workers throughout the surrounding countryside. As the firm has been required to extend its "bus routes" into the hinterland, time lost in transit becomes more and more of a problem.

With an abundance of good, fertile land and adequate tractors and farm equipment, Mum Gardens has in recent years planted and cultivated, at company expense, an employee vegetable garden aggregating some ten acres. A wide variety of common garden vegetables—peas, beans, corn, tomatoes, etc.—are grown for the sole benefit of employees. In addition to the permanent employees, certain heads of households and responsible adults among the temporary employees are free to help themselves to crops in season and in reasonable quantity. Employees can, in many cases, supplement their take-home pay to a worthwhile extent by this added payment in kind.

For temporary employees there are no promotion possibilities except as vacancies or new job opportunities are created on the permanent work force. Mum Gardens has found, in answer to inquiries designed to ascertain why persons are not anxious to work there for the summer season, that the potential employee's first interest lies in year-round employment even at lower weekly rates than he might make during the summer months at Mum Gardens. For the most part, except for those returning to the home or to school in the fall, only after an individual has been unable to acquire assured permanent employment elsewhere does he turn to Mum Gardens. This appears to indicate that, to a considerable extent, Mum Gardens is getting the rejects and leftovers in the local labor market.

As previously mentioned, some degree of intelligence and the ability to follow instructions are required of all workers. Workers have to acquaint themselves with certain "rights" and "wrongs" and be familiar with some safety practices. Mack stated that the company safety record was excellent. In the past half-dozen years there had been only one serious accident, and that had turned out to be much less serious than it might have been. Mack went on to explain that all of the cultivated acreage was periodically subjected to saturation by methyl-bromide gas designed to eliminate certain weeds and harmful germs from the soil. The gas, which is a deadly poison, is injected into a plastic tent which is erected on a wooden frame over a segment of ground. On one occasion, during the gas-filling process, a frame had collapsed and an avid workman at the scene had lifted the tent flap and dashed in to right the fallen frame. Due to the quick action of other workers at the scene, and with the help of sufficient breeze to dissipate the gas, the overzealous worker was revived and survived.

No formal safety training was provided workers and none was thought to be necessary. On-the-job guidance provided by permanent employees was considered adequate safety training. With respect to temporary employees, Mack did not feel that such matters as selection, safety training, or training of any kind were particularly important considerations. His principal concern at this time was being able to acquire a sufficient number of temporary employees to staff Mum Gardens for the 1965 summer season.

QUESTIONS

1. In your opinion, could the difficulties encountered in acquiring temporary workers during recent summer seasons be attributed to the absence of a planned, formal recruiting program? Why or why not?

2. Comment on the practice of using permanent employees in the role of first-line supervisors or foremen in charge of temporary employees.

3. What further inducements, if any, would you recommend that Mum Gardens use in its attempts to acquire adequate temporary help?

4. From the information provided what effect has the present wage rate for temporary employees as a deterrent to acquiring sufficient personnel?

5. Would you recommend that Mum Gardens review its wage-setting practices by examining wage patterns paid similar help in similar businesses (such as farming) in Georgia?

6. When general economic conditions are good and employment levels high, where do you suggest that Mum Gardens and other users of temporary labor turn for their personnel needs?

Mum Gardens of Georgia
Organization, January 1965

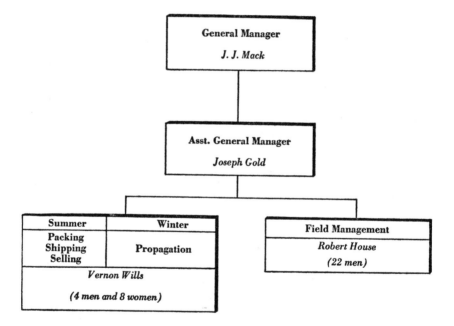

8

Potomac Paper Mill

JAMES BURKE, the administrative assistant in charge of hourly employment at Potomac Paper Mill, received a telephone call from one of the mill's machine-room supervisors, Fred Schmidt.

SCHMIDT: Burke, what's this I hear about Cagle? He tells me he hasn't even been called for a physical, and several guys who applied after he did are already on the job. If my sister's kid can't get on before those newcomers, I don't know what this place is coming to. My thirty years in this mill should mean something.

BURKE: Look, Mr. Schmidt! It's like I told Cagle when he first applied. We have a tremendous volume of applications, and most of the work won't start 'til midsummer. Also, we're trying to select mainly by interviewing and testing in order to get the right people for the right jobs. So far, a job for which Cagle is suited just hasn't opened up.

SCHMIDT: Now you look. I don't care what fancy new methods you personnel boys have dreamed up. You put most of the new men in the labor pool anyhow, and Bart Maynard handles the training and job placement from there. All I'm asking is that you put Sammy (Cagle) in the labor pool and give him his ninety days to prove himself.

BURKE: Well, I'll review his application and test scores and give the matter strong consideration although I can't promise anything.

At this point the conversation dwindled into mild unpleasantries, and Schmidt announced that if nothing were done, he would have to go over Burke's head. When the conversation ended, Burke began mulling over the background and the events at the mill which had caused this conversation and other very similar instances.

Potomac Mill was a large pulp and paper plant located in the mountains of western Pennsylvania. Unemployment for the general area was around 10 per cent of the total labor force. Potomac Mill, owned by a large progressive national paper concern, offered the best employment opportunities in the area. It was a union shop, and had a peaceful record of labor relations, the last strike having been in 1949. Its wage scale was high for the area and slightly above average for all unionized factory work in the entire labor market area. After being hired, employees underwent a ninety-day probationary period. If during this period they showed themselves to be unsatisfactory, the company could discharge them with no union action. After this period, however, the employees became union members automatically, and any discharge or disciplinary action on the company's part was open to grievance through the union. This placed an extra burden on the personnel department to weed out undesirable persons during selection and at least before the ninety-day period terminated.

Due to the large surplus in the local labor market, the personnel department enjoyed a sizeable backlog of applications, and never had to search or to advertise for qualified people. The only problem had been selecting the best qualified from the multitude of job seekers. The final hiring decision usually rested with the supervisors, who requisitioned for the new employees through the personnel department. Hence, the department's main functions in staffing were recruiting and screening. No matter who made the final employment decision, the responsibility for maintaining a high caliber work force was charged to Personnel. Complaints concerning unsatisfactory employees were often brought to Personnel's doorstep.

Jim Burke had been dealing with this situation for two years. He had a Master's degree in personnel administration and undergraduate training in sociology and some psychology. In his tenure as hourly employment manager, he had developed various procedures and instituted several new tests for the screening and placement of job applicants. He believed that he had constructed an adequate and effective system for handling the mill's hourly employment needs. However, in many instances he had discovered that developing effective procedures and instituting them were two entirely different things. His superior, Ralph Schaeffer, the personnel and labor relations manager, had always been receptive to new ideas in the selection area. Yet Burke had long ago learned that Schaeffer could not always be counted on to back up these ideas. Schaeffer's main functions had always involved labor relations and salary administration, and he did not seem to view employment as one of the major problems of the personnel department. However, he was considered successful in his management of personnel and was well respected throughout the mill.

Burke had always found the main obstacle to his objective methods to be the tacit company policy of permitting selection on the basis of kinship and friendship. Due to the rural nature of the area and the existence of large families of long residence, the company had always hired, often unintentionally, many persons with relatives already in the plant (despite inquiries to that effect on the application form). The people in the area seemed to have a strong sense of kinship and were always eager to find jobs for their friends and relations.

The situation which Burke was now considering was all too common. For the most part, the individuals recommended or pushed by relatives and friends in the mill were satisfactory for at least some job at the mill. The number and types of jobs in the mill offered a wide range of possibilities, extending from unskilled menial tasks to skilled mechanical, electrical, and laboratory positions. Hence, Burke had often been able to "fit a job" to the desires of an influential mill person. Yet, he believed that this was an improper situation and in some cases completely unsatisfactory.

He remembered one case concerning the son of one of the general machine-room superintendents. This man had worked his way up from the lowest labor grade to a position fourth from the top of the line hierarchy. His son, upon graduation from high school, applied at the mill. With the exception of his physical examination, the boy would have been completely satisfactory. However, the plant doctor had discovered a defect in the boy's spinal column which would make him extremely prone to injury from lifting heavy objects. Due to employee medical insurance and other union-won health benefits that imposed a heavy cost burden on the mill, Burke had decided to hire the boy for a lab job. Shortly thereafter, Schaeffer informed Burke that the boy was to be placed in a machine room, even though this would involve strenuous labor and a great deal of lifting. Burke soon discovered that the father had gone to the mill manager and stated that if his son could not start in a machine room just as he had, he would quit. Due to this valuable employee's insistent demand, the manager had ordered Schaeffer to have the boy placed in a machine-room position. Thus, Burke had been overruled without having been consulted or forewarned.

With this unpleasant memory in mind, Burke's thoughts now turned to the present bone of contention, Sam Cagle. Cagle had first applied in 1959, but before his application could be fully considered, he had been drafted. Discharged in March, 1963, he immediately reapplied, knowing that the mill's expansion program was creating many new openings. Having been informed of Cagle's relationship to Schmidt, Burke put him through the standard testing and interview procedure. Cagle showed average intelligence and mechanical aptitude in his test results. However, the personality inventory showed definite signs of maladjustment and hostility to authority. The interview reaffirmed these test findings. Though not openly hostile, Cagle seemed suspicious and resentful throughout his talk with Burke. He was very vocal in expressing his dislike for his high school teachers and army superiors. Burke detected several manifestations of emotional imbalance, though he could not put his finger on a specific mental disorder.

Not content to base a conclusion on the test and interview alone, Burke had procured Cagle's high school record and some information about his service performance. Both showed numerous incidents of disrespect and even open insubordination. The evidence now seemed sufficiently definite, and Burke placed Cagle's file in the "dead applications" section. Three weeks had then passed prior to the telephone call from Schmidt.

Unwilling to give in immediately, Burke was preparing to take up the matter with Schaeffer when the latter called Burke into his office.

SCHAEFFER: Sit down, Jim, boy! How's it going? I suppose you know what's on my mind.

BURKE: Yes, I was just about to come to you with this Cagle matter on my own volition.

SCHAEFFER: Back in the 30's, as you know, the foremen did all the hourly hiring. Most of them packed their departments with relatives and friends. Many of them still believe in this policy. When you get right down to it, there's a lot to be said for hiring on this basis. It gives us a good source to draw from and makes for good relations and morale throughout the mill. Anyway, everybody within twenty miles has relatives and friends in the mill.

BURKE: I agree that recommendations from employees are an excellent source. Even though it sometimes stretches my selection rules, I have gone along on similar cases in the past. However, I think it is time to start following the written procedures which have been set or change them to bring this favoritism out into the open. It seems to me that we must draw the line here; Cagle is just too far below our hiring standards.

Burke then retraced the specifics on Sam Cagle for Schaeffer's benefit. He expressed the opinion that Cagle's emotional problems and antisocial attitude would make him a complete misfit.

He further explained to his superior that this man would not only be inefficient as a worker but would also cause tension and decrease the efficiency in his work group. Finally, he expressed the theory that Cagle could be headed for severe mental-health problems in which case the mill might be partially liable for hospital expenses.

Schaeffer seemed impressed with Burke's knowledge and detailed analysis of the man. At the same time, he seemed to be unsure of the action which he should take.

SCHAEFFER: Jim you've done a good work-up on this man. I can definitely see your point, and I'm not going to interfere if I can possibly avoid it. Schmidt has a lot of influence, and he's been pestering me almost continuously. It appears that he knows his nephew is something less than top-grade employment material, and will have great trouble getting and keeping a job elsewhere. If he pushes the point with the brass, I'm not sure I can back up an unfavorable decision on Cagle.

Burke knew that Schaeffer had the formal authority to decide the point himself, or else to back up a subordinate's decision on the matter. However, he also knew that the informal pressures could be considerable.

Schaeffer's concluding remarks confirmed Burke's appraisal.

SCHAEFFER: Technically, this is your decision. I'll back you up as far as is possible. Whatever the disposition is, we must guard against similar recurrences in the future.

Burke left, no further toward a solution, but with a better knowledge of the support he could count on. His next step was a review of the selection systems and policies set up by the personnel office in Pittsburgh. However, the central policies concerning hourly employees were far from precise. The personnel department at each mill was almost completely autonomous in its selection of hourly people. In short, Burke found that hourly employment was almost completely decentralized.

As a last resort for advice, he consulted Bill Streets, who had held the employment manager's position prior to Burke. Presently he was working in safety administration. Burke found that Streets was well aware of the Cagle situation.

STREETS: I know what you're up against, Jim. All I can do is to tell you the way I used to handle it. It seemed to me that strict adherence to hiring procedures like you have set up was futile. You're not going to set the world on fire in that job. So my advice is to bend with the wind and put this guy on up at the wood yard where he can release his tensions on pulp logs.

This advice was succinct and somewhat convincing to Burke. It represented the easy way out, which might have been the best for all concerned in the long run. However, Burke still felt inclined toward sticking to his guns. He knew that employing this man would be wrong. And he felt sure that he had investigated all the angles and sources of advice available to him. With four hundred new men to be requisitioned during the next two months, he saw an excellent chance to apply the selection methods he had devised. Every exception, he was sure, weakened his position. On the other hand, the rejection of Cagle would cause considerable stress, and the decision could well be overturned.

On the following morning Schmidt telephoned again, at this time informing Burke that Cagle had ridden in with him and was at this moment on his way to the personnel office. James Burke, to whom the matter now seemed monumental, realized that the time for decision was at hand.

QUESTIONS

1. How do you appraise a policy of hiring on the basis of relationship as opposed to a basis of straight qualifications?

2. Is Burke correct in discounting his policy mainly because of troublesome exceptions?

3. What do you think of the policy of placing the final employment decision with the line supervisors?

4. How could the line-staff interaction as to communication, organization, and responsibility be improved at Potomac Mill?

5. How much responsibility and authority for decision should be vested in the staff department in the employment area?

6. What could be done to curb the tendency to override subordinates and not back them up on decisions?

7. How could Burke have handled the problem in a manner reflecting effective strategy in problem solving?

8. Would Burke be justified in taking the "easy way out" in this case?

9

Sparkle Bottling Company

THE SPARKLE BOTTLING COMPANY is an international manufacturer of soft drinks. In the United States, each plant that is authorized to bottle and sell Sparkle-Cola is given a franchise. The individual plant is then built through the combined efforts of the parent company and local investors. Stock in the particular plant, representing the investment made by local people, is then distributed to the investors. The daily operation of the plant then becomes the responsibility of the owners of the stock.

The parent company controls the supply of the basic ingredients for Sparkle-Cola at all times. These ingredients are purchased by the local plant as they are needed. The parent company makes periodic checks on each of its plants to insure that quality standards are maintained. The home office aids the individual plants in the development of managerial skills, the payment of their advertising expense, and the combining of several plants' orders to allow purchasing in carload lots. The individual plants, however, are completely responsible for the developing of franchises, the managing of the day-to-day operations of the plant, and all personnel policies.

The Howardsville plant was a small operation owned and operated by a local family. During the Spring of 1963, the position of route manager was under consideration by the manager of the plant, Cal Long. The route manager was in charge of all of the delivery men employed by the plant. It was his job to know all of the delivery routes in order to be able to substitute for any driver who could not report to work due to illness or vacation. He was also responsible for dividing the franchise equally among the delivery personnel and for soliciting and making contracts for the sale of Sparkle-Cola at special events, such as county fairs.

The position did not pay considerably more than that of a delivery man, but it was one of the very few positions to which a delivery man could advance. Thus, from the standpoint of a career worker, the route manager's job was one of his limited chances to become a part of management.

At the Howardsville plant, no policy had ever been enunciated to cover promotion to the route manager's position. Since the plant had been in operation, for nearly thirty years, the position had been filled by the senior delivery man employed at the time. This procedure was considered adequate since the job required only "a fair memory in order to learn and remember the various delivery routes and a pleasant personality in order to get along with potential customers," according to Long. These qualifications were generally considered to be the requirements for a successful delivery man. Hence, it was felt that the position could be used as a reward for effective, loyal service to the company.

The previous route manager, Sam Johnson, had begun work at the Howardsville plant as a delivery man in 1951. He had continued in that capacity until 1957. At that time, the route manager left the company and Sam, being the senior delivery man, was duly promoted to the job. He continued in that position until the summer of 1962, when he terminated his employment in order to take a job with a local gas company. It was generally conceded that Johnson had done an efficient job.

When Johnson left the company, the plant manager decided to discontinue the position and shift the responsibilities of the job to the office manager and the delivery men. The additional work load placed on these individuals would not be considerable since Johnson had left the delivery phase of the operation in good order.

In April, 1963, the office manager, George Harris, had a talk with Long. Harris stated that as a result of the closing of certain stores and the opening of new ones, the quantity of work being done by the individual drivers was becoming imbalanced. It was Harris' opinion that the distribution of stops among route men should be changed in order to correct the situation. Harris felt that he did not have the time to perform such a task and requested that the position of route manager be reinstated. After considering the problem, Long agreed.

Six men were at that time employed by the Howardsville plant in a delivery man capacity:

John Clark

John, age twenty-nine, had been employed as a route man since 1953. He was quiet, friendly with the customers, and seemed to get along quite well. Clark lead a rather boisterous life off the job but had never been in any legal difficulty. He had been married three times in the past six years. Partly owing to his fourth-grade education, John was perfectly content to be a route man for as long as he was physically able.

Roger MacKenzie

Roger was an army veteran who had worked for the company for five years. He was the same age as John Clark. Long felt that Roger "is the most dependable route man we have had in a long time. He has never missed a day of work in five years that I can recall, excepting vacation time of course." He was an efficient delivery man but he occasionally lost his temper when someone pointed out his mistakes to him. Roger had completed high school before entering the service.

WILLIAM FOSTER

Bill had come to the company in the past two years. He had been enrolled in the state university for two years previous to his employment. He stated his reason for leaving college as insufficient funds to support his wife and child and to pay tuition expenses too. Harris echoed Long's feelings when he stated that "Bill is the most intelligent driver we have. Although he does his work satisfactorily and has boosted sales on his route, he is one of the slower workers we have."

The other three drivers had been with the company for less than a year. Hence, they were not given much consideration for this particular job.

Long, who had been manager of the Howardsville plant for three years, felt that choice of the driver with the most seniority might not be the best way to select a route manager. He did agree that the route manager should be a former driver, though. It was Long's opinion that until the last three years, seniority had been the best method for promoting a driver. The drivers at that time all came from a similar class background and a similar educational background. None of the former route managers, with the exception of Johnson, had a high school diploma. The route men generally had completed grade school but few had finished high school.

In the past three years, the caliber of men available and willing to become delivery men at the Howardsville plant had risen noticeably, owing to a slight recession in the area. Of the three drivers employed in the last year, all had completed high school, one having had a year's education at the state university.

Long felt that when conditions in the area became more prosperous, the more intelligent delivery men would wish to leave the plant and seek jobs in which the opportunity for advancement was greater.

In order to retain at least one of the more intelligent drivers, Long was considering passing over both Clark and MacKenzie and choosing Bill Foster for the route manager's position.

In June, 1963, Long called Bill Foster into his office to discuss Bill's work and his plans for the future. Both Long and Bill agreed that Bill had been doing a satisfactory job to the present time. When asked about his future plans, however, Bill replied that he had been thinking about the subject for some time. "Although I like the work, I feel that the opportunities for advancement here are quite limited. At the present time, I have received an offer to work for an insurance company, and I am giving it careful consideration. The pay is not as good, but the job does contain several opportunities for advancement to better paying positions," Bill continued.

Long, having his suspicions confirmed by the discussion with Foster, brought the subject to Harris's attention to get his reaction. Harris thought the question of promoting Foster to the route manager's position deserved careful consideration, but, he reminded Long of the long-standing, unwritten policy that seniority was the prerequisite for promotion in cases such as these. Long and Harris agreed that circumstances resulting in the high caliber of men employed during the past two years would not last. They felt that this education factor might still be a justification for disregarding the old procedure even though the future might again see men with less education serving as delivery men. They felt that, evenso, the overall educational level in the area was rising so that they would have few applicants in the future with only a grade-school education.

Long soon afterward decided that the wise, long-range solution would be to promote Bill Foster to route manager. In order to minimize resistance to the choice of Foster, Long decided to talk with the driver with the most seniority, John Clark, before making the decision public.

The next day, Long called John into his office after work. They discussed the route manager's job and the qualifications necessary for the position, Long stressing the fact that, in his opinion, a man of above average intelligence should be given priority, regardless of his length of service. John agreed that intelligence should be considered to a degree, but he mentioned the fact that previous route managers had done an efficient job without the benefit of a high school education. Clark did agree, however, with Long that his fourth-grade education would be a hindrance. When this point was established, Long informed Clark that Foster was to be the new route manager. Long asked John to keep the news a secret until he could call a meeting in the near future and make the announcement.

Two weeks later, Long announced that a sales meeting for all drivers would be held at the end of the day. The meeting got under way at five o'clock that afternoon. After a brief sales talk on how to take advantage of the warm weather to sell more cases of soft drinks, Long stated that the job of route manager was to be reinstalled in order to have someone to redistribute the individual routes. He then announced that Foster, owing to his previous educational background, was to be given the job. Long continued, "I know this promotion is contrary to the known policy of the plant, but I feel that Mr. Foster can best perform the job." After asking all of the drivers to give Bill their support, the meeting was adjourned. Long noticed that, as the drivers filed out, Roger MacKenzie seemed to be quite agitated.

As a result of Roger's attitude, Harris suggested that Long talk to Roger in the near future in order to keep him from possibly stirring up discontent among the drivers. Harris felt that such a hostile reaction on Roger's part could prevent the cooperation between drivers and Foster that would be necessary for Bill to perform his new job effectively.

The following week, Long called MacKenzie into his office to discuss the choice of Foster as route manager. When asked for his comments on the promotion, Roger said, "I realize that Bill has had the benefit of a higher education, but I cannot see the advantage of this. From past history, education has had relatively little to do with effective performance on the job." He continued, "John Clark told me that he was not to be promoted because of his lack of education. Thus, I felt that I was entitled to the job. Apparently, good performance means little around here since you took over the management of the plant. Everyone knows that as a route man my work is superior to Bill Foster's." Long felt that it was useless to try to explain his reasoning at the moment considering the emotion displayed by MacKenzie. Therefore, Long terminated the discussion, implying that they would have to get together in the near future to discuss the reasons for Foster's promotion.

Six weeks later, Long, while reviewing the sales of each route, noticed that MacKenzie's sales were less than those of any preceding year. When Roger came into the plant that afternoon, he found a notice stating that Long wished to see him as soon as he had finished loading his truck.

At the ensuing meeting, Long asked Roger about the drop in sales. Roger said that he was doing the best he could. He implied, however, that since there was apparently little reward for doing an outstanding job, there was no reason why he should wear himself out working extra hard in the hot sun. Long remarked that since a route man's pay was partly on a commission basis, he thought MacKenzie should be taking advantage of the warm weather. Roger said he would try to do better.

In the following two weeks, sales on Roger's route did not increase, and he was purportedly sick on two different occasions. Considering the circumstances, Long felt that he had no other alternative than to drop Roger from the payroll. His sales had now fallen to a point where only three of the newest route men's earnings were lower. After two additional weeks with no improvement, Long discharged MacKenzie.

Late in August, 1963, Long and Foster discussed the route managership, it now being almost two months since Bill's promotion. Bill remarked that the new job was certainly more interesting, and he appreciated Long's faith in him as demonstrated by the promotion. When asked about his future plans, Bill would not say anything definite. He asked one question, however, that slightly disturbed Long. He inquired, "Now that I have had the good fortune to be promoted, what advancement opportunities are open to me in the future."

QUESTIONS

1. Did the circumstances resulting in a high caliber of drivers warrant an exception to the unwritten plant policy on the promotion of a driver to route manager?

2. Should the parent company assume more responsibility for policy formulation and administration?

3. Is a higher education background a valid requirement for the route manager's job?

4. Evaluate the plant manager's treatment of (a) John Clark and then (b) Roger MacKenzie.

5. Is it desirable to tell an employee about a management decision before it is announced?

6. Should relatively intelligent men with high school or college backgrounds be hired as route men?

7. Will this promotion decision have any effect on the performance of delivery men in the future at the Howardsville plant? If so, what would you predict?

8. Is there anything Long could have done to help restore MacKenzie's equilibrium and restimulate him?

9. What do you make of the interview between Long and Foster at the close of the case?

10

Campbell Textiles, Inc.

AFTER BUYING THE BASIN CITY MILL from another manufacturer, Campbell Textiles found itself faced with a tight labor market. This fact further complicated the task of converting, organizing, and making the plant an efficient operation. Even though there was some unemployment in the area, skilled workers, needed to get the plant in operation, were hard to find.

Campbell Textiles was a large textile manufacturer that, organizationally, was divisionalized by product or product group. The Basin City plant was purchased for integration as a weaving plant into the Automotive Fabrics Division. The plant was under the direct supervision of a resident manager and had four line departments: Preparatory, Weaving, Mending, and Shipping. In addition, staff departments in personnel, purchasing, accounting, and industrial engineering were set up.

Bill Robinson, the personnel manager, tried to employ men with ambition and ability since there were, and would be for several years, many supervisory positions that would have to be filled.

One of the applications he received was from Frank Stillwell, who applied for a position as a weaver. Robinson was particularly impressed with Stillwell and characterized him as clean-cut, well dressed, and very ambitious. Selected information from Stillwell's application blank follows:

Age	26
Height	5′ 11″
Weight	176
Marital Status	Married
Own home	Yes
Dependents	4
Kind of work desired	Weaver
Hobbies	Boating, Football
Crime Convictions	None
Education	High School graduate; Armed Forces Institute (2 years)
Previous Experience	Weaver—Franklinton Mills (2 years) Weaver—Smith Cotton Mills (1 year)
References	Mr. John Boyd, Vice President Cramerton Bank & Trust Company Mr. Osborne Abernathy, Supervisor Smith Cotton mills

Robinson checked Stillwell's references, and the supervisor of his last job at Smith Cotton Mills gave the following information:

Reason for leaving:	Discharged
Would you re-employ:	No
Additional information:	Employee dissatisfied with company practices

The questionable reference check was far outweighed in Robinson's mind by the labor market conditions and the impressive interview. After another interview, this time with his prospective supervisor, Stillwell was hired as a weaver on the third shift.

The Weaving Department was managed by a general overseer, and each of the three shifts had overseers who reported to him. In Weaving there were two main classifications of workers: weavers and loom-fixers. The loom-fixers were highly skilled workers who handled mechanical difficulties affecting the speed and quality of the work. Each loom-fixer had an average of twenty-four looms to maintain while a weaver ran from six to ten looms. Although operating problems were carried directly to the shift overseer, the head loom-fixer was actually an assistant, and second in authority and responsibility.

Having reviewed several periodic ratings that were very satisfactory, Robinson called in Stillwell for a progress and follow up interview. Stillwell appeared in a grey flannel suit and tie, which was typical of his off-duty dress. Robinson again noted his correctness of speech and his facility in oral expression. He also observed, as even more noticeable than before, Stillwell's driving ambition. When questioned on his job goals, Stillwell replied, "I want Mr. Roger's job (the Resident Manager), and if I have to step over people to get there—well, that's life." Robinson saw that this ambition extended into the social and educational realm, for Stillwell was at that time studying algebra and trigonometry by correspondence. Robinson concluded that this intelligent and resourceful young man would bear watching for he seemed to have all the basic qualifications, excluding experience, for a future managerial or supervisory position.

Managers were given wide authority in selection, in training, and in other functions of personnel administration, because of the decentralization philosophy and geographical dispersion of plants, and it was a definite part of overall company policy that promotions take place within the organization. In fact, the company manual stated: "All supervisors should aid in making our organization strong by encouraging employees to prepare for advancement by making all promotions on the basis of merit. Again, as indicated above, this corporation believes in the policy of 'promotions within the organization.'" Further, the company had unimpeded flexibility in administration of personnel policy and in promotions since the plant was organized. The company policy on promotions was not only stated but in fact carried out, for there were several instances of plant managers who rose through every step in the promotional ladder; staff positions were also open to employees on the basis of merit.

Stilwell's progress fulfilled the expectations of Robinson and other members of management. Soon after receiving a merit wage increase, Stillwell was given the opportunity of becoming a loom fixer-learner. He enthusiastically accepted the job and was placed for training under one of the older, experienced loom-fixers. His progress at this more skilled job was very rapid, and Robinson learned through an informal conversation that Stillwell had bought an old, worn loom and had it in the basement of his home. When questioned as to motive, Stillwell replied, "I want to learn everything there is to know about looms." In November of that year, Stillwell was again given a merit and regular wage increase along with his promotion to loom-fixer. Several months later, his supervisor gave Stillwell a formal warning about work quality. Shortly thereafter, an incident of a minor nature occurred between Stillwell and his supervisor, Barry Voss, the overseer of the third shift. After questioning both men, Robinson and the general overseer concluded that relations between Stillwell and his supervisor were somewhat strained and that Stillwell should be transferred to the second shift. Voss remarked, after the transfer, "This guy is getting more and more uncooperative and is trying to make me look bad on my job."

In September of the following year, Stillwell was promoted to head loom-fixer of the second shift. Soon after this, Stillwell began bragging and telling everyone about what "he" had done for the department. The general overseer counseled Stillwell and in effect told him that management was proud of the plant's progress, but that it was a team effort and not a one-man show.

During this period, Robinson developed and installed an employee suggestion system with cash awards for suggestions that were adopted. He also started an Employees Cooperative Committee that met with management to discuss problems; members were elected by secret ballot of the workers. While two of Stillwell's suggestions were adopted, he was not elected to the committee, for co-workers considered him a "loner."

In early December of that year, Stillwell came into Mr. Robinson's office and asked to be transferred back to the third shift. He stated that he and Voss had resolved their differences. He further stated that he had many ideas that would benefit the weave room operation, but that his present supervisor, Kirk Lambeth, wouldn't let him try them. After consulting with the third shift overseer, Barry Voss, Robinson complied with Stillwell's request and he was transferred back to the third shift as head loom-fixer.

For two months previous to December, management had become increasingly concerned about the problem of quality. Supervisory meetings were held and there was an intense effort to solve the problem.

On the night of January 1 of the current year, Stillwell was in the shop making a reed hook[1] for one of the weavers when the shift overseer told him to stop. He reminded Stillwell of the quality problem and told him there was more important business in the weave room; Stillwell complied with this request. The following night the same incident occurred except that both men lost their tempers. The general overseer was called and Stillwell was discharged. The supervisor's report listed as the cause—"failure to follow instructions."

APPENDIX

Campbell Textiles, Inc.

Record of Minutes of a Meeting Held by Employment Security Commission to Rule on Stillwell's Request for Unemployment Compensation

FACTS: At the time of filing his claim on January 11, claimant had last worked as head loom-fixer on January 2, for Campbell Textiles. On the night of January 1, claimant's supervisor contends that he instructed the claimant to stop fixing a reed hook, but claimant denies this. Claimant contends that he was drilling a hole in a piece of metal and when his supervisor asked him to do something else, he immediately carried out his instructions. On January 2, claimant was fixing a reed hook for a loom-fixer. Claimant's immediate supervisor appeared and used vile profanity and claimant retaliated with words not as disgusting. The general overseer was called and stated that he felt that it would be best for the claimant not to work for Campbell Textiles any longer. The employer contends that fixing a reed hook is not part of the claimant's job. However, the claimant contends that a loom-fixer called him on January 2, and informed the claimant that he could not draw ends without a reed hook. Claimant contends that he has been called on by a number of individuals to do odd jobs and he thought that these errands were furthering his job. Claimant also contends that on the night of January 2, he had fixed a pick for his immediate supervisor, which actually was not part of his job, but thought that this was also furthering his job. The employer feels that fixing a loom reed hook was not part of his job and was affecting the quality of work, but claimant feels that errands of this type were bettering the quality of work if anything. Claimant has filed one continued claim and secured employment on January 18.

---

[1] A reed hook is an instrument used by weavers to pick up broken ends of thread. The cost when purchased from a mill supplier is about $2.00.

QUESTIONS

1. Evaluate the decision of selecting Frank Stillwell.
2. At what stages should Stillwell have been counseled? About what should he have been counseled? How should this have been accomplished?
3. Is there any way in which Stillwell's assets could have been utilized by this company?
4. What is the significance of Stillwell's relationships with his supervisors?
5. Why did the company uphold the supervisor in Stillwell's discharge?
6. What considerations (such as performance, discipline, personality, circumstances, the event or act itself, past events) should enter into a decision on discharge?
7. Was Stillwell's alleged "failure to follow instructions" adequate cause for discharge? Were these two "incidents" plus past behavior just cause for discharge?

11

C. R. Baker Company

C. R. BAKER COMPANY, located in a large midwestern city, has become the largest wholesale distributor of automotive trim supplies and repair parts in its section of the country. Its operations also include the manufacture of seat covers and convertible tops. This line comprises about 50 per cent of the total sales in the trim department. Other major items in trim supplies are artificial leather, saran plastics, automotive upholstery fabrics, and other related items.

The automotive-parts line consists of a complete line of repair parts. Also included in this department are wreckers and other heavy equipment such as wheel balancers, front end alignment machines, hydraulic lifts and jacks, and other related equipment.

The company has four vice-presidents who report directly to the company president. Each vice-president is in charge of all operations in his division. The company does not have a personnel director, and so each division head is responsible for all personnel functions within his division. The company organizational chart is shown below.

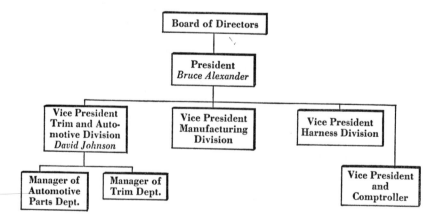

All sales are made by a staff of thirty salesmen. The salesmen report directly to David Johnson, vice-president of the trim and automotive division. Johnson feels that all of his salesmen are of generally high quality. Each salesman sells both trim supplies and automotive supplies. The salesmen make their sales calls on almost every size business from large discount department stores to service stations. The primary outlets for trim supplies are automotive trim and seat-cover shops. Automotive repair parts are primarily sold to service stations and automotive repair shops.

In August, 1963, the management of C. R. Baker Company decided to change the operations in the automotive parts department. It was decided to discontinue the present line of automotive repair parts and begin selling a new line of parts being produced by one of the "big three" automobile manufacturers. It was also decided to have the repair parts distributed to local warehouses instead of directly to the user of the parts. The function of a warehouse distributor is to stock a complete line of automotive repair parts and to sell them to retailers such as repair shops and service stations in a local area.

The management planned to hire two salesmen initially who would begin selling the new line in Minnesota. The present salesmen were no longer to sell repair parts; therefore, they could begin concentrating their sales on trim supplies and equipment. The sales volume and earnings of most salesmen were not expected to decrease, since they would have more time to call on the larger accounts in their territories. The new salesmen had to be highly qualified since they would be selling the idea to warehouse distributors of discontinuing their present line of repair parts and taking on the new line which C. R. Baker Company was selling. They would also be holding sales meetings and clinics and were to use any other means of promoting the sale of their warehouse lines.

The problem of whom to employ for the two new sales positions had to be solved. Mr. Johnson knew of three men who, he thought, would be qualified for the job. One was presently a salesman with Baker Company and another was a former salesman with the company. The third was a young college graduate who represented a large industrial manufacturer from which Johnson had been purchasing automotive parts for his division. A fourth prospect was being considered by the president, Bruce Alexander. This man was presently a salesman for a competitor and was selling to warehouse distributors in a job similar to the one Baker Company was creating.

The four men were contacted and each was very much interested in the opening. Each was thought to be well qualified and capable of being successful on the job. All were invited to visit the head office and were then interviewed by Johnson and later by the Board of Directors. In this case, the Board was going to give final approval for the men employed.

The involvement of the Board indicated the importance which the company was placing on this change in its operations.

Johnson was faced with the problem of recommending two men to the Board for their approval. The applicable information on each man is listed below.

1. JAMES E. VICTOR
   Age: 35
   Education: High school graduate
   Appearance: Acceptable
   Ability to communicate with others: Good
   Psychological tests: Results such as to recommend hiring
   Present employment: C. R. Baker Company for past 5 years as salesman
   Previous experience: Hardware store stock and delivery, 1 year (right after high school); service station attendant, 6 months; auto mechanic helper, 1½ years; air force, motor pool and auto mechanic, tech. sgt., 4 years; salesman, auto parts store, 3 years
   Marital status: Married, 3 children (ages 2, 6, 9)
   Interests: Civic club, church, gardening

James Victor is a salesman with the company in northern Minnesota with residence in Duluth. His sales volume is the third highest of all the company salesmen. He has been extremely successful in his territory and is well thought of by the company management. Victor is enthusiastic about obtaining the promotion.

2. JOHN R. WOOD
   Age: 46
   Education: 1 year of college
   Appearance: Fine—distinguished looking
   Ability to communicate with others: Good and possesses excellent vocabulary
   Psychology tests: Results such as to recommend hiring
   Present employment: Owner and operator of small automotive repair shop; was employed for 8 years as a salesman and terminated his employment in July, 1963
   Previous experience: Salesman, used cars, 5 years; army combat, captain, 4 years; salesman, new cars, 10 years
   Marital status: Single—bachelor
   Interests: Sports watching, golf

John R. Wood turned in his resignation to C. R. Baker Company in May, 1963, because he had planned to purchase an automotive repair shop. The shop was bought in May. The company requested that Wood continue to work the territory until they found a satisfactory replacement. By the end of July, a salesman had been trained and Wood terminated his employment. During the period from May to July, Wood had been working for Baker Company and running his new business.

In August, Johnson approached Wood and asked about his interest in the job. Wood indicated that he would definitely be interested, commenting to Johnson that he would plan to retain his automotive shop even if he were hired. While employed by Baker, Wood had been eminently successful. He had increased the sales volume in one territory to double its previous volume. About one year before resigning, he had been working a large and better territory in eastern Minnesota and had increased sales in this area by 20 per cent in his first year. For the last three years that he worked for Baker Company, he had the second highest sales volume among all the salesmen.

3. ROBERT R. SMITH

Age: 48

Education: High school graduate

Appearance: Satisfactory

Ability to communicate: Good—Easy, ready conversationist with excellent sense of humor

Psychological tests: Results such as to recommend hiring

Present employment: Sales representative for Gopher Automotive Parts Company, a competitor of C. R. Baker Company, for 15 years

Previous experience: Assembly-line worker and foreman, automobile manufacturing, 8 years; army, clerical capacity, 4 years; salesman, automotive lubricants, 3 years

Marital status: Married, 4 children (ages 10, 14, 17, 18)

Interests: Gardening, hunting, fishing

Smith has fifteen years' experience of selling to warehouse distributors. He is presently a sales representative for a competitor in a job similar to the one which Baker Company is creating. He is an excellent salesman and possesses this added experience which none of the other three applicants has.

4. FRANK P. PRIVETTE

Age: 30

Education: College graduate

Appearance: Tall and handsome

Ability to communicate with others: Excellent—earnest and convincing

Psychological tests: Results such as to recommend hiring

Present employment: General Parts Corporation, 3 years as salesman

Previous experience: Navy (ensign to lt.j.g.) 4 years, football coach and physical education, preparatory school, 2 years

College activities: "C" student; fullback on football team, catcher on baseball team; fraternity president

Marital status: Married, 2 children (ages 3, 5)

Interests: Officiating at sports, sports announcing for radio, watching TV

Frank Privette had become known to Johnson since he represented the company from which C. R. Baker Company purchased a large volume of its automotive parts. He was recommended because he had impressed Johnson in his dealings with Baker Company. He seemed to be aggressive and to possess excellent qualities for a salesman. Johnson had not contacted General Parts Corporation nor had he requested references concerning Privette since he did not want to jeopardize Privette's job with General Parts. Privette's experience was in the area of selling automotive parts, and his customers were well established when he took the job. Johnson did not know about his ability to increase sales and generate new customers.

In September, 1963, Johnson decided to employ Smith, his recommendation having the approval of the Board of Directors. In October, Johnson had to select the additional salesman from among the three remaining applicants.

QUESTIONS

1. What observation can be made concerning the company organization?
2. Should a man who has resigned from a company be considered for re-employment at a later time?
3. What qualities of each applicant should Baker Company consider as the most important for the positions that are open?
4. How much should the fact of Privette's educational level be weighed in reaching a decision?
5. How sound was the selection of Smith as the company's first choice?
6. Which man from among the remaining three should Johnson decide to employ and recommend for approval?
7. What additional information concerning the candidates would be helpful to have in reaching a decision?

12

Midwest Insurance Company

THE MIDWEST INSURANCE COMPANY was founded in the early 1930's and has since become one of the largest casualty underwriting companies in the country. Company management has credited this growth to a "spare-no-expense" policy in developing only the most advanced insurance techniques and using the latest office equipment available. In its earlier days, the company had sold only automobile coverage, but at present it sells all types of casualty insurance. One of the company's regional offices was located in a large Midwestern city. This office had been established in 1941 with a branch office manager and four employees. The present branch office manager, Ralph Maddox, had been transferred to this position in July, 1952. He was responsible for complete policy service to all policy-holders in a seven state area.

Exhibit 1 shows the organizational chart as of January, 1964. Five unit managers were allocated duties on a division-of-state basis. Each unit was a service department in itself, complete with its own office staff of approximately 28 people. The section supervisors were considered first-line supervisors for each division within the unit. The number of employees working in each section varied slightly, depending upon the number of policyholders for the states assigned to the unit.

The branch office had a written policy providing for the training of new personnel who were expected eventually to fill the position of section supervisor. These prospective trainees were selected by Maddox after being recommended to him by the personnel department. Maddox and the other executives in the branch office had agreed that the trainees would—as far as they could determine at the time—eventually be capable of fulfilling the job of branch office manager after progressing successfully through the other levels of management. A trainee received his first "merit increase" after three months. After an additional six months, he received another increase. A third increase was given after eighteen months with the company. If the trainee were placed on duty as a section supervisor prior to the third scheduled increase, he received the increase at the time he was removed from the training status. Maddox was responsible for scheduling the program for the trainees and passing on salary reviews of all employees in the branch office. The trainees were usually assigned to different units on a rotation plan under the supervision of the unit manager and his assistant. It was unusual for a trainee to remain in the same unit during the entire training program, but this did occasionally happen.

The Standard Procedure book published by the home office stated that the hiring and discharging of employees would be one of the responsibilities of the unit manager. In the 1961, 1962, and 1963 yearly audits of the branch office by company vice-presidents, Maddox had been criticized for not delegating this authority.

The "personnel department" consisted of Stella Mason. Stella tested and interviewed all job applicants after written requisitions for new employees were forwarded to her by the unit managers. When Stella received these requisitions, she would place an advertisement in the local papers, interview applicants, administer prescribed aptitude tests, evaluate the results, and recommend the applicant to Maddox.

Stella, attractive and pleasant, had been with Midwest since 1947. Prior to her transfer to the branch office in 1954, she had been a typing supervisor in the home office. Because of her length of service with the company and her wide knowledge of company operations, Stella had been made personnel manager by the previous branch office manager. The unit managers believed that Stella was quite capable of making the primary selection of prospective trainees from the applicants who responded to the advertisements in the local papers.

In December, 1963, Maddox received a notice from the home office that George Preston, supervisor of the accounting section in unit three, was to be transferred to another branch office in the following August or September. There were no supervisory trainees in the office, and Maddox told Stella to find an acceptable applicant. Stella interviewed two applicants and gave the prescribed tests. After an evaluation, she decided to recommend John Steed.

Steed was twenty-two years old, single, and living with his mother and stepfather. He was a high school graduate with a good scholastic record and had just completed a three-year enlistment in the Army. Stella made her selection in view of Steed's outstanding record of achievement in school and his high scores on the aptitude tests. Even though Steed was young in appearance, Stella felt he would eventually be capable of becoming a branch office manager. Stella entered these remarks on Steed's temporary personnel record and gave the record and her recommendation to Maddox.

After talking informally with Steed for some time, Maddox told him he was accepted for the trainee position. Maddox then explained the supervisory training program, general company policies, the organization of the branch office, and the "merit increase" program. Steed accepted the offer with a great deal of enthusiasm. Maddox then took Steed and introduced him to Harry Lever, the manager of Unit Three. Lever and his assistant, Jim Olsen, worked out a training program for Steed which would cover all phases of work in the unit. Steed's first assignment was with the accounting section under the direction of George Preston. Preston immediately placed Steed with Ruth and Lois, two adjusters who were to help Steed become acquainted with their work.

Two weeks after Steed started with the accounting section, Ruth and Lois complained to Lever that Steed was "causing a lot of confusion and trying to change everything around." They felt that he was too eager to criticize their work and point out their errors. Lever called Steed to his desk and explained that it would be necessary to make a real effort to get along with the girls because he was going to be there for only a short time. Steed promised "to try to do better," but made no further comment. Lever felt that Steed was learning the work quickly and that he was progressing satisfactorily. He recorded the incident and forwarded it to Stella to be placed in Steed's personnel records. Approximately one week later, Lever overheard Ruth and Lois arguing about one of the customer's policies. He called the girls to his desk and asked them what the commotion was about. Both girls complained excitedly about Steed's highhanded methods and said that he was still trying to change the whole section around. Lever told the girls they would have to work things out among themselves and "settle down within thirty days or be discharged." Ruth and Lois returned to their work without further comment.

Lever called Steed to his desk and told him that the girls were upset about the way they were being treated. He warned Steed that he would have to make much more of an effort to get along peaceably with them. Steed explained that he just wanted them to try out some of his ideas and he had experienced a little trouble explaining what he wanted the girls to do. Lever reminded Steed that he was only a trainee and should not be trying to impose his ideas on the department. He terminated the interview by telling Steed he would begin working with Amy on the following day. Amy was a poster in the accounting section.

Thinking about these incidents, Lever felt Steed might be "playing the girls off against each other," because everyone in the section had been getting along fine before Steed was assigned to Unit Three.

Two days later, Amy and Preston, head of the accounting section, came to see Lever. Amy was crying and explained that Steed had been speaking harshly to her while criticizing her work. Lever told Amy that he would put Steed in another section for a few months, and—according to Lever— that seemed to please Amy.

During the next five months, Steed was sent from one section to another

in Unit Three. Lever and Olsen, his assistant, observed that Steed's work
was satisfactory in sections where men were predominent, but where
Steed had to work with the women there were complaints from section
supervisors. During these months Lever conferred with other unit managers, the section supervisors in Unit Three, and Maddox. Most of these
discussions centered on Steed, progress, and how he got along with other
employees.

In July, Steed's stepfather told him he would have to move out of his
home and live with someone else. Steed had confided in Sam Williams,
the assistant manager of Unit Five, about his personal problems. Williams
was also a bachelor, but he was about ten years older than Steed. When
told of Steed's predicament, Williams offered to let Steed live with him
for a short time. In the evenings, Steed and Williams talked about Steed's
family problems and the progress he was making in the training program.
Williams became interested in Steed's training progress and talked with
Lever and Maddox about Steed's personal problems. During these talks,
Lever became convinced that perhaps part of Steed's problem might have
been brought about by his unusual family situation. However, when he
discussed this possibility with Maddox, the latter expressed his belief that
this did not seem likely.

Early in August, 1964, Preston was transferred to another branch office,
and Maddox reviewed Steed's personnel records. He remembered that he
had granted Steed a three-month wage increase, but he was somewhat
surprised to see numerous incident reports attached to Steed's personnel
records. He reviewed each report and reached the conclusion that in spite
of the unfavorable reports, Steed had apparently received enough training to be promoted to supervisor of the accounting section. He told Lever
of his decision to promote Steed and then called Steed to his office. Maddox
told him that he was no longer in the training program and would be
responsible for the functions of the accounting section. Maddox and Lever
believed that Steed was not too impressed with the news. Lever returned
with Steed to the accounting section and told the girls of the promotion.

For a two-week period following Steed's promotion, Lever felt there
was an easing of tension in the accounting section. On the third Wednesday of the month, the supervisors of the Claims and Underwriting sections came to Lever and told him Steed was causing a lot of trouble with
the people in their sections. Before Lever had a chance to call Steed in
for another conference, four section supervisors from other units and two
of the unit managers told Lever that Steed was interfering with the work
of the rest of the office personnel. Lever immediately picked up Steed's
personnel record, and with Maddox, reviewed the new incidents and
Steed's records. They concluded that Steed should be given only thirty
days "to conform or be discharged." Lever had at first insisted that Steed
be given no longer than two weeks, but Maddox believed it would be

more fair to give him a little longer. In addition, Maddox reminded Lever that the extra time would be the minimum time needed to prepare someone else for the job. Lever then went to Steed's section and told Steed he was being placed on a thirty-day notice and would have "this last chance to conform to accepted office standards of conduct." Steed acted quite surprised at this sudden notification. He declared that he felt his work had been satisfactory, and it did not seem fair that after all this time he could not be shown a little consideration. Lever told Steed to see Maddox if he did not like the decision. Without answering, Steed immediately entered Maddox's office.

Ten minutes later, Steed passed by Lever's desk and said, "I guess I'll be around here for a while after all. I'm not on any thirty-day probation!" Lever was not sure how he should interpret this remark, but resisted the temptation to call for an immediate conference with Steed and Maddox.

Two days later when the weekend had arrived, Maddox had still not called Lever to his office to offer any explanation, and Lever decided that he had waited long enough. He walked into Maddox's office.

Maddox looked up from his desk when Lever entered the office. "What's on your mind?"

Lever told him, "I'd like to know about Steed."

"What about him? Didn't he tell you what I had decided?"

"He told me he wasn't on a probationary notice, but I feel that you should have at least talked with me again before you told him he wasn't going to be put on probation. If we were wrong in making our original decision, I'd like to know your thinking about it."

"Look, Lever, I can change my mind without asking for your permission. I told Steed we would give him another chance without the probationary threat hanging over his head. I'm satisfied that he'll shape up, and as far as I'm concerned, that ends the matter."

QUESTIONS

1. How would you evaluate the relationships between:
   a. Lever, Olsen, and Preston?
   b. Steed and Williams?

2. What significane do you attach to the "temporary easing of tensions" after Steed's promotion?

3. In what ways might the counseling of Steed have been improved?

4. Why do you think Steed acted as he did in
   a. installing new methods as a trainee?
   b. interfering with other departments?

5. How should Maddox have acted in the probationary matter and the change thereof?

6. What do you think of the continued forbearance exercised by Maddox with regard to Steed?

7. Analyze organizational aspects of this case.

8. What do you make of Steed's family situation? What do you think of Maddox's evaluation thereof?

9. If you were hired as a consultant by Maddox to revise the selection and training procedure, what would you recommend?

10. What other concepts or principles of personnel management are suggested in this case?

EXHIBIT 1

Midwest Insurance Company

Branch Office Organizational Chart

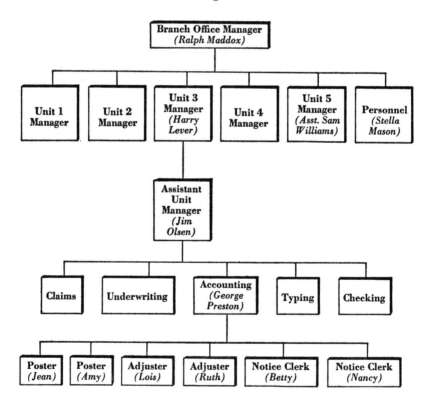

SECTION III

Training and Development

ONE OF THE APPALLINGLY REMISS AREAS of personnel management centers around knowledge of learning theory. At both employee and management levels, indoctrination, training, and development programs are executed with all too little attention to the way people learn.

Indoctrination is the time when a new employee is becoming part of the organization or else is being conditioned against it. Studies of separations have supported, again and again, the key place of effective induction since an inordinately high percentage of separations transpire within the first six months of employment (for college graduates this period might be extended somewhat).

Training in specific job assignments has undergone little improvement in the past twenty years, limited mainly to progress in refined analysis of tasks for instructional purposes and in the introduction of programed learning. But learning by management trainees retains many of the old, glaring weaknesses of passive learning, observational learning, and time waste through poor assignments.

Development has probably received more attention than any other area of personnel management during the past two decades, and yet the planned growth of employees is still largely on a sporadic, disjointed, hit-or-miss basis. Here, too, a great deal more work needs to be done in planning, relating to learning concepts, and evaluating.

SECTION III

Training and Development

13

The Brady Harris Department Stores

THE BRADY HARRIS DEPARTMENT STORES are medium size department stores located in Reading and Wilkes-Barre, Pennsylvania. The original Brady Harris was founded in Reading in 1885 by two young merchandisers, W. F. Brady and W. H. Harris. W. H. Harris opened another store in Wilkes-Barre, Pennsylvania in 1902. W. F. Brady retired in 1907 and W. H. Harris managed both stores until his death in 1920. Following his death, his son, John H. Harris, became head of the two stores. He remained president until 1946. In 1946, both stores were purchased by Richards Realty Company, Inc. of Reading. Upon retirement of Harris, Paul White became president of Brady Harris.

Brady Harris handled all types of medium- and higher-price merchandise normally found in department stores and was considered one of the most profitable stores in eastern Pennsylvania. The stores weathered the depression of the 1930's and by 1964 had a sales volume of approximately $2,500,000.

In 1955, James Brown joined the staff of the Reading store, and after ten years of service he held the position of manager of the first floor. The store was divided for management purposes by floors, each floor having a separate manager. Brown was a graduate of one of the larger universities in Pennsylvania and before joining the Brady Harris staff had taught in the public schools of Scranton.

In 1962, when Brown was promoted to the position of first floor manager, he drew up a training program for salespeople on his floor and also a training program for new employees. Prior to 1962, the company did not have a training program for its salespeople and relied on the old employees, with the help of the floorwalker and floor manager, to train new employees. The two programs as drawn up by Brown were submitted to top management for approval and were adopted not only for the first floor but for all floors.

The new employee training program utilized a sponsor from the department in which the new employee was to work, who was charged with the responsibility of introducing the new employee to his or her job. (The responsibilities of the sponsor and the compensation received by the sponsor for this work are outlined in Exhibit 1.) New employees, all women, were hired as sales clerks after taking a series of tests designed to measure the interest and intelligence of the individual. There were no definite educational requirements for employment with Brady Harris, but the store preferred high school graduates. All salespeople were paid a salary plus a bonus for all sales above an established amount.

The training program for all salespeople as introduced by Brown was as follows: Each month of the year was designated a special month. As an example, the month of April was designated as "Professional Selling Month at Brady Harris." Once a week during each week of the month, all of the salespeople came to work one-half hour early for a training period. At these meetings, all of the employees were given a copy of the subject matter to be discussed. Exhibit 2 through 9 are examples of the type of material presented for discussion. The floorwalkers were given the training material the day before the meetings, and they were in charge of these meetings. After the salespeople read the material, a discussion was conducted on what had been presented. The employees were not compensated for the extra half hour in the morning, although it was mandatory that all salespeople attend.

The program as introduced by Brown remained in effect for two years. In 1964, Brady Harris, along with other stores, started the practice of staying open late on certain days. The longer working day created by this practice forced Brady Harris to stagger their work force to keep the total working hours per week the same as before. With this staggered arrangement, all of the employees never reported at the same time in the morning. Unable to work out a satisfactory meeting arrangement, the training program was dropped. The sponsor system for the new employees, however, was not dropped.

Brown felt that the program had been a success and that both the store and the employees had benefited from it. Therefore, in March of 1965 he was considering ways of getting all of the employees together again and continuing the program. He felt the same type of program that was used in the past should be continued. Even though the store employed a personnel director, Brown felt that it would be his responsibility to get the program started again.

EXHIBIT 1

The Brady Harris Department Stores

Sponsor System

Congratulations—

YOU HAVE BEEN CHOSEN by your divisional merchandise manager with the approval of the personnel director and the general manager to serve as sponsor of your department!

You are no doubt in a fog wondering just what this position entails; it is the purpose of this meeting to explain to you just what a Sponsor System is, how it operates, and just how you fit into the picture.

Purpose

To welcome your new associate and start to make her feel at home. Your interpretation of the policies and systems of Brady Harris, as well as its spirit of service to the customer will greatly influence the newcomer to our organization. The new person's impression of Brady Harris and her desire to do a good job will largely depend upon her reception in the department.

New employees need encouragement, assistance and a sense of direction. You are to be friend, counselor, and hostess.

This will shorten learning periods and achieve standards of efficiency more quickly through a planned system of job induction.

It will also strengthen the link between the initial training received in the classroom and training received on the job. It will further stimulate the efficiency of the regular employees and promote good department morale.

What is a Sponsor?

A sponsor is a *hostess,* who welcomes the new person and makes her feel at home in new and strange surroundings.

A sponsor is a *teacher,* who must be able to organize material, and present it convincingly.

A sponsor is a *supervisor.* In addition to the formal organized instruction which she gives the first few days, she maintains a casual but watchful eye over the new person. She corrects mistakes before they become habits, and directs wherever she can and makes suggestions.

Responsibilities of a Sponsor

It is recommended that you concentrate on your sponsoring in the early morning and late afternoons, and give only necessary instructions when it is required during the busy hours of the day.

A. GENERAL INFORMATION

1. Where to keep personal belongings.
2. The new person should meet: divisional merchandise manager and his assistant and others in department.
3. Explain the proper method of punching the time card, morning, noon, and night.
4. Show the new person the department layout, tubes, central wrapping desk, information desk, where supplies are kept, etc.
5. See that she is supplied with sales books, pencil, tax card and other necessary supplies.
6. See that she knows the location of various forms.
7. Tell new salesperson if similar merchandise is carried in any other department in the store.
8. Go over information on price tickets.
9. If additional information is needed on the sales ticket other than listing the merchandise and price, explain what is necessary and WHY.
10. Give a general idea of the merchandise layout in the department. Explain arrangement of stock according to size, color, price or other methods and where additional stock is kept.
11. Instruct in specific merchandise facts. This should include: advertised merchandise, fashion highlights, materials, price justification, color fastness, launderability, and durability.
12. Teach new employee selling techniques, suggestive selling, trading up, how to greet customers, etc.

B. SYSTEM INFORMATION

1. Explain the system for handling exchange and returns.
2. Show new person the disposition of each copy of salescheck.
3. How to handle special orders and deliveries.
4. Telephone orders.
5. Alterations, monogramming, engraving, repairs, etc.
6. "Will Call" merchandise or hold items, gift wrapping, control of price tags, and other special methods.
7. Lost sale slips.
8. Check with new employee to make certain that she understands thoroughly the operation of the tube system.
9. Explain Brady Harris manner of answering the telephone (answer phone promptly, give department and name. Speak clearly and in a friendly tone).

C. STOCK RESPONSIBILITY

1. Stress the importance of being a good housekeeper and explain the fact that each salesperson must do her share of stock work daily.
2. Explain how orderly stock arrangement aids selling.
3. Emphasize the fact that clean, neat stock impresses the customer.
4. Show how to display the merchandise most effectively for selling; for example, how to fold, how to hang, etc.

5. Explain the duties that are to be done in the morning, during the day and in the evening . . . demonstrate how it should be done and WHY.
6. Make sure the salesperson understands and sees just what her stock is and knows that she is directly responsible for the care of that stock.

D. OTHER RESPONSIBILITIES

1. Morale building. The sponsor usually has a definite responsibility to build morale and store spirit among both new employees and those who have been on the job for a longer period of time.
2. Follow-up work. Sponsors have follow-up duties. Their close contact with new people puts them in an advantageous position to follow up on training and personal adjustment of the employees to the job.

How is Sponsor compensated for her work?

You will receive $2.00 for each new full-time salesperson whom you train. A record will be kept in the personnel department of the number of people trained by each sponsor; at the end of each month a tally will be made and you will be compensated at the above rate.

For how long a period is the Sponsor responsible for the new employee? Are there any written reports to be made?

You shall be responsible for the new employee for a period of two weeks. At the end of that period you are requested to turn into the Personnel Department a "Sponsor's Rating of New Salesperson." The new trainee will also fill out and turn in a "Questionnaire."

If you should have any questions or should any problems arise, don't hesitate to contact the personnel department for assistance!

EXHIBIT 2

The Brady Harris Department Stores

April Is Professional Selling Month at Brady Harris

Is PERSONALITY MORE IMPORTANT THAN INTELLIGENCE in professional selling? It is more important in getting along in the world. When a good brain is matched against a good personality, the latter will usually come out on top. Intelligence will provide the tools for getting along, but personality provides the real thing.

The reason personality is more important is that you can do something about personality control, but you can't do anything about your quota of intelligence. High, low, or average, you have to make out with what you have. But if you have the desire and determination, you can work over undesirable personality traits and turn them in the direction of success.

While it is very difficult to bring about changes in basic personality patterns, it is not so difficult to change habits and attitudes that go against personality development. Such weak personality traits as carelessness and laziness can be overcome. Valuable attributes such as steadfastness, and cheerfulness are acquirable habits.

H. Chandler Hunt, Connecticut educator, showed that personality qualities are vastly more important than basic technical skills in getting and holding a job. From the records of 4,000 discharged employees in seventy-five different companies, Hunt found that only 400 were let out for lack of specific skill, in work involving shorthand, typewriting, English, bookkeeping, spelling, etc. The remaining 3,600 were discharged for controllable personality faults. More than 1,200 were dropped for either laziness, failure to cooperate, or sheer carelessness. Other causes were lack of ambition, initiative, courtesy and loyalty, of dishonesty, tardiness and nonillness absences.

These are all personality qualities of our own making. We acquired them; hence the power to change them is within our own control.

Personality makes a successful salesperson. Your personality is the most important factor in *your* future; so take time to examine yourself—study your personality.

EXHIBIT 3

The Brady Harris Department Stores

April Is Professional Selling Month at Brady Harris

SUCCESS IN SELLING

SELLING IS A PROFESSION requiring tact and ability, but you do not have to be a genius to succeed at selling.

Develop a professional attitude. Believe in your ability to sell. Good selling is more than the ability to talk—"a gift of gab." It is more than a friendly smile. It is an orderly series of steps which lead from greeting the customer to bidding her good-bye.

First let's set the stage for selling. . . .

Live your part—be enthusiastic, be alert, be interested, be physically fit.
Know your lines—know your merchandise (colors, sizes, prices, styles), use and care, other facts. Know your systems and services.
Have your props ready—know what is advertised, know your window displays, have proper merchandise signs, have pencil, salesbooks and other supplies.
On stage—department neat and orderly, ready to greet customer.

How to sell. . . .

Welcome the customer—promptly, individually, and courteously, put her at ease with a friendly smile, find out her needs, show a personal interest in her needs.

Present the merchandise—be selective, show the best choice from your stock for her needs. Demonstrate it effectively—dramatize. Stress value points related to her needs. Show enough merchandise to help the customer but not confuse her. Get merchandise into customer's hands.

Reach a decision—develop an interest in personal ownership, repeat key selling points in value, use and care.

Meet customer's reservations.

Close the sale.

Suggest related items, additional items, etc.

Test the sale—Did you satisfy the customer?

Did you build good will for the store?

Will the customer come back to you?

IF THE CUSTOMER IS SATISFIED YOU HAVE *SUCCEEDED*

The ability to sell successfully is not born in you. It is learned by study and practice. No matter how much you know, there is always more to be learned. No matter how little you know, you can learn to sell successfully if you work hard at it.

EXHIBIT 4

The Brady Harris Department Stores

April Is Professional Selling Month at Brady Harris

THE DREAM SALESPERSON or
MARKS OF THE PROFESSIONAL SALESPERSON

LET'S EXAMINE some of the personal characteristics of the Brady Harris Dream Salesperson or Marks of the Professional Salesperson.

She is interested in her customer and in her store. She is loyal to her store and proud of her merchandise. She is sincere and dependable, straightforward and fair. She can be counted on to do her best without supervision; she thrives on responsibility and takes new duties in her stride. She likes new merchandise, new ideas and better ways of doing things—she is open-minded.

She is not easily irritated and does not often "fly off the handle"—she is even-tempered. She is consistent and maintains high standards at all times. She is not afraid of work and sticks to a job until it is finished. She loves her work and enjoys doing it. She takes pride in knowing her job thoroughly and learns everything she can about her department so she can take advantage of promotions which may come her way if she is qualified.

She is stable, emotionally mature and is not easily excited, confused or embarrassed. She is courteous both to her customers and her fellow workers. She believes action speaks louder than words and therefore never brags. She is cheerful even in difficult situations and looks for the best in people.

She is skillful in presenting merchandise to customers effectively and she is ready with suitable suggestions. She handles even difficult customers with calm, dignified efficiency.

Honesty is important to the professional salesperson, in her dealings with her employer and her customer. She is honest with time, merchandise, and service, just as she is with money.

Analyze yourself; find out on what "Marks of the Professional Salesperson" you need to work and sincerely try to improve.

You are the best—but could You be better?

EXHIBIT 5

The Brady Harris Department Stores

April Is Professional Selling Month at Brady Harris

You CAN OPERATE a good department store in a tent, if the service is outstanding. Service, whether in a department store, hotel, airlines, or any other business, is often the factor which tips the scale FOR or AGAINST success.

Brady Harris, for instance, must compete with other stores which have demonstrated ability to operate with efficiency and dependability and which offer quality merchandise—sometimes the same brand.

But what does the customer want when she goes into a store? She wants courtesy, friendliness and to be given the feeling that she is SPECIAL and her needs are important, not only to her, but to you—the salesperson.

Now, here are two points to remember—good salespeople have an instinctive feeling toward this business of giving the customer that little extra or special attention and she has the habit of making customers feel like an individual and not just another customer. Make your customer feel special, call her by name, select merchandise for her needs, be a good listener. Such a courteous act makes customers feel important—creates good will.

The most lasting impression made by any store are the "human impressions" —the friendliness, warmth, and personal interest of the salesperson who answers the phone, the salesperson who provides the merchandise that satisfied needs, the salesperson who gives that little extra or special attention. . . .

These factors are more important in salespeople than individuals in business or industry. Salespeople represent their company. The impression they make stands for their company more than its advertising, displays, or products.

Some of the merchandise we carry may be similar to that of a competitor, but if we, the salespeople, are friendly, sincere and genuinely interested in our customers, that is the way customers will remember the store and the warm feeling the customers have as a result will be reflected in their preference for our store's merchandise.

So be a professional salesperson and REMEMBER—the service of selling is the selling of SERVICE.

EXHIBIT 6

The Brady Harris Department Stores

May Is Economy Month at Brady Harris

. . . . So LET'S REMEMBER that store profit is measured in *pennies*.

Let's just suppose that you owned and operated a department store similar to Brady Harris. Your store sold thousands and thousands of dollars worth of merchandise during the year. The end of the year, you and your bookkeeper sit down together and look over the operating figures to see how much money you have made. To make it simple, you break it down to each dollar, that is, find out how much profit you made out of each dollar of the store's sales. Here is what you find:

Your *cost of sales* on each dollar is 63 cents. This is the cost of merchandise, mark-downs, stock shortages, freight or postage.

Your *direct expenses* are 15 cents. This includes salaries and your newspaper advertising.

Your *indirect expenses* are 19 cents. This is your rent, lights, supplies and all other operating expenses not included above.

You then add all these expenses up: 63 + 15 + 19 = 97 cents. This is your cost of doing business for the year for each dollar in sales.

You are surprised and discouraged to see that when you subtract this 97 cents from $1.00, you get only *three cents profit* on each dollar and this is even *before* Uncle Sam gets his share in taxes—which you know is a big chunk.

You decide that you must do better next year because you realize you could put the money you have invested in the store in the bank and draw more interest than the profit you've made.

But—you like retailing and are determined to keep trying; so you make the following New Year's Resolutions:

1. Starting right now, I'm going to *train* my salespeople and buyers to do a better job. I'm going to have classes and meetings every week.

2. I'm going to cut my *cost of sales* by being sure my buyers buy the right merchandise, in the right quantities, at the right price and time. I'm going to see that they are on their guard against stock shortages and too many mark-downs. I'm going to have them learn and use the most economical ways to have their merchandise shipped to the store.

3. I'm going to cut my *direct expenses* by training my salespeople to sell more, to trade up, to suggest. I'm going to be sure my buyers spend their advertising money wisely.

4. I'm going to cut my *indirect expenses* by talking *economy* day in and day out to everyone in the store who uses store supplies. I'm going to emphasize the high cost of these supplies and show them how wasting them can keep my store from making a profit.

5. I'm going to show them that a store's profit is measured in pennies and how they, through carelessness, can wipe out this profit very easily.

After I do all these things, I feel better because I know I will have a strong, growing store that can give my employees job security for years to come.

EXHIBIT 7

The Brady Harris Department Stores

May Is Economy Month at Brady Harris

. . . . So, TO BE FAIR, let's talk about something we all have the same amount of. It wouldn't be wealth, youth, love, happiness; we all have these in different amounts. There is one thing, however, that we all have in equal quantities. This is TIME. The richest, the poorest, the oldest and the youngest —all have 24 hours in each day. We are certainly all equal in this respect.

There is a big difference, however, even in this equality of time. That difference is How We USE This Time. Our time is a natural resource that is very valuable. All of us here have found we must sell some of our valuable time so that we may have the means of enjoying the rest of it.

For instance, here at Brady Harris, we sell the store about 7 hours a day, 6 days a week. The store buys this time and pays us for it. Therefore, the store has a moral and legal right to tell us how the time should be used.

Brady Harris' policy toward this time it purchases follows; (you will note how closely it follows our merchandising policies)

1. *Top Resources*—Brady Harris buys time from only those it feels will sell that time honestly and willingly.

2. *No irregulars*—Just as Brady Harris refuses to carry "seconds" or inferior merchandise, it dislikes to buy time from employees whose time is not the very best they have to offer.

3. *Satisfaction guaranteed*—Just as Brady Harris guarantees everything it sells to customers, so does it guarantee the time spent in courteous, efficient, friendly service to that customer.

4. *Economy*—Just as Brady Harris teaches economy in the use of store supplies, so does the store expect a minimum of waste in the time you sell the store.

. . . . So let's all remember *time is Money*, Brady Harris' money. We are expected to spend it wisely and well, just as our buyers spend their merchandising dollars. Let's give full value for every minute, every hour, and we will be rewarded with more sales, bigger bonuses, promotional opportunities, and a feeling of a job well done.

EXHIBIT 8

The Brady Harris Department Stores

May Is Economy Month at Brady Harris

IT'S IN THE BAG!
(or box, ribbon, paper, tissue, tape and other store supplies)

BY THE ABOVE STATEMENT we mean that profit or loss is often affected by what you as a salesperson do after you make a sale.

Test yourself by the checklist below and see where *you* stand.

Profitable Sale, if you
1. use smallest bag possible
2. don't offer gift box unless asked
3. Conserve ribbon, tape and tissue, etc.
4. Care for supplies as you do your merchandise
5. maintain proper supplies in your department

Possible loss, if you
1. use first bag you see regardless of size
2. assume it's a gift and it isn't
3. waste these items
4. are careless with store supplies
5. never have proper size box, bag, etc.

Remember, "Profits Are Measured in Pennies," so don't let these pennies be lost in your department through soiled bags, damaged gift boxes and any other waste of costly store supplies.

EXHIBIT 9

The Brady Harris Department Stores

May Is Economy Month at Brady Harris

... So LET'S ECONOMIZE by bringing all our good habits to work with us. For instance:

When we buy our groceries, we are careful to stay within our budget; we make good buys, depend on known brands. Let's be sure we follow the same principles in our buying here.

We try to keep our homes spic and span in case friends drop in. Here, we *know* friends are coming to see us, so let's be ready for them.

We try to keep drawers, closets, desks, etc., neat and orderly at home. It's a bigger job here, but it's just as important.

At home we conserve time, lights, food and clothing, as a matter of good sense. It makes just as much sense here in supplies, time and merchandise.

In our home, we show our guests the very best in gracious courteous hospitality. It's of tremendous importance that we treat our customer guest the same way here.

If a guest calls at our home, we stop what we are doing and greet them. Let's remember this in our department if we happen to be busy with stock when a customer approaches. When we are expecting guests for dinner, we wouldn't think of not being at home when they arrive. We know customers are coming; let's "be at home" in our departments when they arrive.

We don't discuss family matters and problems or argue in the presence of our guests at home. This is a fine policy to follow in front of our customer guests, also.

In other words, let's not *waste* these good habits we have learned over the years. It will be both economical and profitable to apply each and every one of them to our jobs, as well as our homes.

QUESTIONS

1. What is your opinion of the sponsor system as outlined in Exhibit 1?
2. What do you think of the compensation per new employee sponsored?
3. If you were an employee, how would you feel about having to report to work one-half hour early for the training class?

4. Do you think the floor managers should have been in charge of the training class instead of the floorwalker?

5. What would you suggest to Mr. Brown about arranging for a new time to conduct the training class?

6. How do you evaluate the quality of the material presented during the training class? Would you add to or subtract from the material presented?

7. What are your views on the way the training classes were conducted in the past? If the program is started again, how should the classes be conducted?

8. What do you think of the policy of having a training class every week of every month?

9. How do you react to the statement that "even though the store employed a personnel director, Brown felt that it would be his responsibility to get the program started again"?

14

State Farm Supply, Inc.

STATE FARM SUPPLY, INC., operates more than 50 retail farm supply stores in a two-state area of the Midwest. The stores sell primarily feeds, seeds, and fertilizers, but also carry a wide variety of other supplies used by farmers and gardeners. These other lines include insecticides, fencing, hardware, paints, oil and grease, tires, batteries, stock medicines, electrical appliances, and milking machines. Some of the stores operate an egg-marketing service, and most of the stores buy grain from local producers and resell it locally or to the company's feed mill. The sales of the stores vary from $25,000 per year for a few of the smaller stores up to almost $1 million for the largest.

The individual stores are generally named for the county in which they are located. Each store is operated by a manager who is responsible directly to a store supervisor. The company has four store supervisors, with the 50 stores divided about evenly between the four. The managers are relatively independent, having to get approval from their supervisor only on decisions involving policy changes, large purchases not covered by the store's budget, or salary increases for employees.

State Farm Supply has experienced exceptional growth, starting with just one store less than 25 years ago. Managers for the various stores have been obtained in many different ways. During the early growth period many managers were hired with little or no previous managerial training. Managers at some stores developed into excellent managers, while some stores have had a chronic problem of high turnover of managers. This high turnover, plus a policy of opening one or two new stores each year, has placed a burden on the company in finding qualified managers. In the past the company was able to promote some of the men who originally started to work as helpers in the store. This policy has largely been discontinued since it is seldom that a man qualified to assume the increased responsibilities of a manager can be found in this manner. The difficulty of promoting from within has been compounded by recent attempts of the company to raise the standards of its managers.

State Farm Supply has no consistent method of recruiting, selecting, or training new managers for its stores. Men who wish to apply for a manager position do so through the personnel department of the home office. The personnel department consists of the director, who is a college graduate with a major in personnel administration, and one assistant. Present store managers, store supervisors, and other executive personnel are encouraged to recommend persons whom they consider to be prospective manager material. A number of additional applicants hear about job openings or know of the company and apply at the home office for manager jobs on their own. No other type of recruiting is done. When an opening occurs and there is no one to fill it, the company generally promotes an assistant manager from one of the larger stores. As pointed out, this has not been an entirely satisfactory procedure and contributes to the fact that only five of the company's store managers are college graduates.

A person who applies for a position as store manager fills out a personal history form and attaches any letters of recommendation he may have. His first interview is with the personnel director. If the director finds that the applicant shows promise and meets the company's minimum requirements (a high school education is required; some experience in agricultural work is desired; managerial experience is an asset but is not an absolute requirement), he is referred to the director of marketing, under whose jurisdiction all the store managers fall. The director of marketing interviews the applicant and reviews the personal history form. If the man receives approval here, he is started in the Manager Training Program.

The Manager Training Program is an on-the-job period of training in one of the stores, lasting a maximum of one year. Usually the trainee is sent to a store that has profitable operations with a manager who has shown willingness and ability to instruct trainees. Since the salary of a trainee is paid by the home office, most managers are anxious to have trainees. The older managers in the larger stores usually do most of the training. Sometimes, however, the trainees are sent to fill vacancies at small, less efficient stores where the manager needs a good assistant. Even when a trainee is sent to one of the larger stores first, he may be transferred one or more times to alleviate manpower problems in the stores. The company feels that working in different sorts of store environment helps the trainee as well as the company. Trainees are never transferred without their own consent, but the trainees generally accept a transfer for fear of jeopardizing their career with the company.

During the one-year training period a trainee may be promoted to store manager whenever there is an opening. The store manager under whom he is training, the store supervisor of the district, the director of marketing, and the personnel man must all concur before a trainee is promoted, in most instances. If a man has not been promoted to manager at the end

of the one year, one of three courses of action is followed. First, if the man
has the qualities to be a manager, but an opening has not occurred, he is
offered an extension until there is a place for him. Second, if the man does
not have the qualifications to become a manager, but has shown special
aptitude in some phase of a store's operations, he is offered a permanent
job in that capacity, with the understanding that he is no longer a manager trainee. Third, if the man has not shown enough of the qualities the
company is looking for, or does not choose to stay under conditions
offered him, he is released.

DADE FARM SUPPLY

The Dade Farm Supply, with annual sales of about $400,000, is one of
the State Farm Supply's medium-size stores. In 1950, the manager of the
Dade County outlet for the previous ten years left to enter business for
himself. Since that time the Dade Farm Supply has had a total of five
managers. In each case of a manager change it has been at the request
of the company. All of the managers that were released had been through
the training period of the company's program.

Bill Sherrill, the fifth manager of the Dade store, was also a product
of the Manager Training Program. Sherrill was 34 years old, married, and
the father of one child. He was a high school graduate. After returning
from military service in 1946, Sherrill worked on his father's farm for a
few years, and later as a salesman for a furniture store. Sherrill first came
into contact with State Farm Supply through his brother-in-law who was
one of the more successful store managers for the company. Sherrill
received his first six months of training at his brother-in-law's store, but
when a manpower shortage developed in the small Lance County store,
Sherrill was transferred there. When the opening occurred early in 1959
at Dade Farm Supply, Sherrill accepted the job offer of manager.

After a few months as manager of the Dade store, Sherrill was convinced that one of the chief reasons this store had failed to operate
efficiently was the caliber of employees at the store.

Sherrill announced to all the employees that he would request salary
increases for all of them just as soon as the store's operations improved
to the point of showing a profit. No amount of the prospective raises was
specified nor was the length of time it would take before profits could
reasonably be expected.

Charles Mitchell

Charles Mitchell had been at the Dade Farm Supply for almost four
years. He was a high school graduate, married, and the father of two
children. After service in World War II, Mitchell worked as a machinist
and welder for several years. For the three years prior to coming to Dade

he had worked in a farm supply store for another large firm in a neighboring state. At the insistence of his wife, Mitchell returned to his home town, where he obtained the job at the Dade store. Mitchell weighed only 145 lbs. and found it difficult to do much of the heavy manual labor involved in general warehouse work. Consequently, he became accustomed to working almost exclusively in the salesroom. His experience with farm supply products made him the best qualified of the employees for this work. When Sherrill's predecessor was requested by the home office to designate an assistant manager for the store, the manager had selected Mitchell. No increase in pay was given Mitchell, and his duties remained the same as before.

Sherrill was not pleased with the performance of Mitchell. A point of particular objection was Mitchell's aversion to warehouse work. Sherrill realized that Mitchell was not suited for continuous manual labor, but felt that he could assist at times when a truck had to be loaded on short notice or some other emergency arose. Sherrill felt that Mitchell was not as proficient in the salesroom, either, as he should have been, due chiefly to the fact that he wasted too much time in idle talk with customers while other customers waited for service. He also felt that Mitchell did not show the proper interest in the store's operations for a man with the title of assistant manager.

Mitchell complained a good deal, principally about the fact that he had received only one small raise in his four years at Dade Farm Supply. He also felt that Sherrill did not entrust him with enough responsibility. Sherrill resented the complaining of Mitchell. While Mitchell did not go directly to the manager, Sherrill knew that Mitchell was dissatisfied. Sherrill felt that the complaining of Mitchell was making the other employees dissatisfied also. Sherrill concluded that Mitchell was lazy, disinterested in his work, and lacking in the leadership qualities needed in an assistant manager. Although he did not want to fire Mitchell, Sherrill secretly hoped he would quit.

Curtis Daniels

Curtis Daniels was 31 years old, married, and the father of four children. Daniels, who had not finished high school, had worked in a grain elevator on the night shift before coming to Dade Farm Supply on a full-time basis. When Sherrill became manager, Daniels was working during the day at Dade, but leaving a little early each night in order to get some sleep before going to work at midnight at the grain elevator. Even though he was working a total of almost sixteen hours per day, Daniels was one of the best employees at the store. He was ambitious, interested in the work, dependable, and courteous to customers. Sherrill persuaded Daniels to leave his job at the elevator and work full time at the store. Sherrill often placed work under the supervision of Daniels rather than Mitchell, the assistant manager.

When an egg-marketing program was established shortly after Sherrill became manager, Daniels was given the responsibility for delivering the eggs and contacting new customers. Daniels was proud to be in charge of egg sales and was conscientious in his work. However, he found it increasingly difficult to get time away from his other duties to devote sufficient time to the egg program. He felt that he wasn't doing the job expected of him. In addition to the egg-marketing job, Daniels drove one of the regular delivery trucks, clerked in the salesroom, and worked in the warehouse. Several times he requested the manager to allow him more time for the egg program, each time receiving from Sherrill a promise for the time. But conditions seemed never to improve along this line. After two incidents with the woman who graded the eggs, Daniels requested that he be relieved of the responsibility for the egg job.

Frank Whirlow

Frank Whirlow was the "old-timer" at Dade Farm Supply. Frank, who had not finished high school, was 37 years old and single. He lived alone in a one-room apartment, usually spending his evenings at the American Legion Hut and his weekends hunting for Indian arrowheads on the farms of some of his many friends. Frank was known by a large percentage of the adult population of Dade County and was regarded by many as something of a "character." He had been with Dade Farm Supply as a truck driver for about 11 years. During this time he had worked for six different managers. While he had at one time been an excellent worker, Frank became less and less efficient. He often took several hours to make a 20-mile delivery, made mistakes in billing merchandise, and delivered the wrong merchandise. On several occasions Sherrill spoke to Frank about some of these mistakes, whereupon Frank became irritated and "talked back" to Sherrill. When Frank made no improvement Sherrill did not try to correct him further. Sherrill did not want to fire Frank for fear of unfavorable reaction from many of Frank's customer-friends.

Clayton Forbes

"Buddy" (Clayton) Forbes, 17 years old, had quit high school at the end of the ninth grade and had gone to work in a pulp-wood yard near the Dade Farm Supply. On occasion Forbes had helped unload boxcars at Dade. During a busy period Forbes worked most of one week. When he asked Sherrill for full-time work, Sherrill decided to use Forbes in the warehouse until the busy period was over. However, when business did slack off, other work was found for Forbes, and he stayed on. Occasionally he waited on a customer in the salesroom. Almost without fail, the customer left the store obviously dissatisfied with the slow, lackadaisical service he received, and one of the older clerks often had to complete the sale and make change.

Mrs. Ruby Hilliard

Mrs. Ruby Hilliard was originally employed to fill in for the regular bookkeeper who was on maternity leave of absence. When the regular bookkeeper did not return to work, Sherrill persuaded Mrs. Hilliard to remain. She agreed to do so on condition that she could leave early enough each day to be home by the time her children arrived there from school. Mrs. Hilliard did excellent work but sometimes found her job conflicting with her responsibilities at home. Work in the office piled up as a result. On occasion the posting of accounts receivable was as much as five days behind when Mrs. Hilliard had to be out for a day or two. Mrs. Hilliard was not happy in her work, mainly because she found it so difficult to keep it up to date. She asked Sherrill several times to find someone to replace her. Sherrill said that he was satisfied with her work and not to worry if it was not always up to date.

Mrs. Margaret Clifton

Mrs. Margaret Clifton, the egg-grader for Dade Farm Supply, had previously worked as an egg-grader for one of the large meat packing firms in the city. She was proficient in her work but took something of a superior attitude to Curtis Daniels, who she felt did not know very much about the egg-marketing business. Twice she and Daniels had gotten into heated arguments over the operations of the egg program. Her final argument in each case was that Mr. Sherrill was her boss. The second argument had resulted in Sherrill allowing Mrs. Clifton to leave for the day after she had broken into tears. Sherrill then talked to Daniels and told him not to argue with Mrs. Clifton, but in any future differences of opinion to come to him for a decision.

* * *

At the end of 1964, the Dade Farm Supply was operating only slightly better than before Bill Sherrill became manager.

QUESTIONS

1. How would you analyze the situation involving Charles Mitchell?
2. What could Sherrill have done incentive-wise to increase productivity?

3. Evaluate the following as to potentiality for development:
   a. Curtis Daniels
   b. Frank Whirlow
   c. Clayton Forbes
   d. Ruby Hilliard
   e. Margaret Clifton
4. How well qualified was Sherrill to cope with these situations?
5. What is the function of the store supervisor for Dade Farm Supply?
6. Evaluate Sherrill's handling of Curtis Daniels.
7. What would you do, how, and when, if you were Sherrill?

15

Dobson Botanical Drug Company

THE DOBSON BOTANICAL DRUG COMPANY was founded in New York in 1903 by Charles Dobson. He had started work as a laborer in an import house, but because of his business ability, he soon became general manager of the warehouse. He saved some money during this time, and with the help of the bank, he then built a small plant and imported and processed botanical drugs. In time he developed it into a substantial organization with factories in three Northern cities, one in the South, and an international purchasing organization. At the present time the Dobson Drug Company has a sales volume of $15 million per year and a total employment of 650.

Charles Dobson retired in 1948 and left the business to his son Edward. Charles Dobson was still active in an advisory capacity since he knew the import business as well as anyone in the entire industry. Edward Dobson was made president of the company at this time. He was brilliant, energetic, and well liked by the other members of management, although at times they thought him to be "bull-headed."

A few years ago Dobson employed a general, company personnel manager, John Whitehurst. Whitehurst received a bachelor's and a master's degree in psychology at Yale University; Dobson felt that this, along with his other qualifications, made him suited to be the overall personnel manager.

Most of the executives of the Dobson Drug Company were not college graduates. Many had started working with Charles Dobson as laborers when the business was young and had eventually worked up to the top positions in the company. Even though these executives were not college graduates, they were capable men and were also extremely valuable to the company. Most of these executives were approaching or had passed retirement age, however, and both Dobson and Whitehurst realized that they should begin developing new men.

The Dobson Drug Company had never had an executive-training program, nor did the management have much of an idea about how to develop one. Most of the executives believed that the best training was on-the-job training, since this was the method under which they themselves had grown.

Dobson and Whitehurst decided that they would select one promising young college graduate every six months and put him through an executive-training program. They planned the program carefully, trying to include every detail that would be important to a future executive. They agreed that knowledge of the product was the single most important requirement for a drug executive. They then decided that the trainee would spend the first two or three months at the company's mill in Tennessee which ground and processed native botanical drugs.

There he would be taught how drugs were processed and how a mill was managed. The trainee would be under the supervision of the assistant plant supervisor, reporting directly to him. The trainee would also make two or three oral reports a week to the general manager of the mill. At the end of his stay there, the trainee would be expected to turn in a written report about the operation of the mill, giving his evaluation of this phase of the training program. The general manager of the mill would make oral reports from time to time on the trainee's progress to the management of the Dobson Drug Company.

For the second part of the training program, the prospective executive would operate out of the main office in New York. Here there were three Dobson Drug Plants within a radius of one hundred miles. One was for the distillation and percolation of drugs, one for milling gums, and one for milling a wide variety of imported botanical drugs. The trainee would be required to spend a minimum period of two months in each plant. During this stay he would work on and would learn to operate each machine in the plant. He would be directly responsible to the foreman in the department in which he was working. On Saturdays the trainee would be shown how orders were scheduled. At the completion of the two-month period, he would spend a week in the office of the respective plant. There he would learn how orders were received and processed and how production schedules were determined. In addition to this, he would be required to submit a written report to the supervisor of each plant, explaining the operation of each machine in the plant and the types and grinds of drugs that could be processed by each machine. Each supervisor would then submit a report to Whitehurst on the trainee's progress.

After the recruit had completed his training in the third plant, he would have a comprehensive interview with Whitehurst. They would review the entire training program thoroughly. Whitehurst would tell him honestly what the reports on his progress had been. If most of the supervisors had given the trainee poor reports, then he would be released. The trainee would ask any questions he might have and then would be asked to make constructive criticisms for the improvement of the training program. If the trainee were to stay with the company, he and Whitehurst would talk over the areas of work which the former could enter and would discuss where each job might lead. Whitehurst and Dobson felt that the trainee should have, by that time, a good idea of what he wanted to do. The trainee would then talk to Dobson. They would further discuss the field which the trainee had selected and would consider the future of that field and the future of the trainee in general. Dobson would then start him officially as an administrative assistant, in salesmanship, or in purchasing. If the trainee decided to go into the selling field, he would make several rounds with a regular salesman and then be assigned to a territory of his own.

With plans for the training program nearing completion, Whitehurst decided that it was time to find his first trainee. He contacted the placement services of most of the surrounding colleges, and all of these said that they would be glad to make arrangements for his interviewing students who would soon be graduating. He resolved to try Rutgers University in New Jersey first. Rutgers' graduates had good reputations in the state, and the school was known to have high academic standards. Rutgers' graduates who went into business frequently joined large national corporations after graduation. Whitehurst realized this, but he still felt that the Dobson Drug Company had a lot to offer that national corporations could not offer. Therefore, he believed that he could recruit a promising graduate. Dobson was prepared to offer a starting salary that was as high as any in its geographical area for a trainee, and the company could also assure the trainee that he would be working near his home if he lived in that general area. Whitehurst decided that he would not limit his interviews to prospective graduates concentrating in business or economics but that he would interview anyone interested in going into business who was graduating that June.

After many interviews Whitehurst became paraticularly impressed by Alfred Wellons, who also seemed much interested in the Dobson Drug Company. He was an average student, well liked by his classmates, and came from a prominent family in the state. Wellons and Whitehurst had a lot in common and soon developed a friendly relationship. Wellons scored high in the intelligence test that Whitehurst gave him; in fact, he rated well up in the superior group. Aptitude tests showed that he was well suited for administrative and management work in selling, finance, or production. Whitehurst had a lot of faith in these tests and consequently was pleased when Wellons performed so well on them. Wellons also had excellent references from his professors, from former employers, and from prominent citizens in the area. After interviewing and testing were completed, Whitehurst asked Wellons to come to the main office in a few weeks for further interviewing. He accepted the invitation, and while he was visiting the company, he was offered the opportunity to become the first trainee of the Dobson Botanical Drug Company.

Wellons felt that this was an excellent opportunity. He had always wanted to work in a smaller company in which there was a good chance to progress rapidly and thought that this offer to become Dobson's first management trainee was too good to pass up. He believed that since so many of the executives of the company were ready to retire, he would move ahead in whatever area he found himself most interested. Yet he knew that he must make a good record in order to do this. Because of a knee injury, Wellons had no military obligation, so he told Whitehurst that he would start in the training program on the first of July.

Wellons was told to report to the mill in Tennessee on the first day of July. Since the mill was eight miles away from a town, the management of the mill had built a small lodge that would provide meals for the administrative staff of the mill and rooms for any visitors or executives of the Dobson Drug Company who might want to spend the night at the mill. Wellons was told that his room and board would be provided by the lodge.

When Wellons arrived at the mill, he found that the lodge had been closed, and he was told that he would have to get room and meals in town at his own expense. This angered him, but he was determined to overlook it in his desire to make a good impression. Dolph Morgan, the general manager at the mill, met Wellons when he arrived and introduced him to David Lockland, the plant supervisor, to Brantly Burns, the assistant supervisor, to Conrad Bellamy, the head salesman, and to the other members of local management. Morgan discussed the training program with Wellons and told him to learn all he could about the mill by walking through the plant and asking questions of the workers. Morgan also told Wellons to report to him three times a week to discuss his progress. He then turned Wellons over to Burns, the assistant plant supervisor.

Burns' field was mechanical engineering. He had studied this subject in his only year in college. He had been forced to give up college after one year in order to support his family. He had kept up with the study of mechanical engineering after he had left school, and he probably knew more about his field than most graduates in engineering. Burns' main job was to care for the wide variety of grinding mills and tumblers operating from line shafts and individual motors throughout the two-story manufacturing plant.

Burns was not happy when he was told that it would be his job to look after Wellons and to teach him about the mill. He believed that he was the busiest person in the company, and he felt that Morgan and Lockland were always piling unnecessary "dirty work" on him. Thus Burns told Wellons to walk around the plant and learn what he could from the workers during the first week. Wellons did this, but he did not feel that he was learning much because the complexity of grinding operations was difficult to gleam from laborers in the mill. The processing of botanical drugs is difficult to observe since mills were in constant operation, and the vital parts of each mill were enclosed. The workers made it clear to Wellons that he was in the way when he tried to ask questions.

Finally Wellons persuaded Burns to take him through the plant and explain the process of milling and tumbling. The next three weeks of Wellons' stay at the mill were spent in going through the plant and helping Burns to make repairs, more as a helper to hand him parts and tools. Having been out of town most of the time, Morgan was able to hold few conferences with Wellons. He had reason to think that everything was going smoothly until Wellons came into his office one day and said that he did not feel that he was learning anything and that he was sure that he was wasting his time wandering aimlessly through the mill. Morgan told Wellons that he would see what he could do about improving the training program.

Morgan called Lockland and Burns into his office at the end of the day to discuss the problem. Burns said that Wellons had complained to him, too, about not learning anything. Burns said he thought that Wellons lacked initiative and was lazy and Lockland was inclined to agree. Both admitted, however, that they could improve their training methods and promised to do so, although they said that it would of course be difficult to find time for training with the amount of work that needed immediate attention. The next day Burns took Wellons through the plant again, explaining in detail the milling and grinding process. Wellons spent the remainder of his two-months' stay wandering around the mill looking for things to do. Before he left for the main office, he submitted a written report to the management of the mill explaining the processing of botanical drugs. Morgan sent a report to Whitehurst saying that he thought Wellons would make a good executive for the Dobson Botanical Drug Company if he would develop some initiative.

Wellons began his second phase of training in the distilling and percolating plant. This division was not the largest but was by far the most complex of the three divisions. Whitehurst and Dobson believed that if Wellons learned drug-manufacturing operations thoroughly, he would have little trouble with the other two divisions. Wellons' first assignment was to work in the vitamin compounding plant. His job consisted of helping to operate the mixing and pressing machines. The workers in this plant did not have to be constantly on the job as the workers at the mill did, and so they found time to answer Wellons' questions. Wellons continued this type of training as he went through the fish-oil department, the cough-syrup department, and the packaging department. He turned in a good report to Whitehurst and at the end of his stay in the division the supervisor gave him a good recommendation.

Wellons told Whitehurst that he thought the training program at the main office was much better than the one at the mill, but he afterwards added that he thought it was all too slow. He insisted that a person could learn all he needed to know about drug operations in two weeks instead of two months. He said that he was anxious to get started in an administrative job. Whitehurst told Wellons to be patient, but he added that it was a natural thing for trainees to get discouraged about the pace of a training program and that he should not worry about it. This seemed to convince Wellons and he entered the insecticide division with much enthusiasm.

Most insecticide business is in the summer months, and so the winter is a busy season for this division. During the seasonal buildup, Wellons was used as an extra worker and was put on operations that needed additional help. After the training in the insecticide division, Wellons was sent to the gum division. The supervisor of the insecticide division sent his report to Whitehurst saying that he thought that Wellons understood operations well enough but that he detected a lack of drive in Wellons which was essential for one who was to be a successful executive in the Dobson Drug Company.

Wellons spent two months in the gum plant doing about the same type of work as he had done in the other two plants. At the end of the period, he went in to have an interview with Whitehurst. Whitehurst told Wellons that he had done an average job as a trainee and no better. Wellons admitted that he had not put his "whole self" into the program, but he said that he was sure he would be much better as an administrator than as a trainee. They then discussed Wellons' future with the company. Wellons said he would like to go into the international or selling fields. Whitehurst said that he knew that a good man in either of these fields would have a strong future with the company.

Whitehurst had to leave town on a special assignment with Edward Dobson for a week. He told Wellons to spend the week in the office and to try to learn how orders are processed by observation and asking questions of the staff. He also told Wellons that when he returned they would talk further about his future with the company.

Midway during the week, Arthur Ridgeway, the vice-president in charge of production, called Wellons into his office ad told him that Dobson had just called and wanted Wellons to go to Tennessee where a new milling machine was being installed. This was a new, large investment for the Dobson Drug Company and Ridgeway told him that it looked like an excellent learning opportunity for a young man just starting with the organization. Wellons was not very enthusiastic about the idea, because he was not too interested in production, but he accepted it as a challenge.

Wellons' first week in Tennessee was spent helping Burns get the milling machine ready for production. The second week was spent "getting the bugs out of" the machine while it was in production. The third week Wellon sent a letter to Dobson submitting his resignation. He told Dobson that he regretted having to resign, but he did not feel that he was suited for the botanical drug business.

QUESTIONS

1. How could the management of the Dobson Drug Company have improved their training program?

2. What do you think of the company's selection process?

3. What steps should Wellons have taken to get more out of the training program?

4. Should Dobson or Whitehurst have been the one to tell Wellons of the opportunity in Tennessee?

5. Since the Dobson Drug Company had been successful in their noncollege men, should they limit their hiring to noncollege men?

6. What is your evaluation of Wellons as you see him in this case?

7. What training or development principles are illustrated in this case?

8. Should Wellons have resigned? If not, what were his alternatives?

9. What do you make of the recurring criticisms of Wellons' lack of drive?

16

Evelyn Penrose, Buyer

For Six Years Miss Evelyn Penrose had been at the Bon Marché in the
Bonmar Shop in the ready-to-wear departments. While in high school she
did stock work in the summertime and on Saturdays and began selling at
Bon Marché after completing one year at the State College for Women.
After three years in the Bonmar Shop, the buyer, Mrs. Laggerly, told
Miss Penrose that she was to do the unit classification job and that if she
kept up her good record some day she might be considered for eventual
promotion to buyer. Three years later and four years before she was due
for retirement, Mrs. Laggerly died of a heart attack while on a market
trip. The assistant buyer, Mrs. Rivers who was forty-eight, was appointed
to succeed her. In six weeks she resigned suddenly because of her husband's unexpected transfer to another city.

When Lamont Montague, the divisional merchandise manager, talked
to Mrs. Rivers about a replacement, he said, "I'm really concerned about
the Bonmar Shop. Who could ever have foreseen this situation? Personnel
has suggested Mrs. Henderson from Infants as a replacement, but I can't
go along with it. She was an assistant in Bonmar once but is doing fine
just as she is and Infants is such a specialized department anyhow. What
are your suggestions?"

Mrs. Rivers told Montague that Miss Penrose was her own choice. She
said:

> I realize that she did not finish college or enjoy as much recognition and
> status as the Executive Squad people get but we just couldn't have run the
> department without her. She has continued to sell as much as possible in
> addition to her unit classification work. The truth is, she really has been
> doing the assistant Buyer's job but without the title—and I think she certainly
> deserves a chance. No one else really *knows* the department like she does.

Montague sighed, shook his head, and said:

> Well, I agree that she has ability and is a good girl but do you think she is
> an executive at heart? I was considering making her the assistant buyer for

her accuracy and knowledge of the classifications, but *this* would be *quite* a leap. However, I recall she did have initiative to go on a market trip with you as part of her vacation, didn't she? I have my fingers crossed on this one, but if you think she has the capacity to become a buyer, I'll put her with you for as long as you can stay to help train her.

After Montague and Personnel notified her of her appointment as acting buyer, Miss Penrose "trained" with Mrs. Rivers for three weeks. Montague observed her work closely and at the end of the second week complimented her and said he wanted her to have a good, full-fledged assistant. He said that Montford Smith, executive vice-president, had stressed the importance of good leadership and trained people in a recent luncheon speech he made to the Junior Chamber of Commerce.

He and Miss Penrose approved a Marian Dohme who had joined Bon Marché as a recruit to the Executive Squad the previous June. Miss Dohme had been a fabrics major in college. Not long after, the training supervisor for ready-to-wear asked Miss Dohme to help work out a course on fabrics. Miss Dohme said if they wished to pursue the project they better ask Miss Penrose—she had been very vocal in disapproving the idea and was not willing for Miss Dohme to do it because of the time involved. "Teach *our* girls if you want to teach."

About the same time Mrs. Blosser, the department head in the Winsocki Valley Store—Bon Marché's only branch, received a notice to attend a seminar in merchandising arithmetic handled by the Control Division and the Training Department. Miss Penrose received a copy of the notice. She immediately phoned Mrs. Blosser and said she thought it a very poor time of year to get involved in that. She added, "I don't see why you branch people who have your merchandising done for you should get pulled off your job when we're short anyhow." Mrs. Blosser told Miss Penrose she had not asked for the course but was pleased to be included and intended to go. "I want to learn more about store operations including merchandising."

The following week the Sales Promotion Division and the Training Department worked out a week-long program for all salespeople to hear three leading manufacturers and two magazine representatives give a program on better fashion selling through better personal appearance. The floor manager was responsible for scheduling the people in his area. Miss Dohme helped him in suggestions for the schedule and said,

I'm so excited about this program. I want to see *how* they go about relating personal appearance and better fashion selling." The second morning of the program Miss Penrose came in at 10:30 after a doctor's appointment. She saw only one salesperson on the floor, went in the stockroom and saw only one salesperson there. Miss Penrose turned to her and said, "How does anybody expect us to sell anything or get anything done if there's nobody here to do it? I'd like to know how much farther they're going to strip me with all these idiotic meetings. *I* didn't have all this claptrap—I just worked hard and stuck with the job.

QUESTIONS

1. When Miss Penrose "trained" as a buyer, what all should have been included in her program?
2. How long should a development program for a buyer continue?
3. Since a buyer not only purchases but has some responsibility for sales, what do you think should be her main qualifications?
4. What is Miss Penrose's real difficulty?
5. Who is responsible for development in an organization?
6. Who is responsible for integrated training?
7. What is the team role of line and staff functions in this kind of situation?

17

Futuro Electronics Corporation

THE EASTWOOD PLANT of the Futuro Electronics Corporation is located in the midwestern part of the United States. The plant was constructed about two years ago with the expectation that it would eventually provide employment for 1,500 workers. At the present time, about 800 are employed, and there is a long waiting list of skilled, semiskilled and unskilled persons desiring work. It is expected that increased production will take place gradually and that, eventually, the plant will be filled to capacity. (See Exhibit 1 for plant organization chart.)

The primary products of the plant are high quality television sets and transistor radios, products in which the company has always pioneered and led in sales.

The plant is of modern design and is fully air-conditioned and well lighted. Administration offices are located in a separate, but connecting, building at the front of the plant. Raw materials are received and stored at one end of the plant, and finished products are moved out the other end. Machine tooling, stamping, milling, plating, printing, molding and assembly operations are all necessary to the manufacturing process, as well as the usual support elements of maintenance, control, inspection, and storeroom operations. (See Exhibit 2)

Four assembly lines are operated with three being used regularly for standard products, the other for special orders. Only very large orders can be accepted of a special, nonstandard nature since production changeover is extremely costly.

The corporation has always been proud of its personnel program and places strong emphasis on fair and friendly treatment of all employees. Employees are guaranteed wages equal to or better than those paid within the community and area by comparable employers for similar work; the wage system is tied in with the Bureau of Labor Statistics' Cost of Living Index with employees receiving proportionate wage increases as the index advances. Seniority and personal qualifications are used as the bases for transfers and promotions.

John Matthews, industrial relations manager of the plant, upon being interviewed, stated that he was pleased with the operation of the personnel program within the plant and felt that workers were generally satisfied and happy. As evidence of the workers' job satisfaction he pointed to the results of several elections which had been held to gain union recognition as bargaining agent for the plant workers. In each election, the workers had voted overwhelmingly against the union. Matthews believed that his open-door policy for employee grievances had been successful in preventing unrest among the workers, and he pointed to the up-to-date medical facilities, large cafeteria, pleasant lounges, and ample parking lots as evidences of the company's interest in its employees. Liberal benefits such as group insurance, pension plans and overtime pay, and paid holidays, vacation, and jury time are provided. Prompt and fair handling of grievances is assured by management, and the company pledges to make every effort to provide year-round employment.

Matthews was reluctant to concede that there were any serious problems in the administration of personnel. Upon questioning, he did say that a few troublesome situations had come to his attention, but he felt that all had been satisfactorily handled. He mentioned two, both involving the Industrial Engineering Department, which he thought were interesting:

The first case involved Andy Morse, a young, highly skilled machine repairman in the plant Engineering Department. Andy was twenty-two years old and had gained considerable experience in electrical machine and equipment repairing during his army service and while working in several other factories. He had been employed at the Eastwood plant for about six months, and, along with four older men, was used as a "troubleshooter."

The first special order accepted by the company was for 75,000 transistor radios. The Engineering Department had designed the transistor, and necessary layout work and assembly arrangements had been made in order to meet the tight production schedule of this rush order. After manufacturing operations had begun, it was found that a special jig would be needed in the assembly operations in order to insure safe handling of the delicate materials. Harold Reilly, manager of the Engineering Department, and his assistant, Jack Williams, worked several days and nights to design the specifications for the jig. They called on Jack Davis, plant maintenance engineer, to assign one of his specialists to build the jig. Davis selected Andy Morse for the job since he had previous experience in working at a company where special production work had been done.

Andy was assigned a separate bench in his department and furnished with the necessary tools and materials designated in the specifications. Reilly impressed on him the necessity for completing the job as rapidly as possible since the rig was for use in the rush order, and he indicated that Andy should be able to finish the job in two or three days.

The next afternoon, Andy came into Davis' office and the following conversation occurred:

ANDY: Mr. Davis, you know that jig I'm working on?

DAVIS: Yes, Andy, what about it?

ANDY: Well, that thing won't work. I've looked at some of the plastic cases over in storage, and when that clamp is put down its going to be too tight. I'll bet it will break or chip the base, and besides, it's too clumsy to be handled right.

DAVIS: Well, Andy, you know I didn't do the specifications for that jig. Why don't you go to see Mr. Reilly about it.

Andy went to the office of Harold Reilly, head of the Engineering Department.

ANDY: Mr. Reilly, that jig you designed isn't going to work.

REILLY: What do you mean? We were very careful about it.

ANDY: Well, I've been looking at some of the plastic cases that the jig is supposed to hold, and when that clamp is closed, it's going to be too tight and break the cases wide open. Besides that, the jig is too big. I've figured out how to make it a whole lot better.

REILLY: Nonsense! We checked that design against the cases and it was okay. Now you quit stalling and get that jig finished. We need it for assembly in three days.

ANDY: Okay. I'll do it, but I don't promise it'll work.

The next day, Davis was going by Andy's bench.

DAVIS: Are you about finished with that jig, Andy?

ANDY: Well, sir, I'll be through with it tomorrow morning, but I still don't think it's going to work.

DAVIS: Didn't you see Mr. Reilly about it?

ANDY: Yeah, but he just said that it would be okay and to hurry it up.

DAVIS: Well, let me know when you get through. I've got a couple of repair jobs I need you to do since all the other troubleshooters are busy.

ANDY: Okay, Mr. Davis.

The next afternoon, Reilly came into Davis' office and complained that Andy wasn't through with the jig yet and that he was wasting time in trying to change the way the clamp worked. He also said Andy had argued with him about it.

Davis called Andy into his office.

DAVIS: Andy, Mr. Reilly tells me you're trying to change that jig and that you're wasting time.

ANDY: Well, Mr. Davis, I told you it wouldn't work.

REILLY: What do you mean by that? I designed that jig myself.

ANDY: I don't care who designed it. It won't work with that clamp.

REILLY: You must think you know more about engineering and design than I do!

ANDY: No, sir. Mr. Davis, can I go back to my repair work?

REILLY: You just do that, and I'll finish screwing that jig together myself. It won't take me long to do it. (Mr. Reilly left the office.)

DAVIS: Andy, maybe you better go on back to your regular work. See your foreman and tell him you're to work on that stamping-machine repair job.

ANDY: Yes, sir. Thank you.

Andy found his foreman, Buddy Pate, and told him that Davis said for him to work on the stamping machine.

PATE: Did you finish that jig okay, Andy? I saw Mr. Reilly over there talking to you awhile ago.

ANDY: Yeah, I finished making all the parts, but I hadn't put the clamp on it. Mr. Reilly got mad at me when I told him that clamp wouldn't work right.

PATE: Now, Andy, when are you going to learn to do just like they tell you and let them take the blame if something goes wrong?

That afternoon, Davis called Pate into his office.

DAVIS: Buddy, I want to ask you some questions about Andy.

PATE: Okay, Mr. Davis. What do you want to know?

DAVIS: What do you think of Andy as a worker?

PATE: He's the best repairman I've got, and he's mighty smart about figuring out ways to fix things in a hurry. But, he does like to do things his own way.

DAVIS: What do you mean?

PATE: Well, sometimes when we're doing a repair or maintenance job according to the book, he'll suggest a different way of doing it that he thinks would be better. Then, if we don't do it his way, he'll get all fired up and say for us to go on and do it that way and that he'll just go on to another job. And he does.

DAVIS: Why didn't you let me know about this before? I would have made him stop that, or else laid him off!

PATE: The thing about it is, Mr. Davis, that Andy's almost always right. He's been responsible for a lot of the improvements we've made, and he's always figuring out ways to save us time on jobs. As far as I'm concerned, Andy can change from one job to another whenever he wants to, smoke when he wants to, and take a day off whenever he likes. He gets more work done than any of the other men, and he can do any job in the shop better and quicker than anyone else. As you know, we don't have enough good troubleshooters now, and I can't afford to lose him and still get my work done.

DAVIS: Okay, Buddy. That's about all I wanted to know for now.

Reilly finished assembling the jig that night. It was placed on the special assembly line the next day and assembly work was begun from the parts already produced. Additional parts were being turned out continuously from a special production-line setup, and the move men were complaining about the crowding in the temporary stockroom arranged for these parts.

After several hundreds of the transistors had been assembled and were being inspected prior to packaging, one of the inspectors noticed a tiny, hair-line crack in the case of one of the devices. Upon further checking, it was found that every transistor produced so far had a similar tiny flaw in the case. All the devices had to be discarded. The special assembly line was closed down and its workers temporarily reassigned. It took about a week to have a new jig designed and made.

Matthews explained that he knew about the trouble on the special assembly line and that the workers had to be temporarily reassigned, but said he didn't know about the episode involving Andy Morse until Andy came in to see him one day several weeks later. Andy said that he had heard about the "open-door" policy and had come in to see Matthews because one of the "bigwigs" had been picking on him. He said he didn't think it was fair and felt like quitting. Matthews questioned him further and Andy said that he had a run-in with Mr. Reilly. He explained that ever since then, Mr. Reilly had been picking on him and making slighting remarks about him and his work in front of Andy's foreman and co-workers. Andy stated that he kept his mouth shut when around Mr. Reilly and felt that Mr. Reilly had no right to try to "make a fool out of me."

Andy then told Matthews all about the episode involving the special jig. Matthews told Andy that he would look into the situation and see what he could do. He advised Andy to just go about his work, and, if Reilly had any more to say to him, to talk to Mr. Davis about it and then come to the personnel office if they couldn't work it out. Matthews stated that he asked Davis about the incident and verified Andy's story, but that he never heard anything more about it from any of the individuals involved. While checking through Morse's personnel file he discovered that Andy and his foreman, Buddy Pate, were first cousins. It was against company policy for members of the same immediate family to be employed at the same plant, but this rule had never been applied to cousins. Matthews said that he decided not to mention this fact of the kinship to anyone.

The personnel manager recalled another incident which had given him considerable concern for awhile.

Michael Wade was a young electrical engineer just three years out of college. He served in the Navy for two years and came out a lieutenant, junior grade. Wade then applied to Futuro Electronics Corporation for a job, was accepted, and placed in the training program at the company's main headquarters for approximately six months. The usual procedure was for the trainees then to be assigned to several of the different divisions of the company for which they were best qualified, to work for about six months in each of several plants. It was felt that this gave the men time to learn more about the company and to decide in which division they wanted to be and were suited to be placed. After the trainees completed this period of gaining experience and made their preference known, it was the usual policy to assign them within the division of their choice if a requirement for this preference existed and if their work had been satisfactory.

Matthews explained that all technical and executive personnel were initially employed through the company's main personnel offices and that only production workers and clerical personnel were hired locally at the plants.

Michael Wade was the first of these technical trainees to be assigned to the Eastwood plant of Futuro Electronics for some of his seasoning experience. Matthews stated that he had been very favorably impressed by Wade and had taken considerable care to see that he secured satisfactory housing in the town and was made to feel welcome at the plant. He introduced him to the plant manager and to many of the executives and staff. Wade was assigned for duty to the Engineering Department, and Matthews asked Reilly, the manager of the Engineering Department, to take particular interest in his training. Reilly said that he was always glad to get a new man and would look out for Wade.

About four months later, Matthews made an appointment to have lunch with Wade one day. During the meal, Matthews told Wade that he had just got another monthly progress report on him from the Engineering Department, and that the report indicated that Wade was progressing very well in his training and doing good work. Wade became red in the face and said heatedly that any monkey could do just as good work as he after doing the same thing for four months. Matthews expressed surprise and asked what he meant.

WADE: I know that you have been very nice to me here, Mr. Matthews, and so I have been reluctant to come to you and complain about anything. Since you ask, though, I'll tell you just how I feel.

MATTHEWS: Please do, Mike.

WADE: As I understand it, I'm supposed to be here to learn all about this plant's operation and the engineering involved in getting out our products. Since the first day I went to work in the Engineering Department, though, I have been assigned to only one job. We completed that in about five weeks, and ever since then Mr. Reilly won't assign me to anything new. I've been to see him at least once a week, but he just keeps telling me to stick with it, and he'll come up with something. He and all the other engineers stay busy all the time and are always complaining about being overworked. I keep volunteering to help them, but they all say that Mr. Reilly will have to okay it before I can work on any plans. And do you know what he has me do now every day? For three months I've been checking the daily reports from the inspection section on the performance of the wiring used in our TV sets. Even the secretaries could do that in about five minutes per day. Mr. Reilly says for me to spend the rest of my time reading company literature and manuals about products produced in other Futuro plants.

Mr. Matthews, I want to get in with the other men and use some of my knowledge and abilities in working on our new product designs. Frankly, I'm fed up with the situation here.

MATTHEWS: Needless to say, this is all news to me, Mike, and I am very much surprised. I have read your monthly progress reports and thought that you were getting along just fine and were receiving good training. I'm going to look into this situation and see what I can do to correct it.

Matthews said that he went to see Reilly that same afternoon and inquired how Wade's training was progressing. Reilly said that, as far as he knew, Wade was coming along all right. Matthews then told Reilly about his conversation with Wade and said it seemed the boy was being done an injustice in not getting enough chance to work on electrical engineering projects. Reilly gave Matthews a hard look.

REILLY: John, I've always tried to go along with all the company policies and cooperate with you personnel boys; but don't you try to tell me how to run my department. I've been an engineer with this company for twenty-five years, and I've never had any serious complaints about my work. Now don't tell me that anybody can take a hot-shot college kid and teach him everything about engineering for this plant in six months. He'll just have to come to work every day and keep his nose to the grindstone like everybody else until he gets settled somewhere. I could use another man in my department, but I need somebody with experience.

MATTHEWS: Don't get all excited, Harold! I know you fellows are overworked, and I thought that Mike Wade could be a help to you. Why don't you try him out on another project? He might surprise you.

REILLY: Well, I will if I can find one he can help on. But don't you come checking up on me anymore, John, or I'll tell Harry (Flowers, plant manager) that you are interfering with my department.

The interview was terminated very shortly thereafter. Matthews called Wade a week later and found out that he had been assigned to work on the design for a new TV set to be used in closed-circuit TV's. Mike was pleased with this development and much interested in the project. About a month later, Matthews again called Wade, and Mike told him that the project had been completed a week before and he was back to reading manuals again. A week later, Mike came by Matthews' office and said that he still wasn't doing anything. For several days, Matthews considered seeing Flowers, the plant manager, about the problem; but in the meantime, a letter came from Futuro's main headquarters directing that Wade be sent on to another plant. Matthews decided to let the matter drop. When Wade left, Matthews told him that he hated to see him leave, but that maybe he would find more interesting work at one of the other plants. Privately, Matthews resolved to keep a closer eye on any other trainees who came to the Eastwood plant and make sure that they got better training.

QUESTIONS

1. What aspects of motivation are present in this case?
2. Analyze factors in job satisfaction revealed by this case.
3. What should Matthews do, if anything, to help Andy Morse?
4. Is there any significance to the implied nepotism involving Morse?
5. How could Matthews have prevented the situation involving Michael Wade from arising?
6. What action, if any, should Matthews take with the departure of Wade?
7. What do you think is the cause of difficulty with Reilly?
8. How can one in another staff capacity relate effectively to a man like Reilly.
9. What should be done to assist with Reilly's development?

EXHIBIT 1

Futuro Electronics Corporation

Organization Chart, Television and Transistor Radio Division

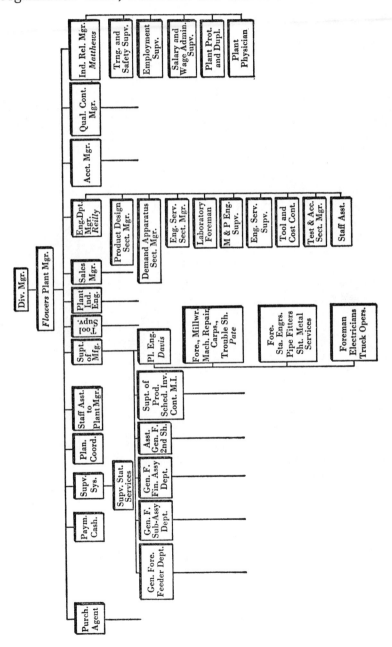

EXHIBIT 2

Futuro Electronics Division

Plant Layout Chart and Flow Diagram, Television and Transistor Radio Division

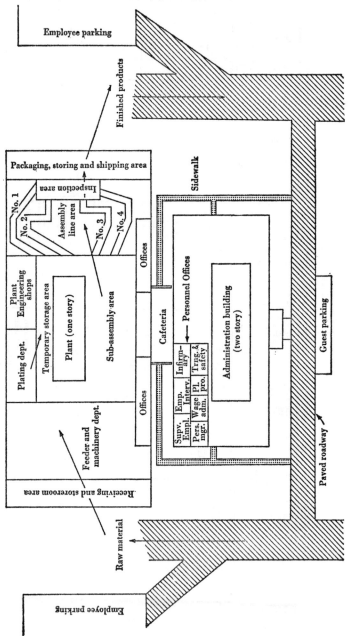

18

Grand Haven Table Company

THE GRAND HAVEN TABLE COMPANY was established in Michigan in 1918 by Edward Detrich. Detrich was a young carpenter who had a hobby of making and refinishing tables in his garage. He took great pride in his workmanship and soon many of the people in the surrounding area were asking him to make tables for them. He became so involved in his table work that he gave up his carpentry work to devote full time to making tables.

By 1910, he had moved out of his garage and had bought an old warehouse. By 1925, he had about fifty people on his payroll. All his resources were now tied up in this table-manufacturing plant. He had his financial difficulties, but his insistence on high quality gradually built up the reputation of his firm so that he was mostly concerned with getting funds for expansion.

In 1930, Mr. Detrich decided that his company could make more money if it could mass-produce high quality tables. He felt that there would be a demand for high quality tables at less than the custom price. With this goal in mind, he continued to expand his operation. By 1959, he had a medium-sized furniture factory located outside Grand Haven, Michigan. The company employed from 200 to 250 people. In addition to numerous types of high quality tables, a medium-quality line of tables had been added.

The company has had a successful record of growth and in 1964, sales were expected to increase by 10 percent. The present management of the firm felt that at least a 10 percent increase in sales could be expected for every year for the next seven to ten years.

Mr. Detrich retired from active management in 1958 at age 70. He still had an active interest in the company and still maintained a small office in the downtown display room of the company. He had one son who was a doctor and who had no interest in the business, except that some day he would inherit the 70 percent stock interest that his father now had.

Mr. Detrich for a long time had been aware that his son had no interest in the furniture business and hence had decided to build up a core of professional management personnel who could continue to successfully and profitably operate the Grand Haven Table Company for his son.

With Mr. Detrich's leadership, management developed long-range plans to build strength into the organization. Management had developed a policy of providing an understudy for each management position so that in the event a "manager" should suddenly leave, die, or be retired, his position could be easily filled with present employees. This went along with management's philosophy of promoting from within.

The president of the company, John Rich, had just had a survey made of the understudies available for taking over the position of production foreman. In reviewing this survey, he found that there was no trained replacement available for Ralph Stith. With some anxiety, he called in Jim Roberts, the personnel manager to find out why there was no replacement available for Stith.

Mr. Rich patiently but firmly explained to Roberts his strong feelings about always having someone available or in training to take over, just in case. Mr. Rich reminded Roberts that Stith's job was no simple first-line foreman's job, and that continued production accompanied by the maintenance of high quality was something that the company could not afford to sacrifice.

To emphasize the seriousness of this problem and to check to see if there was anyone else in the organization who could take Stith's job, Mr. Rich briefly reviewed Stith's job description with Roberts.

Stith supervises approximately sixty to seventy employees, mostly unskilled and semiskilled personnel. He directs the work of three to four leadmen in addition to the hourly paid employees. He is responsible for a great deal of paper work and department records. He must be familiar with every type of table manufactured by the company. He must be able to recognize flaws in the wood or finishes. Hence, he controls both production and quality and is the last man to approve the quality of the product before it is shipped to dealers. Stith himself has said that even if a person were familiar with the products and the manufacturing process, it would take him a good six months just to learn the details involved in the record-keeping and the helpful "tricks" necessary to insure the quality of the finished tables.

Roberts thumbed through his personnel files and admitted that no one was available at the time and that it would take a minimum of six months to train someone.

Mr. Rich momentarily lost his composure and threw his pencil on the desk and said, "Roberts, Stith is 60 years old! He could die or retire tomorrow! You know the company policy. Just what have you been doing in the personnel department?"

Roberts, a bit shaken, pulled out Stith's personnel folder. Mr. Rich was rather surprised at the thickness of the folder and asked if Stith had been a problem. Roberts said that Stith's work had been satisfactory, but that he seemed unwilling to pass on the knowledge of his job to any of numerous assistants that had been placed under him for that purpose.

Roberts then scanned some of the pertinent data on Stith:

He is sixty years of age. He is married with grown children. He has completed a grammer school education. He has forty years of practical experience, and is an excellent production and quality supervisor. He gets along well with subordinates and superiors as well as with associates in the management level. He is considered to be loyal and conscientious. He has been employed with the company for over twenty years, having been with the company since the organization was considered small in size up to the present enrollment. He came to us from a southern furniture manufacturer. His wife is a native of Michigan and at the time he was employed, he had returned to settle some family matters and then decided to stay on with us.

Until 1961, we always had a leadman who could have taken over Stith's department. The third leadman was due to retire in three years. Bob Smith, a promising young employee with a high school education was promoted to leadman. He did such a good job as a leadman that in the middle of 1961, we assigned him as an assistant to Stith. After six months as assistant to Stith, Smith was transferred to another production department. Stith had recommended this transfer, as he felt that Smith was not yet ready or able to do a foreman's job.

Early in 1962, we hired Joe White. Joe had considerable experience in working with a new finishing process that we were considering using on our medium-quality tables. To familiarize Joe with the job requirements for a foreman with Grand Haven, we temporarily placed him as assistant to Stith. Joe worked in this capacity for thee months and then was promoted to foreman of his own department. Joe was a hard worker and well liked by his superiors and subordinates, but the production and quality standards of his department never reached the company standards. Ron Collins, our production manager at the time told me that he had to spend much of his time with Joe, teaching him some of the basic details which he should have already learned. Joe left us last year (1963). In an exit interview, Joe stated that no one in the company wanted to tell him anything. The production manager didn't have the time to spend on little details and his three month training period with Stith was useless.

Shortly after Joe White left us, I had the opportunity of placing one of our college trainees in Stith's department. Mike Rounds had recently graduated from the University of Michigan and was well thought of. He was a hard-working boy who seemed to have a promising future. I assigned Mike as an assistant to Stith. I personally requested Stith to help Mike in learning his operation. At the same time, I requested Mike to submit a monthly written report to me telling me what he had learned in Stith's department. Mike had submitted reports on all his previous training and so this part of his training was nothing new to him. Mike's work progressed well for the first few months. He learned the general knowledge of Stith's department rapidly. After he had acquired this general knowledge, he seemed to run into a stumbling block. In reading his third monthly report, I realized that he had not learned anything new. He questioned many facets of the operation. I felt sure that Stith knew the answers to most of the questions raised by Mike.

I called Mike in for a conference to talk over his third report. I asked him if he were having any trouble learning what Stith did. Mike said that at first Stith answered all his questions, but recently, Stith never seemed to have the time to answer any of his questions or give him any guidance at all. Mike said, "Frankly, I think Stith feels that you are going to force him out and he doesn't want anyone to have a complete knowledge of his job." We transferred Mike to another department shortly before the completion of your manpower survey and hence, there now is no available replacement for Stith.

The problems arising from these three people who were supposed to have been trained by Stith seemed to indicate an unfavorable pattern. I talked with several of our older employees who were friendly with Stith. I even had an occasional chat with Stith. I learned that Stith had developed the attitude that any replacement he might train to succeed him will take his job before he reaches retirement age. The feeling that apparently exists is that in years past, perhaps in his association with another company, outside employees were brought in and offered better job opportunities within the company over presently employed personnel. In addition, supervisors who trained men for their assistants ended up with the assistant being given the job of the supervisors who had trained him.

I have been concerned with a replacement for Stith ever since Mike Rounds was transferred from Stith's department, which was only three weeks ago. Stith has been a satisfactory employee with the exception of his unfavorable attitude toward training anyone who could have taken over his job. Actually, Mr. Rich, I am not quite sure what to do.

QUESTIONS

1. Do you think Roberts was negligent in the performance of his job as personnel manger?
2. Do you think the president, Mr. Rich, should have acted the way he did?
3. What was Stith's problem?
4. If you were Roberts, what would you do with Stith?
5. Do you think Stith was justified in having the attitude he had?
6. What could be done to prevent the development of such attitudes?
7. Should Roberts have detected Stith's attitude earlier?

SECTION IV

Supervision

SUPERVISION is an area of personnel management which properly follows selection, training, and development. A traditional aim of personnel administration has always been "to establish, develop, and maintain an efficient work force." The day-to-day task of supervising is concerned with *maintaining* such a work force through effective direction of subordinates.

These six cases deal with some of the problems in supervision. Most of them are individual, interpersonal relationship situations, but two of these situations have to do with the intricacies of group relations. Grievances, discipline, resistance to change, and relations with other supervisors are among the major focal points in these cases.

Running through all of this section is the thread of communications. So many problems exist because of communication failures, differing perceptions of communications, and plain lack of communication. The supervisor's own role in communication is bound to include counseling. Often passed off as a superficial task, counseling becomes quite complex when employee problems have their origins in deep-seated behavioral difficulties. What the supervisor and personnel administrator should do in such situations is well worth exploring. So it is that the first two cases in this section suggest counseling problems along with other involvements.

COMMUNICATION

19

Mr. Johns

ROBERT STARK was the newly appointed assistant to the Industrial Relations Officer of the Civil Service Commission on a small military base in the West. It was his duty to investigate all employee complaints and to recommend possible solutions to the officer in charge of industrial relations. He had recently received a complaint from Mr. Sauers, chief supervisor of the Roads and Grounds Section. Mr. Sauers had voiced his complaint on the telephone two days previously. The conversation had gone something like this:

SAUER: Mr. Stark, are you aware of the plot of the "wheels" in Maintenance to force Mr. Johns off on me?

STARK: No, I'm not. Suppose you start from the beginning and tell me all about it.

SAUER: Well, in a week my timekeeper-typist is leaving since her husband is being discharged, and I will need to replace her. Last week I notified the employment section that I would need a replacement and asked them to start sending qualified applicants as soon as possible. Several days later three applicants came to my office to be interviewed. After checking their qualifications and talking to them, I was all set to hire one of them yesterday morning. That's when it happened—Ralph Richards who, as you know, is the chief supervisor of all the maintenance departments on base called me and said he had just learned that I needed a timekeeper-typist. He suggested that Mr. Johns from his office be considered for the job. At first I thought he was joking and laughed. When Richards said he had never been more serious in his life, I couldn't believe my ears. Richards and I have gotten along fine for the past ten years, but that ended it. I told him I would not hire Mr. Johns under any circumstances. Richards said that I might not have any choice in the matter and hung up.

Mr. Stark, you know as well as I do what's happened since—Mr. Richards has gone to Colonel Williams, who is in charge of Maintenance, to get him to pressure the employment office into sending Johns down here over my protests. According to Civil Service regulations, I'm supposed to be able to hire whom I choose, but you know those big-shots can easily forget the regulations when some military brass hat puts the pressure on them. Mr. Johns will poison my entire organization if he comes down here; most of my men know him and dislike him already. Besides, he's not qualified for the job since he can't type.

STARK: Other than not being able to type, just what is so terrible about this Mr. Johns? I'm not acquainted with him.

SAUERS: That's right. You're new here. Why, he's so bad that he's been transferred all over this base because no one can stand to work with him. He can't get along with his fellow workers because he's underhanded, very uncooperative, a sneak, and has a superior attitude. He has a running feud with half the supervisors on this base and treats the office girls like they were cheap hussies.

I've got the friendliest, most cooperative group of leadingmen of any shop on base, and I intend to keep it that way. My leadingmen have to work in close cooperation with the timekeeper-typist on sick and annual-leave records, equipment records, requisitions, and correspondence. With Johns in that position, there would be nothing but trouble.

STARK: All right, Mr. Sauers, I'll check on it. Give me a little time. You'll hear from me soon.

After talking to Mr. Sauers, Stark sent for Mr. Johns' employment record in order to get a better picture of his personal background and previous work on the base. From the employment record Stark was able to ascertain that Johns was forty-eight years old, married and had two daughters aged fifteen and seventeen. He was a college graduate and had been the principal of a small high school in a nearby town prior to coming to work for Civil Service. His record of Civil Service work indicated that he had worked on the base for six years and that his present rating was GS-4. During the six years, Mr. Johns had worked at various jobs including timekeeper for the payroll section, bookkeeper in another part of the payroll section, had had two different jobs in the fiscal unit and had been in the office at Maintenance for two years as fiscal accounting clerk. According to the job description the fiscal accounting clerk recorded the time, money, and labor expended on every maintenance job on the base, from fixing a door hinge to building a new building. The records came in every day from eleven shops and represented work done by some five hundred workers.

To get further information on Johns and the other side of the story, Stark called Ralph Richards at the Maintenance Office. Richards told him that Johns' work was highly satisfactory but that he wanted him transferred for the good of his whole office. Richards said Johns created an atmosphere of ill feeling in the whole office by his open feuds with other employees, his silent contempt for his supervisors and his censorious attitude toward the girls who worked in the office with him. When Stark asked him to elaborate, Richards related that Johns had a habit of staring disparagingly at the girls in the office. On several occasions office girls had come to Richards and asked to be transferred or for Mr. Johns to be transferred or placed in a different office. Recently one of the office girls, Jane Weldon, came in tears to Richards stating that if she weren't given a job away from Johns, she would resign. Richards stated that this girl was a very efficient worker and not the type to become easily disturbed. He talked to several of the other girls in the office who told him that Jane had worn a snug-fitting sweater to work that morning and that Johns had stared at her all morning as if he thought she were a cheap hussy. Finally Jane had burst into tears, gone over to Johns' desk and told him, "If you don't like the way I look, then keep your slimy green eyes off me!" On another occasion Faye Bratton, a girl from another office who frequently came in to chat with the girls in Johns' office and to round them up for coffee break had told Johns that she was sick and tired of the way he looked at her with "hate in his eyes" every time she came into that office and that the next time he did it she was going to slap his face. On both occasions Johns had made no reply but had just looked smug as if he had just heaped burning coals upon the heads of the unrighteous. Richards said that he knew it must upset the girls to have someone stare at them all the time, but he couldn't do anything about it. He said he would feel like a fool telling Johns not to stare at the girls in a disparaging way.

Richards further stated that all the girls in the office disliked the way Mr. Johns treated Sara Gibson. Sara was thirty-two years old, a college graduate and had the same Civil Service rating as Johns (GS-4). An attack of polio had left Sara partially paralyzed from her waist down. Although it was difficult for her to move about, she was able to continue her job which entailed mostly sitting at the same desk all day making entries in a ledger. Due to the crowded conditions of the office and since Sara and Johns had similar duties, their desks had been placed together. The telephone was on the top right corner of Johns' desk and could not be moved since the cord would reach no farther. When the telephone rang, Johns would just ignore it thus forcing Sara to get up and walk around Johns' desk to answer it. Sara had at first asked Johns to answer the telephone and explained her difficulty in moving about, but after seeing Johns continue to ignore the ringing telephone, she had decided that if the telephone were going to be answered, she would have to do it. And even though they worked only a few feet from each other all day long, Johns never spoke to Sara unless it was absolutely necessary.

Mr. Richards also told Stark that Johns hated his supervisor, Mrs. Gladen. Mrs. Gladen was thirty years old, a high school graduate, had worked for Civil Service for the past eight years, and had a rating of GS-6. In Mr. Richards' opinion, Mrs. Gladen was a very intelligent, well-liked and capable supervisor. Although Johns never outwardly showed it, it was thought by all the other workers that he felt nothing but resentment and silent contempt toward Mrs. Gladen. He never spoke to her unless it became necessary and never missed a chance to belittle her to the few people he talked with. On several occasions he had gone to Richards to point out mistakes and discrepancies in his department which would reflect as poor supervision on the part of Mrs. Gladen. Mrs. Gladen had, on several occasions, told Richards that Johns' attitude and actions resulted in unpleasantness, inefficiency, and lowered morale among the employees in her section and asked that he be transferred. Richards had tried, but to no avail since there had been few jobs open in his classification. He was interviewed for several of these jobs but was not hired because the supervisors knew of his reputation.

According to Richards the twenty some employees in the Maintenance Office were a friendly and gregarious group. They usually had a big dance at Christmas and several parties during the year. The girls had showers when one of the other girls got married or had a baby. It was the custom to stop work twenty mintes early on an employee's birthday while everyone gathered around the coffee urn for coffee and birthday cake—that is, everyone except Mr. Johns. He steadfastly refused to take part in any of the social activity of the Maintenance Office.

Richards lived near Johns and had known him for several years before he came to work for Civil Service. He was able to tell Stark some interesting aspects of Johns' personal life. Richards said that Johns had been forced to resign his position as school principal when the parents of the community had presented the school board with a petition signed by practically every parent who had a child in high school. They demanded that Johns be fired, charging that he was too strict on the pupils, meddled into the personal affairs of the female students by condemning lipstick and certain types of clothing, and was uncooperative with the parents. They further charged that several good teachers had resigned and moved to other schools because they could not get along with Mr. Johns. Richards said that Johns had two daughters in high school and that he would not allow them to date, wear lipstick, nor wear high heeled shoes on any occasion and that he forced them to wear dresses and skirts with the hems much longer than was the style.

Richards further stated that Johns was an avid church-goer. He was well thought of in his church and had been elected a deacon. He was often called upon to pray in the services and prayed beautiful prayers usually centered around brotherhood. The people of his church were very critical of the people in the nearby town for forcing Mr. Johns to resign as high school principal there. They felt that it was all politics.

Johns suffered almost constant pain from arthritis all over his body, and one leg joint had become so stiffened that he walked with a limp.

Richards ended his conversation with Stark by saying that he believed Johns' trouble stemmed mainly from having a woman for a supervisor and his inability to get along with the girls in the Maintenance Office. He said he thought it would be best for all concerned if Johns were transferred to Roads and Grounds where he would be under Mr. Sauers and would work only with men. (The present timekeeper-typist was the only woman in the Roads and Grounds Section.) He further stated that any typing that needed to be done at Roads and Grounds could be done at his office. He suggested running a truck down to the Roads and Grounds Section twice a day to pick up material to be typed and deliver the finished work.

Stark was at a loss as to how to solve the problem of Mr. Johns. One thing was certain, Johns could not be fired since his work was beyond reproach and since he had attained Career status with Civil Service. (After a Civil Service worker has worked for three continuous years, he attains Career status and dismissal can be reviewed by the Civil Service Commission in Washington, D. C.) Stark knew that sending Johns to Roads and Grounds would solve the problem in the Maintenance Office but might create an even larger problem at Roads and Grounds. Also, sending Mr. Johns to Roads and Grounds without Sauers' approval would be in violation of Civil Service employment regulations and would reduce the efficiency of that shop by depriving it of a typist.

Stark knew that he had to do something about Johns very soon before the Maintenance Officer pressured the employment office into transferring him to Roads and Grounds.

QUESTIONS

1. If you were Stark, what recommendations would you make to the industrial relations officer and why?
2. What do you feel are the behavioral factors behind Mr. Johns' inability to get along with his fellow workers?
3. How do you account for Mr. Johns' censorious attitude toward the female employees in the Maintenance Office and his treatment of Sara Gibson?
4. If Mr. Johns remains in the Maintenance Office, what recommendations would you make toward lessening the ill feelings between Mr. Johns and the female employees? Between Mr. Johns and his immediate supervisor, Mrs. Gladen?
5. All things considered, do you think it would be better for Mr. Johns to be retained in the Maintenance Office or transferred to Roads and Grounds?
6. What, if anything, can Stark do to circumvent the collusion between the "military brass" and the employment section?
7. Why do you think Mr. Johns' superior, Richards, had not counseled with the man?
8. Who do you think should conduct counseling with Mr. Johns?
9. What approach should be used in counseling with Mr. Johns?

20

Transoceanic Airlines, Inc.

Bob Kemsey had been recognized for his ability as a line navigator with Transoceanic Airlines, Inc. He had amassed over 1800 hours of flying time in less than two years, and had touched down at every base from which the company operated in Europe, North Africa, South America and North America. In January of this year, however, Kemsey was removed from flying status as a result of a temporary physical condition. He would not be allowed to fly again for at least a year.

The company's headquarters was located in Miami, Florida, and all flights originated from Miami International Airport. For obvious reasons, the primary maintenance facilities were located there also. They were organized in three separate sections: the Field Section, responsible for all required shop and specialty work; the Flight Line Section, responsible for all through-flight maintenance; and the Periodic Section, responsible for the periodic inspections required every 160 hours on each of the eighty-four aircraft in the fleet.

The Periodic Section employed about 450 personnel, and at the time Kemsey was removed from flying status, this division needed a personnel assistant. The company did not like to lose qualified flying personnel, and since Kemsey seemed to get along well with people, it was decided that he could fill the vacant position. Kemsey reported to the maintenance superintendent, James Condon, although his staff superior was the general manager of personnel for Transoceanic, Marvin Lee, and he worked most closely with the supervisor of the Periodic Section, line chief Roy Neatherly.

After two years of college at the University of Florida, Kemsey had joined the Air Force. He entered the Aviation Cadet Program, obtained his wings as a navigator, and flew three years with the Military Air Transport Service prior to joining Transoceanic Airlines. Kemsey was totally unfamiliar with personnel work, and equally unfamiliar with the work performed in the periodic maintenance section. As he put it, "my job is flying airplanes, not keeping the grease-and-oil boys happy."

The line chief, Roy Neatherly, a gnarled veteran aged 55 with twenty years' service at Transoceanic, had been asked to acquaint Kemsey with operations on the flight line. He agreed to do so and said that he would take Kemsey through "just as if he were an airplane getting inspected." The two of them, Kemsey and Neatherly, went first to the wash pit. This was where the aircraft were cleaned, drained of gas and oil, and readied for dock work. Next, the two men went to one of the eight nose docks where the aircraft, as Neatherly stated, "were taken apart and put back together again in less than 48 hours. It pushes us a little bit sometimes," said Neatherly, "but according to the analysis boys, this is how long if should take to complete a periodic inspection. Those fellows are really busy. They have put out a book that tells us every move to make, when to make it, how to make it, and they change their minds about it every day. They organize, reorganize and then organize some more. The problem is that they don't know what goes on down here, but they damn well expect you to follow that book and explain to others why it's a good thing."

After the 48-hour inspection, the planes were gassed and oiled again, and towed to the "runup" area. This area was some distance away, and as the two men walked across the ramp, they were discussing some of the pros and cons of the centralized maintenance concept. "The good old days of crewing your own airplane are gone," said Neatherly. "The men, under the centralized maintenance concept, have no more regard for one airplane than they do for another; they just talk of them in terms of numbers. I remember when people had some pride in what they did; they worked together; everybody was out to have the best ship in the fleet or bust."

Suddenly, one of the smaller towing vehicles seemed to appear from nowhere. Neatherly yelled, and the driver just missed running over both of them. "What in the world was that guy doing?" asked Kemsey. Neatherly laughed and said, "I don't know what I'm going to do with that nephew of mine." He went on to explain to Kemsey that his nephew, Roger Anderson, had come all the way from Michigan to learn about airplanes. He did not understand the difficulty that Anderson was having in developing as an aircraft mechanic. "After all," said Neatherly, "he was an expert automobile mechanic before coming here and the transition should not be too bad."

Kemsey and his escort reached the run-up area and noticed that several mechanics had pulled a maintenance stand up under the number four engine of a DC-8. "This is where we test them after dock maintenance," said Neatherly, "and, then, if everything's okay we turn them over to you glory boys to shake down upstairs." About this time, one of the mechanics stepped on a wrench that had been left on the deck of the maintenance stand. He would have taken a bad fall had it not been for a lending hand from one of his fellow workers. Neatherly quickly found out which mechanic had left the wrench, called him down off the stand, and proceeded to chew him out in the fashion normally expected of a line chief.

All the way back to the maintenance office Neatherly cursed "the idiots" he had working on the line. "We've had a lot of bad accidents lately," said Neatherly, "just because some goof ball like that kid back there won't watch where he puts his tools down." Kemsey thanked Neatherly for the tour and returned to the personnel office.

In the following months, Bob Kemsey felt skeptical on more than one occasion about his qualifications for personnel work. At the same time, he found the work both intriguing and challenging. And it took only a few experiences for him to develop a wholesome regard for maintenance men and for the problems with which they had to contend.

It was not long before Kemsey had the opportunity of meeting Neatherly's nephew in person. A credit agency in Michigan wrote a letter concerning a loan that Roger Anderson failed to clear up before coming to Miami. They stated that the payments were several months in arrears, and although small, they would appreciate Transoceanic bringing the matter to Anderson's attention. Kemsey called Anderson to his office to discuss the letter.

Anderson appeared to be embarrassed over the fact that the company had received a letter of such a nature. He claimed that he had absolutely forgotten about the loan and would take care of the back payments on the following payday. During the course of the interview, Kemsey noticed that Anderson had difficulty sitting still; he seemed to be thinking about something entirely apart from the conversation being conducted. Kemsey attributed this, however, to Anderson's embarrassment and did not pursue the matter of his manner any further.

Several months later Kemsey received a letter from a local grocery store requesting information concerning the whereabouts of Roger Anderson. The store manager indicated that after building up a substantial account, Anderson had not been seen or heard from for several months. Before calling Anderson to his office about the debt, Kemsey decided to check the records. He found from the personnel data folder that Anderson was 35 years old, married, and claimed three dependents. His formal education had terminated at the eighth grade, and Anderson had become an automobile mechanic. Kemsey also noticed that Neatherly's nephew had received treatment on three separate occasions at the company's first-aid station. The treatments had involved cuts and bruises incurred seemingly through negligence.

Upon reporting to the personnel office, Anderson appeared to be even more embarrassed than before and at the same time much more withdrawn from the conversation. Again, Anderson stated that he did not remember charging anything at the particular store in question but would see the manager that afternoon. When the interview was over, Anderson thanked Kemsey and said he hoped that this would not happen again. He looked around and stood still momentarily, almost as if he did not remember from which direction he had entered the room. The situation troubled Kemsey, and he decided to investigate the case further.

That afternoon Kemsey went to see Anderson's immediate supervisor, Paul Owens, who was in charge of Dock Four. Owens had an assistant foreman, and the two of them supervised the 24 men assigned to the dock. Owens did not hesitate to give Kemsey information concerning Anderson.

> That fellow [he said], has about as much mechanical ability as my two-year old. Neatherly assigned him to me as a first-rate mechanic, but so far he has only performed menial tasks around the dock—sweeping up and that sort of thing. That's all he'll ever do as long as I have him; I don't care whose nephew he is. Everything he does goes wrong and nobody wants to work with him. The boys kid him and ride him a lot, especially George Hampton; he's the dock's funny man. That guy Anderson is really stupid. I don't think he realizes that nobody likes him. Of course, everybody knows why he is still around, but somebody should get rid of him. Only yesterday, the boys tell me, he almost walked into a propeller.

Kemsey decided that he had better talk to Anderson again. He was convinced that the man was really a troubled individual and thought that maybe he could help him. Kemsey asked Owens to send Anderson down to the personnel office that afternoon and he would see what he could do.

After some time and patient questioning, Kemsey was able to find out from Anderson that his financial difficulties were much worse than they appeared. For several months now, he had been borrowing from one loan company to pay another. He also found that Anderson's mother-in-law lived in the house with him and his wife. "She can't do much of anything," said Anderson. "She has got arthritis pretty bad."

Kemsey asked Anderson if his wife worked in order to help out with the finances. At this point, Anderson was much more at ease and talked without hesitation. "My wife is pretty fat," he said, "and she's kind of self-conscious about it, and doesn't want to be anywhere that people can see her. She doesn't do much to help matters either. Why, I've known her to eat as much as fifty dollars worth of chocolates in a month." Admittedly, Anderson did not know where it would all end. He said that he intended to keep coming to work every day, and that he was going to be an aircraft mechanic if it killed him.

Kemsey asked him if he could not make more money as an automobile mechanic in one of the garages downtown. Anderson said that he really didn't know much about cars. "Sure, I've worked on the assembly line at Chrysler," Anderson said, "but that doesn't teach you much about cars. I'd go back up there and work, but my brother-in-law says that they are laying people off as are other automobile companies because of a seasonal slump. Besides, I like my work here and nobody's complained about the way I do things."

The next morning Kemsey went to Dock Four to tell Owens what he had been able to find. When he arrived, he noticed that there was very little activity in the dock. The men were clustered in small groups and appeared to be talking among themselves. Some of the men would leave one small group and move to join another; and little, if any, work was being accomplished. Kemsey moved through the dock toward the small office located in the rear.

Owens and his assistant were both in the office, seemingly unaware of the situation that existed within ten feet of them. Kemsey stood for a moment in the office before anyone spoke. Finally, Owens looked up and said, "Good morning, Kemsey, looking for your friend Anderson?"

"No," Kemsey replied, "looking for you—what's going on?"

"The boys are upset," answered Owens, "must have been something they ate."

"Okay, okay," Kemsey retorted, "what happened?"

Owens then related what had taken place about fifteen minutes before Kemsey arrived:

Neatherly came in here this morning, [Owens said] just after we towed 544 in. He was his usual self, hollering and screaming around. Well, he was checking the safety lines on the nose wheel and noticed that they weren't secured properly. He asked me who was responsible, and I told him I wasn't sure. Well, he went out and asked for himself. Jim Schmidt told him that he thought he had done it right, but Neatherly wouldn't pay any attention to that. Now Schmidt's a nice kid, Kemsey, and I think, sort of religious. Everybody likes him and everybody knows that he really works hard. He is trying to become a good mechanic. Well, anyway, Neatherly called him a goofball, and a stupid idiot, and finally told him he was the dumbest S.O.B. he had ever known. If it had been me he was talking to, I would have poked him one right there; I've been looking for an excuse to do that anyway. But Schmidt just stood there and took it; he didn't say anything. The bad part is that the cable connection means nothing and the men know it. It's just one of those things that the damn book says to do, and Neatherly probably had it put in the book. Well, anyway, the men haven't done a thing since Neatherly left, and I don't aim to do anything about it. Ralph tells me that he heard one of them say something about walking out. If they do, it would serve him right.

Kemsey turned to walk out and when he did, he found himself facing the whole group. He stopped, took a deep breath, and said, "I assure you that something will be done about this." The men parted and made a path for Kemsey to walk through.

QUESTIONS

1. What should a company's policy be on indebtedness of employees?
2. How should Kemsey have proceeded when he first noted Roger Anderson's detachment?
3. How can Kemsey help Anderson when much of his problem seems to be domestic?
4. What would the approach of a good counselor be when Anderson told him the nature and extent of his personal problems?
5. In the case of a line supervisor on the same level as the personnel man, what can his approach be to
    a. Help such a man with deficiences in supervision?
    b. Bring such deficiences to the attention of Transoceanic management (if at all)?
6. How can Kemsey help Paul Owens?
7. What should Kemsey do in the current crisis involving Neatherly, the Dock Four crew and Jim Schmidt?

21

Jack Norton Restaurants

TWELVE YEARS AGO Jack Norton started a new restaurant called "The Hofbrau" in a university town. The restaurant was situated near a cafe and gift shop belonging to Norton's father. The Hofbrau was an immediate success and its sales increased rapidly. Four years later Norton acquired another restaurant in the same town, and after extensive remodeling, opened it under the name of "The Gourmet." Early this year Norton bought a third restaurant in the town and had it converted into a home-delivery restaurant. This restaurant was called "The Stork." All of these specialty restaurants were successful, both volume and profit-wise. Yearly sales grew progressively and from the original employment figure of 10, the group's employment now reaches, with some fluctuation dependent upon the season, an average of 85 to 90 employees.

Legally the three restaurants are separate corporations, and each operates under a full-time manager. The managers are allowed considerable freedom of decision, but Norton takes an active part in their management, visiting each place several times every day.

Norton is now thirty-eight years old. He holds a degree of B.S. in chemistry and has completed a considerable amount of work towards a master's degree in business administration. Prior to opening "The Hofbrau" he helped his father operate the cafe and gift shop. He is married and has two boys aged seven and nine. Active in the town's community projects, he has acquired a site for developing a shopping center sometime in the future. Norton is a man of considerable business acumen under whose direction the three restaurants have become the center of the town's busy restaurant and catering trade. The restaurants are considered by many to be the finest in this town of 15,000 and are recommended highly by touring and dining guides.

The restaurants employ men only, both white and colored. Relations between employees of both races are cordial with no difficulties experienced in this connection. Norton has strongly liberal feelings socially, politically, and in religion; towards employees his attitude is mildly paternalistic. He strongly disapproves of drinking and smoking, but has the reputation of being tolerant and understanding of employees' failings.

Each employee is carried on the payroll of the restaurant employing him but, when necessary, some work part of the time in other restaurants within the group. In a few cases men are, more or less regularly employed by two, or even all three of the restaurants. There is, in fact, considerable flexibility within the organization which, in part, explains the success of the venture. Of the 85 employees currently on the payroll, only 23 are full-time employees, the others being either part-time college student employees or men holding other part-time and even full-time jobs. Among the latter group a substantial number work at the university hospital. Of the employees, around twenty are white, the rest colored. Except for managers, the white employees are students at the local university.

At all three restaurants, experience with regard to rate of employee turnover has been good. Among the full-time staff separations rarely occur, and even the part-time and second-job employees do not experience a rate of turnover higher than is usual for the trade and for this part of the country.

New employees are usually hired by the managers, but some are occasionally employed directly by Norton. In most cases however, Norton interviews the new employee subsequent to his selection by the manager. This "second interview" frequently takes place only when the new employee is transferred from one restaurant to another. The organization has no standard employment application form, but under Norton's influence, a rough procedure for an employment interview is in general use. The applicant's personal data are obtained; he is asked whether he smokes; his drinking habits are closely questioned, and he is asked whether he has had any "trouble with the law." He is, if white, also asked whether he would object to working under a colored supervisor. A positive answer to that question terminates the interview. (In two of the three restaurants, colored men supervise certain phases of restaurant work.)

Information obtained from the applicant is checked in a variety of ways. His previous employers are contacted; inquiries are made through employees of the three restaurants who are usually able to supply management with detailed information about the applicant's character and about local opinion of him. In cases where it is not possible to check upon the applicant in the above ways, information is sought from the police. After the man has been hired very few personal records are kept by any of the three restaurants.

Management is of the opinion that the hiring procedure is, on the whole, effective but also feels that there is room for improvement in both interviewing and checking on applicants.

After the man has been employed he is subjected to a sort of "stress test." The restaurant trade is famous for frequent "crisis" situations, and a new employee is made to work under pressure for long hours. The idea is to find how he would behave under stress conditions. Norton is a firm believer in long hours of work and feels that the success of his venture is, at least partly, due to this policy of having employees work long work-weeks. This enables him to hire fewer men than would otherwise be necessary and he is also able to pay higher total weekly wages than his competitors. No clear-cut promotion system prevails, but in general the management believes in promotion from within the organization.

Disciplinary problems are not serious, but management is somewhat concerned over inconsistencies in dealing with breaches of discipline. No written set of disciplinary rules exists; most of them are "assumed to be known." In The Gourmet a notice is posted, warning employees of fines for lateness. The fines, however, are seldom imposed and employees are evidently aware of laxity in applying this rule.

The organization is not troubled seriously by absenteeism, but occasional "rashes" of absence cause irritations on busy days, and Norton and his managers are aware that they take different actions in the event of absences. When a man fails to show up and does not produce a valid excuse, such as a doctor's certificate, the management's reaction is colored by the way in which his absence was felt, business-wise. If an employee fails to come on a slack day the offense is, more or less, overlooked. He receives no pay; he may be admonished, and, very occasionally, he may be laid off for a short period of time—but no serious disciplinary action is taken because of the offense. Managers sometimes even welcome such absences since they mean labor savings on slack days. However, if the employee is absent on a busy day, the management's reaction is likely to be far more drastic, even though the excuse offered is a reasonably valid one. Cases have occurred when the employee was dismissed outright for such an offense. Norton gives his managers full freedom in the matter of firings and invariably backs them up in cases of appeal.

Three years ago, George Manning, then aged thirty, was hired as dishwasher by the manager of The Hofbrau. Manning is married, has children, and, as far as the management is aware, has no serious troubles in his personal life. The man is somewhat limited in his capabilities, but, within his limitations has performed satisfactorily and has shown some desire to improve his job status. At his request he was assigned as a trainee short-order and grill cook. His work was satisfactory but he did not show sufficient promise of becoming a skilled cook. It was accordingly decided to transfer Manning to The Gourmet where he would work full-time as dishwasher and general kitchen helper. Subsequently he was retransferred back to The Hofbrau, again as dishwasher and kitchen helper. At the same time he continued to work part of his time at The Gourmet.

Manning continually asked for more hours of work in the week but was unwilling to report before noon. Even so, in response to his request

Gill Goring, manager of The Stork, arranged for Manning to work additional hours at that restaurant as kitchen cleaner, his hours at The Stork being from midnight to 3 a.m. each night. Manning's duties at The Stork consisted of cleaning the kitchen and utensils and helping the baker for about half an hour. The baker worked in the kitchen all during Manning's three hours there but needed his help for only a short period. Manning performed his work quite well or, in Goring's words, "as well as could have been expected of him." His work was important since restaurants are subject to inspection by state health authorities, and a dirty kitchen can cause them to order a close-down or a down-grading in the State Sanitation Certificate. A down-grading would have been serious for a restaurant in The Stork's class.

On a Tuesday, early in February of this year, Manning left The Hofbrau at about 11 p.m., slightly earlier than usual. He reported for duty at The Stork at 1 a.m., though, instead of at midnight. One of the Hofbrau's employees told Goring next morning that, during the intervening two hours, Manning had been drinking somewhere in town. Goring was absent on the night in question, and Manning reported to Bob Cleary, the assistant manager at The Stork. Immediately after reporting to Cleary, Manning went to the telephone and made a call. Cleary, who was counting the day's receipts, overheard part of the conversation and his impression was that Manning was talking to a woman. Cleary remembers Manning's closing sentence, which was: "I'll see you in half an hour maybe."

Having made his call, Manning approached Cleary and "mumbled" rather indistinctly words to the effect: "I have brought along another man to help me tonight as I want to leave early." Cleary does not remember the exact words spoken by Manning but noticed that Manning had with him another employee from The Hofbrau. Cleary normally did not work at The Stork at such a late hour but he was generally aware that Manning had to clean the kitchen. To the best of his recollections he replied: "I do not care what you do, but the place must be cleaned up." Before Cleary left The Stork, Manning started to assist the baker, as he was supposed to, but almost immediately after Cleary's departure, Manning also left the restaurant, leaving his friend behind. The baker reported the next morning that he "knew" that Manning was drinking and that he went to see a girl. The baker said he warned Manning not to go away and, later, told Manning's friend that the kitchen must be left clean. Manning's friend made some attempts to clean the place but, since he was not skilled, the work was not well done.

At 3 a.m. Manning returned to The Stork but did not go inside the restaurant and made no attempt to check his friend's work. He simply picked his friend up and they both went to a neighboring town where they lived.

In the morning, Goring came to work and found the kitchen filthy. It was in such a bad state that Goring was sure that the restaurant would have been closed up had it been inspected on that particular morning. He had to delay opening for over an hour and had the cook clean the kitchen. Goring was upset by the incident and immediately instituted a searching inquiry. Having received reports from the baker and other employees, he talked to Cleary. Cleary said that he was not aware that Manning intended for his friend to substitute for him and was emphatic on the point that he instructed Manning to clean the kitchen.

Goring reported the matter to Jack Norton and, during the afternoon, Norton and Goring interviewed Manning. Prior to the interview the supervisor at the Hofbrau warned Manning that he was "in trouble."

The interview was conducted mainly by Norton, who first told Manning what the management knew about the incident and then asked him for his explanation. Manning denied strongly that he had been drinking or seeing a woman and said: "I would not tell you a lie, Mr. Norton. You know me. I had permission to be off and it was an emergency. I am telling you the truth. My wife run out of oil and now I have a wife and children freezing to death in this cold weather. Last night I went to borrow some money to buy oil with. This is the truth and I am not telling you a story."

Manning repeatedly asserted that his was the true version of the incident, but Norton did not believe him and told him he was fired. Manning pleaded with Norton, but the owner refused to change his mind.

Goring was uneasy about the incident and thought that Manning had been treated too harshly for what, after all, was his first offense. Accordingly he again talked to Cleary and asked him to recollect what exactly transpired between him and Manning during the night. Cleary said that he could not remember the precise words used by Manning. He was also not certain whether his reply was not so phrased as to give Manning an impression that the substitution was authorized.

Goring discussed the incident with Stanley Foster, manager of The Hofbrau, where Manning had been on the payroll. Both managers came to the conclusion that Norton's reaction to the incident was probably influenced by the largely unsubstantiated evidence that Manning had been drinking and "stepping out on his wife." They both further agreed that Manning was a good employee and that they would like to have him back. In the meantime Manning approached several employees of the group and asked them to intercede on his behalf with the management.

About a week after Manning's dismissal Goring and Foster talked to Norton and asked him to rehire Manning and give him another chance. Norton replied: "Do what you want to do. I fired him and cannot rehire him myself."

A supervisor of The Hofbrau was accordingly instructed to get in touch with Manning and rehire him. Manning was warned that he was on indefinite probation and is now working as kitchen helper at The Hofbrau and The Gourmet. He is, however, no longer employed as kitchen cleaner at The Stork.

QUESTIONS

1. What is your opinion of the method used by Norton to interview Manning after the incident?

2. Do you think Manning's discharge was justified?

3. What do you think of the recommendation of the two managers that "they would like to have Manning back"?

4. What do you think of Norton's statement: "Do what you want to do. I fired him and cannot rehire him myself"?

5. Do you think that a written set of disciplinary rules would be beneficial to the Norton Restaurants?

6. What effect do you think increased discipline would have on the employees, who have been working under an informal system with only a few formally prescribed rules?

7. What would you do to eliminate the inconsistencies in dealing with disciplinary problems?

8. What advantages and disadvantages to both employees and management do you see in the frequent temporary transfers among the restaurants?

22

The Lone Star Manufacturing Company, Inc.

THE LONE STAR MANUFACTURING COMPANY was a large scale producer of women's dresses, suits, and other outer garments, employing some 600 workers in its main plant which was located in the suburbs of a fairly large city in the Southwest.

The company drew its workers from the city and the surrounding area. The labor supply was adequate numerically and consisted mainly of individuals of Spanish and Indian descent. About two-thirds of Lone Star's workers were in this category, a few of them having only recently arrived in this country from Mexico. The vast majority of the workers were women.

The main plant was not a modern establishment, using old sewing machines, cutting equipment, and methods in its various manufacturing processes. Nevertheless, the company was able to maintain a fairly sound competive position against more up-to-date competitors principally because its pay rates were lower than those existing in other parts of the industry. Then, too, there were no other garment manufacturers in the particular region where Lone Star was located. The company attempted to keep its pay rates close to but below other manufacturing firms in the area and had a reputation for steady work.

Lone Star was not organized. A recent election among the workers resulted in defeat of an attempt by a nationally known union to organize the plant. Lone Star's plant manager attributed the union's defeat to the company's fair and equitable treatment of its employees. A representative of the union had been quoted by one of the local newspapers, however, as attributing the defeat to management's "coercion" of the workers.

Production at the main plant was so organized that garments moved through the various stages of production from the raw cloth to finished product by truck from department to department. The cloth went first to the cutting department where it was cut into various shapes as required for the particular pattern being used. The various pieces then went to the sewing department where the principal sewing operations were completed and then to the finishing department which added any trim or ornamentation required.

At 4 p.m. on March 28, Rosemary Mason, who supervised eight women engaged in cutting sleeves for dresses, approached the assistant Cutting-Department supervisor, Mary Falconer, and suggested that action be taken to discharge Rosita Garcia, one of the cutters who had been employed in her section for almost two years. According to Mason, Garcia had failed to report for work with the second shift that day and had not notified her that she would be absent. In addition two of the other cutters were absent due to illness (both properly excused). As a result the Sleeve-Cutting Section was falling behind in its work and was unable to keep pace with the other cutting operations. Furthermore, Mason alleged that this was the fourth or fifth time to her knowledge that Garcia had failed to report for work without notifying her and that she had "no need for cutters who could not be depended on."

Work within the Cutting Department was specialized to the extent that one section and the workers therein might cut nothing but sleeves, another nothing but collars, etc. Lack of modern equipment made this pretty much a hand operation. While specialization permitted personnel with limited training to do an acceptable job there was, nevertheless, a considerable degree of skill involved and performance above standard did not come, generally, until a year or more of experience. Since the flow of work to the Sewing and other departments depended upon the speed with which the cutting work was performed, a steady rate of production here was essential to the smooth functioning of the entire production process.

Falconer agreed that discharge seemed to be the only solution and stated that she would take Garcia's case up with the personnel office and recommend her discharge. This she did in a telephone conversation with George O'Rourke, the personnel director, the following day.

Rosita Garcia was a forty-six-year-old widow. Her records indicated that she had received some six years of schooling as a child in Mexico. Upon the death of her husband over twenty years ago, she had left her home in a rural community of Mexico and brought her young son to this country in the hope of finding employment which would permit her to support both of them. She worked as a domestic servant in various households during her earlier years in this country and had subsequently been employed for two years by a laundry as a seamstress to repair damaged clothing and for three years as a cook's helper in a restaurant. She was originally employed by Lone Star as a janitress in the cutting department some seven years ago. While performing her janitorial duties there over a period of some five years, she became familiar with the simpler duties of a cutter and occasionally assisted in the actual cutting operations when the workload was especially heavy or when one of the regular cutters was absent. When a vacancy occurred in the Sleeve-Cutting Section two years ago, she was promoted to this vacancy and had been employed there ever since.

After receiving the call from Falconer, O'Rourke examined Garcia's personnel folder and found that on two previous occasions during the past year she had been suspended from duty, once for three days and once for one day, for failing to report for work and also failing to notify her supervisor that she would be absent. In each of these two unexcused absences a letter had been written to Garcia signed by Falconer advising her of the suspension and of the reasons for it. In a second conversation with Falconer the same day, O'Rourke learned that Garcia had also been absent without prior notification on October 1 last year and again on February 12 of the current year. The absence of October 1 had resulted in a verbal reprimand by Mason. The February 12 absence had been subsequently excused as being due to illness.

While employed as a janitress Garcia had been absent from duty on rather frequent occasions as indicated by the payroll records. Her personnel folder, however, contained no indication of any of these absences having been unexcused nor of any evidence of any disciplinary action having been taken against her during this period. When queried by O'Rourke as to whether any of Garcia's absences during the period of her work under his supervision were unexcused, Manuel Spinoza, a janitorial supervisor, stated that he could not recall any such incidents.

On April 2, Garcia received a letter from O'Rourke notifying her that she was being discharged effective April 9 for excessive absences without proper authority (see Exhibit 1). On April 8 a letter was received by the personnel office addressed to a Mr. Nelson (there was no one by that name on duty in the personnel office) in which Garcia requested that her case be reviewed and that she have an opportunity to be heard (see Exhibit 2).

The grievance committee at Lone Star was composed of five supervisory employees, one of whom was O'Rourke's assistant who served as the non-voting recorder. In line with company policy, the committee could hear employee grievances, question such witnesses as deemed appropriate, conduct investigations when such were necessary to establish facts, and make a recommendation as to action it felt should be taken. The proceedings of the committee together with the recommended action were furnished O'Rourke who then made a recommendation to his superior, the plant manager, as to whether the committee's recommendation should be accepted or rejected. Final decision rested with the plant manager.

On April 9, Garcia, Mason, and Falconer appeared before the grievance committee. Pertinent extracts of the ensuing testimony follow:

CHAIRMAN: Miss Mason, will you please tell us what your reasons were for recommending Mrs. Garcia's discharge.

MASON: Well, there were four or five times she didn't show up for work without telling me she wouldn't be there and I can't keep my section running without workers.

CHAIRMAN: Could you give us the exact dates Mrs. Garcia was absent without properly notifying you?

MASON: (After examination of some papers she had before her) She was absent on the 17th and 18th of April last year, again on the 21st of April last year, again on the 1st of October last year, and this last time was the 28th of March this year.

MEMBER: What action was taken against Mrs. Garcia as a result of these unexcused absences?

MASON: She was suspended without pay for three days for the first time she was absent last year and suspended without pay for one day the second time. I just talked to her about being absent last October and told her it had better not happen again. When she didn't show up for work the other day and I didn't hear anything from her, I told Mrs. Falconer she ought to be fired.

MEMBER: What procedure do you require your employees to go through in order to be properly excused if they must be absent from work?

MASON: The ones on the second shift are supposed to call me or Mrs. Falconer before 3 o'clock—that's when the shift starts—and let us know they won't be here so we can make arrangements to cover for them.

MEMBER: Do all your workers know about this requirement?

MASON: There is a notice on the bulletin board that tells them what to do and nobody but Mrs. Gracia seems to have any trouble doing it.

MEMBER: Did you ever personally explain the procedure to Mrs. Garcia?

MASON: Yes, I told her every time she was absent that she should have called me.

MEMBER: Did Mrs. Garcia ever call you and inform you of the fact that she would be absent from work?

MASON: She never called me beforehand like she was supposed to but a few times she called some of the other girls in the section and once or twice she called me later in the day to tell me why she didn't show up.

MEMBER: Do the other girls in your section often leave messages with their fellow workers when they have to be absent from work?

MASON: Well, sometimes they do. You see, there's only one telephone on the floor where we work and whoever happens to be the closest answers it when it rings. Sometimes they just tell whoever answers the telephone to tell me, but they're not supposed to.

FALCONER: If they can't get Miss Mason they're supposed to call me in my office, but I don't remember Mrs. Garcia ever calling me.

MEMBER: Did Mrs. Garcia ever explain any of her unexcused absences to you after her return to work?

MASON: When I would ask her why she didn't show up, she would give me some excuse about being sick or claim she had told one of the other girls she wouldn't be here, but she never could remember just who she had talked to so I never could check on her story. One time I remember sending her to Mrs. Falconer for being absent and Mrs. Falconer checked with her doctor and found out she really had been sick so we didn't do anything about her not showing up that time.

CHAIRMAN: Other than these absences has Mrs. Garcia's work been satisfactory?

MASON: Well, not always.

CHAIRMAN: In what way is she inefficient and have you talked to her about it?

MASON: Several times I have had to get after her for being fifteen or twenty minutes late for work.

MEMBER: Do you prepare efficiency ratings on the employees in your section?

MASON: Yes, I do.

MEMBER: Have you mentioned any inefficiency on Mrs. Garcia's part in any of these ratings?

MASON: I don't remember whether I did or not.

RECORDER: According to the record here both ratings given to Mrs. Garcia by Miss Mason were "satisfactory" and there is no mention of any deficiencies. The last rating was in December last year.

GARCIA: When I was absent in October Miss Mason told me she was giving me another chance because I was a good worker and got along with everybody.

CHAIRMAN: Mrs. Garcia, would you like to give us your side of the story now?

GARCIA: The first time I was absent was because they changed me from the first to the second shift and didn't tell me about it. The two days I took off were the two days I was supposed to have off on the shift I was working on then. The first thing I knew about being changed to the second shift was when I came back after my two days off and checked in at 7 o'clock in the morning and one of the girls told me I wasn't supposed to be there because I had been moved to the second shift two days ago. She took me to the bulletin board and showed me the notice because I thought she was joking. I tried to tell Miss Mason what happened but she just told me I was supposed to read the bulletin board and she was going to suspend me. When I got the letter telling me I was suspended it made me so nervous I couldn't come to work that day and I got laid off another day for that. Some of the other girls missed days without anything happening. I don't know why Miss Mason had it in for me.

CHAIRMAN: Miss Mason, would you explain the matter of the shift changes and how the workers are notified of such changes?

MASON: Nobody much likes to work on the second shift so after anybody has been working on it for sixty days they can ask to be put back on the first shift and we move a replacement from the first to the second shift. We keep up with who has been on the first shift the longest and when we have to move someone to the second shift they are the ones we move. It was Mrs. Garcia's turn to move to the second shift and Mrs. Falconer's office put a little note on the bulletin board telling her about it which is what they always do. She just didn't bother to look at the bulletin board or claims she didn't see it.

GARCIA: That was the first time I had been put on that shift and nobody told me about it and I didn't know it.

MASON: We used to talk to them about going on the second shift but we got all kinds of excuses about why they couldn't go on it so we just started putting the little notes on the board a year or so ago.

CHAIRMAN: How about the absence in October, Mrs. Garcia?

GARCIA: That time was while I was on the second shift and I had some pork chops to eat and they made me sick. I called in and talked to Mary Gonzalez who lives in California now and she said she would tell Miss Mason but she claims nobody told her.

MASON: She couldn't remember who she talked to when I asked her about it and I know nobody told me anything.

GARCIA: That's when she told me if I was absent again without telling her I'd get fired.

CHAIRMAN: Now, the last absence?

GARCIA: My son had gone to see relatives in Mexico and I got a letter from him saying he had fallen off a horse and was hurt. He didn't say how bad it was so I took the bus to go see about him. This was on my day off and I thought I could catch a bus back in time to get to work the next day. After I got there, I couldn't get a bus back in time. When I got back the next day, I was told to go to Mrs. Falconer's office. She told me I was going to get fired and that she was tired of these "Juarez vacations." I tried to tell her why I couldn't get back in time but she just told me I had already had enough chances.

MEMBER: What is a "Juarez vacation"?

GARCIA: That's what they call it when somebody goes to Juarez and has a big time, then can't work the next day.

MEMBER: How old is your son, Mrs. Garcia?

GARCIA: He's 22.

MEMBER: Was he hurt badly?

GARCIA: He didn't break any bones but he had a sore shoulder and lots of pain in his back.

CHAIRMAN: Do you have anything further to say at this time?

GARCIA: Most of the girls don't think I ought to get fired and they told me if I would tell you my story I wouldn't get fired.

MEMBER: Can you read English, Mrs. Garcia?

GARCIA: Not much, but I usually get one of the other girls who can to read me any papers I get so I don't have much trouble.

CHAIRMAN: Mrs. Falconer, would you tell us what you know about this case and just how you fit into the picture?

FALCONER: Well, as I see it, what Miss Mason has said is about all there is to it. I'm the assistant to Mr. Rogers. the man in charge of the Cutting Department. He doesn't like to get involved with the disciplining of women, so I do most of it for him and the section supervisors come to me with their problems and I take care of them.

MEMBER: Is Mr. Rogers aware of the action which has been taken in this case?

FALCONER: No, he has been awfully busy with some production problems he is trying to get straightened out and I didn't want to bother him. He usually leaves problems of this kind up to me.

GARCIA: I tried to see Mr. Rogers but she wouldn't let me.

MEMBER: Is it a policy in the Cutting Department that an employee wishing to see Mr. Rogers must go through you, Mrs. Falconer?

FALCONER: No, but I try to relieve him of as much detail as possible and I saw no reason why Mrs. Garcia needed to see him.

MEMBER: Mrs. Falconer, do you explain to new employees in your department the rules for obtaining authority for an absence?

FALCONER: No, but I'm sure the section supervisors do. Perhaps Miss Mason could tell you more about that.

MASON: I don't have a new worker very often, but when I do I usually tell them what to do. I don't remember how much I told Mrs. Garcia when she was hired as a cutter. She had been working around our section so long she should have pretty well known the rules.

Upon completion of its deliberations the grievance committee recommended that Garcia be discharged. O'Rourke forwarded the case to the plant manager recommending that he approve the grievance committee's findings. After reviewing the testimony and Garcia's personnel folder, the plant manager asked his secretary to summon O'Rourke and Rogers to his office immediately.

EXHIBIT 1

The Lone Star Manufacturing Company, Inc.

Office of the Personnel Director

April 2

Mrs. Rosita Garcia
Cutting Department
Lone Star Manufacturing Co.

Dear Mrs. Garcia:

This is to advise you that it is proposed to effect your discharge for excessive absence without proper authority to be effective at the end of the second shift, 11:00 p.m., April 9.

The specific charges set forth below are made against you in support of the above proposed action:

You have been absent without proper authority on the following dates:

    April 17, 18, last year
    April 21, last year
    October 1, last year
    March 28 of this year

You have been given many opportunities to improve your record. After your absence on October 1, Miss Mason discussed the matter with you and determined to give you another chance. She advised you that there must be no recurrence. As recently as February 12, you failed to call in or report for duty. This absence was charged to illness in the hope that you would not again violate requirements.[1]

Your unplanned absences have caused great hardship to other personnel in your section. As you know, they must work much harder to keep up the flow of material or someone from the first shift must work straight through both shifts.

In accordance with our plant regulations you have the right to answer this notice of proposed removal personally, and in writing, and to submit any and all evidence you may desire. The personnel office will make such records available as you may require for preparation of your reply. Your answer should be mailed or delivered to the Personnel Director on or before April 9.

Careful consideration will be given to your reply.

Yours truly,
/s/ G. O'Rourke
Personnel Director

---

[1] See Exhibit 3 for Lone Star's standard penalties for unexcused absences.

EXHIBIT 2

The Lone Star Manufacturing Company, Inc.

April 6

Mr. Nelson
Personnel Office

Dear Mr. Nelson:

In reply to the letter that was given to me dated April 2 where I see that my removal has been asked for excessive absence.

1-Reason: for being absent on April 17 took two days off by mistake a week before I had been off on Sunday and Monday and I thought I was off the same days for that week. Tuesday when I report to work I had change my clothes when one of girls ask me what was I doing there and I told her I was going to work and she said you are now on second shift. She told me that I had taken the wrong days. Miss Mason came along and said that Mrs. Falconer wanted to see me. So I change my clothes and went to see her she asked me if the notice was still up when I took off Saturday and I said I don't know. She then told me that personnel office had send me a letter and she did not know what they were going to do. I went to personnel office and she told me that the letter was sent to me because I did not show to work and she did not know if I want to work or not. I all so ask personnel office that if I hadn't taken off Sunday and Monday then I would have had 8 working days without a day off. It was the first time that I was going to work over 5 days without days off. And she told me how they work it. That day I went home and I was mad when I got home. Then I got nervous and not work the next day. October 1 had for Supper some Pork Chops and around 8:30 I was very sick at 10:30 I was in the General Hospital very sick for Food Poison. I call personnel office when I got out of the hospital around 4:00 p.m. October 1 and told her, and she ask me if I was going to be able to work that following day and I told her I would that I was weak, but I was not hurting. I could bring prove from Dr. Lee and my bill for $28.30 for that short time I was in the hospital so I do believe I was sick.

February 12, I went up on Mountain when I came down that afternoon I was very sick. I call and said I could not make it. I went to see the Dr. next day, I was going to have a Lab test and if I was sick I was going to let the Supervisor know. But the medicine he gave me stopped me from having pain and I did not take the test March 28. I did not show to work because I have a boy that went to Mexico about 200 miles away for a short visit and he went horse back riding and he fall from the horse, was trying to race with other kids and was hurt. This same boy has been in the hospital twice because has been in wrecks and he pass out for hours. So when they send word to me what I thought was the worse so I took off not thinking of calling or not. The boy was not hurt too bad and I try to come back on the next bus, but I could not make it. When I get here that was at 3:00 to late to report to work, did not call that day because knew I would not do me any good.

Mr. Nelson, why aren't all personnel treat the same? The date that they gave me the letter I was in Mrs. Falconer office when Mrs. Torres had been off for mistake. She told her that for that day she would get no pay. But why not a day suspension along with no pay. That's the way I was treat. Mrs. Torres has been here long and she too made a mistake.

Some of the absence that they have given me are unreasonable and I want to go through the Grievance Procedure feeling that is action is unjust.[1]

I also request a hearing. Please excuse my letter.

/s/ ROSITA GARCIA

EXHIBIT 3

The Lone Star Manufacturing Company, Inc.

PLANT REGULATIONS
NUMBER   8-19   July 1

Section XIV

DISCIPLINARY ACTIONS

TABLE OF STANDARD ACTIONS

7. Absence without authority (Any absence from duty which has not been granted and approved pursuant to provisions of Section XIII)

   First Offense: Official written reprimand or suspension of one to three days with no pay for the absence or the suspension.

   Second Offense: Four to six days suspension with no pay for the absence or the suspension.

   Third Offense: Seven to ten days suspension with no pay for the absence or the suspension, or discharge.

❋ ❋ ❋ ❋ ❋ ❋ ❋ ❋ ❋ ❋ ❋ ❋ ❋ ❋ ❋

JOHN K. BOONE
Plant Manager

---

[1] Under the Lone Star's plant regulations an employee could appeal to the Plant Grievance Committee if he felt that he had been treated unjustly in any action affecting him and the grievance committee would hold a hearing.

QUESTIONS

1. Were the various punishments given the employee in line with the company's table of standard action?

2. How much basis do you think there is for the employee's charge (see Exhibit 2) that punishment is not administered fairly?

3. What can you say with respect to communications between management and the employees in this company? How could communications be improved if such is necessary?

4. What do you think of the company's employee orientation program? What improvements, if any, would you recommend?

5. In what respects does employee rating affect this case?

6. What do you think of the grievance committee as constituted? Give reasons for your opinion.

7. What would you suggest for improvements in the procedure used in this company for the handling of a grievance?

8. What do you suppose the plant manager has in mind discussing with O'Rourke? Rogers?

9. Assuming you are the plant manager, would you approve the recommendations of the Grievance Committee? Why?

23

Thrace Textiles, Inc.

THRACE TEXTILES, INC., located in an eastern state, manufactures rayon fabric utilizing the viscose process, a means whereby wood pulp is converted to rayon thread. The company also has a weaving operation in which the thread is woven into fabric.

Begun in 1920, the company has progressed slowly but steadily since its inception to the point where it could expand on a sound basis. This expansion has taken the form of a new nylon and synthetic fiber division which adjoins the older rayon plant. Having just completed the new plant in June of 1958, August of that same year found Thrace still adding workers needed to operate it. Some of the workers in the rayon plant had indicated a desire to transfer to the new plant averring that the newer plant had better working conditions. Where workers expressed such interest and where they could be fitted into the new operation, the company acceded to requests for transfer.

Workers in the rayon plant had been organized for approximately ten years, and management-union relations, though occasionally disrupted by disagreement of company and union over contract renewal, had been generally good. Only a small number of grievances went to arbitration each year. Though the new plant had not been fully staffed, some efforts were already being made to organize the workers. Top management, still opposed to unionization in principle, if not in active opposition, was anxious to prevent organization in the nylon division if possible.

Morgan West, an English chemist, had founded the company and steadfastly believed that workers were privileged indeed to work for Thrace. He had often been heard to comment that things had never been so good in Britain. Morgan vacated the presidency in 1951 in favor of his son Peter who maintained the same views about unions and about employment with his company.

At one stage of rayon manufacture, wood pulp is converted to small tufts of fiber resembling cotton bolls. These tufts are fed into a hopper from which small, electrically driven trucks are loaded. The trucks transfer the material to another department some fifty yards away where other machines continue to process the fiber.

157

A fleet of twelve trucks is required to keep production moving, and each of the electric trucks has an operator. The route to the trucks' destination is amply wide for passage but because of the trucks' height all six room openings through which they pass necessitate the operator ducking his head. All of the doorways are interlaced overhead with electrical and air conditioning conduits. In addition, humidity control equipment is so extensive that pipes have to be run over the doorways.

One day, some three weeks prior to the scheduled opening of the new plant, a newly hired driver neglected to duck. In the ensuing accident, the driver was knocked off the moving truck and suffered a fractured skull. The driverless truck continued until it rammed into a vat of acid causing a fire to break out which destroyed the truck and vat while damaging surrounding equipment to the extent of several thousand dollars.

Following the accident, one of the plant's safety engineers surveyed the damage and investigated the cause. When it was determined that the operator forgot to duck, the recommendation that roofs be installed over the truck operator's head was presented and adopted.

Approximately two weeks after installation of the roofs, a personnel assistant and the drivers' foreman were discussing the accident at the scene when loud banging and ripping noises were heard coming from the loading room. Investigating, they found all the trucks stopped and the drivers with an assortment of tools at work knocking and ripping the recently installed roofs off the cabs of their trucks. When approached by the foreman and personnel assistant, they stopped and stood expectantly. The foreman asked what was going on and was answered by one of the older men, later identified as the shop steward. The answer given was: "We've all drove these d—— trucks at least five years—, I've drove nearly ten and ain't none of us cracked our noggins yit. We're figgering on gitting a transfer to that new nylon plant and we ain't gonna drive humped over in these here trucks 'til we git moved."

Both the foreman and his visitor noticed that the roof was indeed too low to permit drivers to stand erect; that it *did* require them to operate with their heads ducked down and bodies hunched over. They also found that the doors through which the trucks passed on their way to the other departments were too low to permit a higher mounting of the truck roofs.

QUESTIONS

1. Following the accident, what concepts of group dynamics might have been applied in working with the truck drivers?
2. How does the new nylon plant affect action in this case?
3. What should the foreman have done when he came upon the men ripping off the truck roofs?
4. What action is appropriate in this case and why?

24

Mrs. Janet Williams

PART A

The Wilson Clinic is an autonomous part of the Edmundson General Hospital, which is located in Connecticut. The clinic processes approximately thirty thousand patients per year. This volume is made up of diagnostic referral cases and obstetrical cases.

The medical staff of the clinic consists of approximately fifty doctors, seventy-five nurses, and eight to ten laboratory technicians. Each doctor on the staff is a specialist in his field. To maintain his specialty, each doctor is expected to teach and perform a substantial amount of research in addition to seeing private patients.

In March, 1964, Dr. Victor Buell, chairman of the Hospital Board, announced the appointment of John Driver as personnel director. Driver replaced the former personnel director, Richard Johnson, who resigned in December, 1963. The duties of the Personnel Department in addition to acquiring, developing and maintaining the clinic staff are to supervise all nonmedical activities, such as collection of accounts and administration of a precise appointment system made necessary by the time limit each doctor has to see patients.

The Clinic Board agreed in May, 1964, to employ an assistant for Driver to relieve him of some of the daily routine duties because a large amount of Driver's time was required each week in meetings with the Board. Charles Willis, a June graduate of the M.B.A. program at a major university was employed for this position.

In early July, Driver had an informal chat with Willis and told him that Dr. Buell had informed him that the Board was receiving a large number of complaints from the doctors on the staff concerning the appointment schedule. Upon examination, Willis and Driver found some doctors were complaining that they were finding themselves wasting time, sometimes as much as thirty minutes to an hour, waiting for patients who had been instructed to come in at the wrong time. Often, the complaint was just the opposite; the patient had been instructed to come in too early and subjected to an excessive waiting period. Driver instructed Willis to look into the appointment situation.

Willis first went to Mrs. Shirley Adams, the chief administrative supervisor, and asked what her views were on the situation. Mrs. Adams stated that "the appointment system has always been in a mess here. I hoped that when Mrs. Janet Williams (the appointment secretary) came up here she could have straightened these problems out. She got off to a bad start, though. Mr. Johnson didn't approve her application when she first submitted it so she appealed to Dr. Buell and he got the job for her. Mrs. Williams and I used to get along fine when we worked together downstairs. Since she has been up here, our relationship has been strained."

The next step Willis took was to review Mrs. Williams' file. He found that she was fifty-three years old, had been a widow one year and had a son of college age. The file contained a record of a telephone conversation from Dr. Buell to Johnson in December, 1963. The text of the conversation is as follows:

BUELL: Dick, don't you need someone for the appointment job? How about Mrs. Williams?

JOHNSON: Yes, I do need someone for that job. However, I wasn't impressed with Mrs. Williams' record. You know she was released from downstairs.

BUELL: Yes, I know. However, you don't need a genius in that job, do you? She seems to have the proper qualifications for the job. She knows all of the doctors' names, is middle-aged, knows medical terminology and has a pleasant face and voice. Why don't you put her on?

JOHNSON: Well, if you want her in that position, I'll put her there.

BUELL: I think she is capable of doing the job and would be pleasant to have around.

JOHNSON: I'll call her in the morning.

Willis also found that Mrs. Williams was one of the highest-paid employees in the entire hospital due to her long association with the different divisions of the hospital.

The appointment system as now set up requires a considerable amount of physical manipulation on the part of the appointments secretary. Each time a request for an appointment is received, the secretary must select the book containing the requested doctor's sheet, ascertain the available dates and hours, enter the appointment in the book, and fill out an appointment slip. The process is made more difficult by the size of each book. The books are heavily bound and measure approximately 2'-6" x 1'-6". Since most of the appointment requests are by telephone, the secretary usually has one hand occupied in the receiver while fumbling through the particular book.

Willis observed Mrs. Williams for a full day and found that she was in the habit of making shorthand notes (her own system) on the pages of the appointment book when she was rushed. Mrs. Williams could read her notes but Willis doubted whether anyone else could.

Upon request from Willis, several representatives of office-machinery companies made studies of the system and submitted recommendations for changes. Willis and Driver together selected a revolving file system which they felt would eliminate the physical problem of working with the different books.

Mrs. Adams and the other supervisors were called in to comment on the proposed change. All of the supervisors were in agreement that the proposed system would help to eliminate mistakes.

Willis and Driver then decided to take Mrs. Williams into their confidence in order to have her thoughts on the proposed changes; Mrs. Williams was not impressed with the system. She stated, "I haven't heard many complaints on the system we are now using. This new system has never been tried. Do we have to be the first to try it?" Driver then pointed out that everyone who had been consulted thought that the new system would help to get her job done with less effort. The conversation ended sharply with Mrs. Williams making the statement: "Well, if the new system comes in, I go!"

Driver has postponed action on the proposed change to this date. In a recent conversation with Willis, Driver stated: "I don't know what I'm going to do with Mrs. Williams. She is openly antagonistic towards Mrs. Adams, and appears to be strongly resentful when any change in the appointment system is mentioned. On top of all this, she seems to be a personal friend of Dr. Buell's. He has called me several times to inquire what we are doing to make her unhappy."

QUESTIONS

1. What part should the chairman of the Clinic Board play in the administration of the clinic personnel?

2. What type of problem would you, as personnel director, expect to encounter when someone in a position of authority applies pressure in order to get someone a job? Include in your discussion the probable results if (a) you yielded, and (b) if you did not yield.

3. What problems can a relatively new personnel director expect to encounter when proposing a change of some sort?

4. Why do you think Mrs. Williams objects so strongly to the proposed system?

5. What action, if any, would you, as personnel director, take?

6. What amount of authority would you recommend that a personnel director be given?

7. How would you appraise Johnson's relationship with Dr. Buell?

PART B

On Monday, August 12, 1964, Mrs. Williams approached Mrs. Adams and requested the following Friday off. Mrs. Adams replied, "I am afraid that I cannot approve it right now, but I shall let you know definitely tomorrow. This is our annual vacation period and we have a good number of people out ill." On Tuesday, Mrs. Adams called Mrs. Williams after consulting with Driver and told her: "I cannot approve your request unless it's an emergency, because the clinic is already operating with a skeleton staff." Mrs. Williams, somewhat upset, replied, "In that case, I'll have to tell you, I will not be here on Friday. This engagement is important to me." Mrs. Adams then went to Willis and told him of Mrs. Williams' request, why it was not approved and what Mrs. Williams' reactions were.

Wednesday morning, after an informal discussion concerning the current workload of the staff, Willis and Driver decided not to allow anyone time off until some of the employees who were out sick returned to work.

Willis then went to Mrs. Williams and explained that he and Driver had decided that it would hamper the efficiency of the clinic and place undue hardship on the rest of the staff for anyone else to be out except in the case of an emergency. He further stated, "Friday is especially bad, as you know, since we have most of the O. B. patients in on that day." Though she did not say anything at the time, it was obvious to Willis that Mrs. Williams was not satisfied.

On Thursday morning, Mrs. Williams asked Mrs. Adams if she could go to see Willis. Mrs. Adams stated she had no objection and sent Mrs. Williams in to see Willis. Willis later reported the following conversation to Driver:

"During Mrs. Williams' visit, I was very sympathetic, but firm, in regard to our previous decision. The conversation lasted about an hour and a half and, at the conclusion, Mrs. Williams stated, "Well, then you will explain to Mrs. Adams that I will be off Friday!" I was astounded! I finally managed to tell her that I was afraid she had missed the whole point of our conversation, that I had tried to explain to her why she could not be off Friday. She said, 'Why, Mr. Willis, I did not understand you to say that!' Finally, I told her that was my decision and if she wanted to go to see Driver to please feel free to do so."

Mrs. Williams met Driver in the hall later in the day and asked if she could talk to him. Driver consented and they went to his office. Mrs. Williams renewed her request and explained that she had made arrangements to go to Bridgeport to keep a golf date with Bart Raleigh, Congressional representative for Bridgeport. Driver told Mrs. Williams: "It is my considered opinion that you should work on Friday. It is my main responsibility to keep this clinic adequately staffed. I would suggest that you call Mr. Raleigh and explain the situation to him."

That night, Mrs. Williams called Driver and stated: "I have been unable to get in touch with Mr. Raleigh. May I call Mrs. Adams and explain this to her?" Mr. Driver: "I suggest that you go to Mr. Raleigh's home and leave a note if you cannot reach him by telephone. No, I do not mind if you call Mrs. Adams."

In the telephone conversation with Mrs. Adams, Mrs. Williams explained why she wanted the time off. She told Mrs. Adams of her conversation with Driver and explained that she could not go to his house because of "the way it would look." She further stated that "Mr. Driver said if it was all right with you for me to be off tomorrow, it would be all right with him." Mrs. Adams replied, "Under the circumstances, I said no and I would still have to say no; but if Mr. Driver says it is all right with him, it will be all right with me."

Mrs. Williams did not report to work on Friday. When Driver learned of this, he approached Mrs. Adams and Willis to find out why. He was surprised to find both Mrs. Adams and Willis thinking he had by-passed them and given Mrs. Williams the day off. Driver then explained: "She called me last night and said she had been unable to get in touch with Mr. Raleigh and asked if it was all right for her to call Mrs. Adams. I could see no harm in that, so I said yes. However, I did not give her permission to be off."

Mrs. Williams reported for work on Saturday morning.

QUESTIONS

1. What factors do you think allowed this situation to get to the point of confusion it finally arrived at?
2. Evaluate Mrs. Williams, Mrs. Adams, Mr. Willis and Mr. Driver.
3. What action, as personnel director, would you take concerning Mrs. Williams?
4. What do you think of the organizational relationships in this case?
5. What could be done to see that similar problems do not occur?

SECTION V

Administration of Labor Costs

THE ADMINISTRATION of wages, salaries, and other labor costs is difficult for a number of reasons. To both employee and employer money is a sensitive and important subject. The employee is concerned not only with the absolute amount of his pay but also with the pay he receives relative to others. The employer of course thinks of wages in terms of their importance to costs and to profits; at the same time, he has some appreciation for their meaning to employees and is reluctant to disturb existing wage relationships. But maladministration takes place in wages and salaries for numerous reasons: supervisors are subject to pressures that lead them to make unwise decisions; theory and principle are deficient in this area; it is a phase of personnel management which is vulnerable to bargaining and to ill-considered compromise. As a consequence, inequities and other problems creep into this area of administration.

Cases in this section consider incentives for both wage and salaried employees, wage classifications and wage scales, the relation between supervisors' and subordinates' pay, and various wage and salary policies. The last case deals with the increasingly important labor cost item of employee benefits and services.

25

Termite Control, Inc.

ON JANUARY 7, 1964, at a meeting with the foremen of the Rowe plant of Termite Control, Inc., Mr. Max Smith, vice-president in charge of production, was confronted with the question of incentive wages for crane crews in the shipping department. Smith realized that immediate action must be taken and that he would have to make appropriate recommendations to the executives at their meeting on January 11th.

Termite Control, one of the world's largest wood-preserving firms, produces treated electric and telephone poles, railroad cross ties, piling, lumber, and fence posts. When founded in 1927, the company specialized in the sale of lumber and ties, and as sales increased, a plant was constructed near Rowe, Alabama, a town of 8,000 persons. This plant eventually expanded into the largest pressure-treating operation in the world, and in 1937, another plant was constructed in Stramburg.

General offices are located in Rowe, with sales offices in Washington, New York, and Richmond. Storage yards are operated in Burlington and Rahway, New Jersey to implement distribution along the Atlantic seaboard.

Economic cycles have a distinct influence on sales and consequently on production of the firm. However, the company has maintained a good sales record over the years and has suffered a deficit for only one year since its incorporation.

As a result of growth in the industry and the discovery of a new wood-seasoning process, a sister corporation, Quick, Inc., was spun off from Termite Control in 1959. It holds and administers the patent on the quick-drying process, designs plants for other firms, and engages in a vigorous program of research and development.

As of September 30, 1963, Termite Control had assets of $4,400,000, with those of Quick, Inc. totaling $194,000.

Since its organization in 1927, Termite Control has been, typically, a family controlled firm. The founder is now chairman of the Board and his son is president of both Termite Control and Quick. The Board of Directors is made up of seven men, of whom four are officers of the firm. Policy is dictated to the president who in turn coordinates with the secretary-treasurer and the vice-presidents (see Exhibit 1). These executives meet every Monday morning to discuss problems and to formulate plans for the firm. The vice-president in charge of production, Smith, controls both plants and is responsible for the personnel, production, and engineering functions at each (see Exhibit 1 a).

The wood-preserving process is a very complicated treatment, involving long periods of time and several intermediate processes. Termite Control obtains some of its untreated wood from its own timberlands, but the largest portion is purchased. Four purchasers are employed to travel throughout the South and to locate and obtain timber rights on land. A contract is then drawn up with a timber producer (cutter) who will cut and haul the timber to a railroad siding. At this point a Termite Control inspector closely measures and grades each piece (the term "poles" will be used hereafter) before it is loaded into a gondola. The gondolas are then routed to either plant, depending upon the need for materials.

When the poles arrive at the plant, they are immediately unloaded from the railroad cars onto skids which feed into the pole-peeling machines. Here the remaining bark is removed, and the timbers are smoothed. The poles are then stacked to dry and season for two to three months (Quick's process for cross ties and lumber reduces this to a 24-hour seasoning period). They are unstacked and moved to the pole yard where they are framed (grooved and bored) according to customers' specifications. This is semiskilled hand work and must pass a rigid customer inspection.

The poles are placed on trams by cranes, and the charge (group of poles) is moved to the treating room by diesel electric switcher. Here the charge is pushed into a cylinder approximately 175 feet in length to undergo the actual preservation. Termite Control uses several different types of liquid preservatives, with each treatment generally involving the same processes. The cylinder is made air tight, and the poles are steamed in order to open up the cells of the wood. Then the liquid preservative at about 250° F is pumped into the cylinder and put under intense pressure. This pressure is maintained for two to four hours and a vacuum is then pulled to remove excess liquids. The underlying theory of this empty-cell process is that the cells will be filled with preservative as the pressure is built up. When the vacuum is pulled, the preservative is withdrawn from the wood leaving only the surface of each cell coated or preserved.

After the above treatment is completed, the cylinder is opened and the charge pulled out onto the drying dock. Sufficient time is allowed for cooling, and the poles are then given another inspection, either by the customer's inspector or Termite Control personnel. This involves boring a specified number of poles with a hollow bit to obtain small wood borings.

Each boring is measured for the number of inches of peneration of the preservative, and based on the findings, the charge is accepted or rejected.

After acceptance or retreatment, the poles are either stored in the appropriate customer stockpiles or loaded onto railroad flat cars for immediate distribution.

Termite Control has always had the reputation for being a leader in the wood preserving field and for maintaining a high quality product. This is best exemplified by Lane Laboratories, research division of Miller Chemicals, choosing the Rowe plant for the site of extensive tests. Chemists were sent down from New York, and they worked at the plant over a period of two years. Results of their tests are still published and referred to by the laboratory.

Termite Control employs a total of 385 persons (see Exhibit 2 for breakdown). The office payroll includes the home office employees; supervisors at both plants; salesmen; buyers; and Washington, New York, New Jersey, and Virginia employees, making a total of 99. The Rowe plant payroll totals 184 and the Stramburg plant, 102.

Because of the intense competition in wood preserving and the unskilled nature of the work, the industry has been labeled "low wage." Numerous textile and industrial firms in the Rowe area offer higher wages and consequently bid away the better grade labor. Most of Termite Control's jobs require manual labor and necessitate the laborer working out of doors throughout the year. The climate is extremely hot in the summer months and uncomfortably cold during winter. Also, a wood-preserving plant is usually dirty and the work unpleasant. Most jobs involve hazardous operations, and many prospective employees are reluctant to work under such conditions. For these reasons Termite Control has always been plagued with the problem of having to employ substandard labor.

Prior to Smith's joining the company in 1956, the employment function was a haphazard operation. Each foreman (see Exhibit 1 a) would hire, terminate, or lay off the workers in his department strictly on an arbitrary basis. On many occasions a worker would be cut off from one department and then would be hired immediately by another department foreman.

But Smith established an employment office which centralized all plant personnel relations. An employment director was hired to employ and discharge workers and to direct safety and first aid. A policy of layoff based on seniority was established which created a better feeling of security among employees.

Only once has Termite Control been affected by unionization. In 1948, a group of skilled employees organized a local union and struck for higher wages. Since this was a small part of the entire work force, operations were continued. This led to picketing the railroad spur track and occasional acts of violence when the railroad switch engine crossed the lines. A court injunction was obtained by Termite Control, and eventually the strike was broken. Most of the striking employees were not rehired, and no attempts to form a union have since taken place.

Since Termite Control deals in interstate commerce, the firm is subject to the federal minimum-wage legislation set forth in the Fair Labor Standards Act. The $1.25 per hour minimum and time and one-half for overtime compensation apply to all plant employees, but several different methods of wage computation are used, i.e., hourly, piecework, and group incentive. The reconciling of these various methods has always presented a difficult problem.

When Smith became production vice-president, he contracted with an industrial relations consultant for advice on setting up an incentive plan. After several months of study and investigation, a plan was devised, standards set, and rates published.

The plan was installed but was discarded after two years of operation. It was found that the seasonality of the work hindered the plan and that productivity had not increased as expected. The plan was quite complicated, and it was difficult for the foremen to compute the required payroll data. The executives recognized the plan's shortcomings and eliminated complicated incentive calculations except for crane crews, when the minimum wage was raised from $1.00 to $1.25 per hour. This increase was not an across-the-board $.25 raise for each employee, because the executives felt that those making $1.25 or more should not receive the full amount. Therefore, a wage scale was drawn up and approved whereby an hourly rate is paid for each job regardless of seniority.

The lumber yard, treating room, and shipping department work strictly on an hourly basis; the tie and pole yards are almost exclusively on piecework. This is because the latter are concerned with railroad cars that must be returned to the railroad immediately or penalty charges will be imposed.

Termite Control offers its employees several benefits over and above the usual paid vacation and individual insurance. A profit-sharing retirement plan for all employees provides an incentive intended to produce efficiency and to build up longevity with the firm. A group life and hospitalization insurance plan has been very popular among the workers. Each Christmas a party is given, at which time service lapel pins are awarded and fruit baskets distributed. Pins are given for each five years of tenure, and the recipients are generally proud of their recognition.

The groups of employees remaining on the incentive plan are the crane crews, three on the pole yard, and three in the shipping department. Each crew is made up of a foreman (checker), an operator, and three crewmen.

The shipping foreman, Henry Mays reported to Smith the strong feelings of dissatisfaction among his crane crews because of the incentive plan. In this production foreman meeting, Mays recommended emphatically that the problem be resolved as soon as possible. Much of the discontent stemmed from wage payment methods. Only certain crane jobs were covered by the incentive plan, and the shipping crews are given little opportunity to work on incentive-covered jobs, whereas the pole yard crews were continually so engaged. Morale and productivity of the shipping crews were waning as take-home pay discrepancies continued, week after week.

The incentive plan was retained on the pole yard in order to encourage fast work with untreated materials. The railroad allows one day idle time on the gondolas in the plant without penalty, and under normal conditions the cranes must operate at peak efficiency to meet the unloading deadline. This operation requires that the poles be lifted out of the gondolas, one at a time, and placed on the skid leading to the pole peeling machines. Speed is also important in loading the untreated poles onto trams for movement to the treating room. The production schedule must be strictly adhered to, because each minute of idle cylinder time costs the company $10.

The incentive plan had established standards for the crew jobs with any work exceeding this amount calculated as a percent of the standard. This percent is the amount that production costs were reduced by the crew's actions, and a portion of these increased profits is apportioned to crew members as a percentage of their hourly wages.

But the shipping crane crews were not required to rush their operations. Their objective was to load the finished poles neatly and safely for shipment. Minimum damage and quality of workmanship are the important factors, more skill being required for such operations than for pole yard jobs. Yet the base hourly rate of pole and shipping crane crews is the same:

Crane operator	$1.80
Crane foreman	1.60
Crane crewman	1.30-1.40

The crane operator received an hourly rate higher than the foreman because of his skill and because of labor shortage in this classification. The only incentive job performed by the shipping crews was the removing of treated poles from trams, which required but a small proportion of their time.

In the same meeting with Smith, shipping foreman Mays mentioned the long hours required by his job and that no additional compensation was being received, since he was on salary in contrast to crane foremen who were on an hourly pay basis. He pointed out that foremen come to work at 7 a.m. and normally leave around 6 p.m. The other foremen agreed that this should be discussed along with wage rates and incentives. At the close of the meeting Smith stated that he would bring up both matters at the next Monday meeting of the executives.

Before that meeting Smith felt that he should review the situation and draft notes concerning the recommendations he would make. He realized that this was a difficult situation and that several important factors should be considered before deciding on any recommendations.

Termite Control could not afford to lose any of the crane crews, especially the operators, because they are some of the most highly skilled workers in the plant.

Safety has always been a problem for Termite Control since most jobs are hazardous. The emphasis on speed in the pole yard had recently caused several accidents involving crane crews. The most spectacular occurred when an operator, carrying a group of poles from the stock to the trams, allowed the load to drag the ground while the crane was traveling at 15 miles per hour. The load swung back into the crane, shearing off the top of the cab just above the operator's head.

With these considerations in mind, Smith sat down to make notes and reach a final decision as to what he should recommend to the executives on Monday morning concerning the incentive and supervisory compensations.

QUESTIONS

1. What are the causes of wage problems among the crane crews?
2. What is the connection between safety and incentive plans? How can safety be emphasized under incentive plans?
3. In adjusting wages after an increase in the minimum wage, should an across-the-board increase be granted?
4. Is the benefit plan of Termite Control, company or group oriented? Which is preferable?
5. Should the supervisors be compensated for their overtime? Why?
6. What indications are there to point up the need for an experienced personnel director?
7. What should Smith recommend for solution to the wage payment problems?

EXHIBIT 1

Termite Control, Inc.

Executive Organization Chart

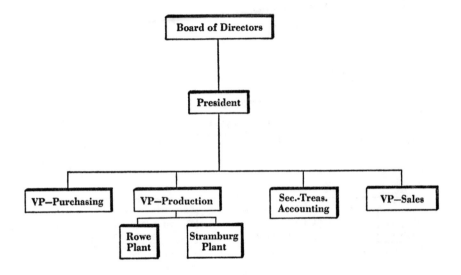

EXHIBIT 1a

Termite Control, Inc.

Rowe Plant Organization Chart

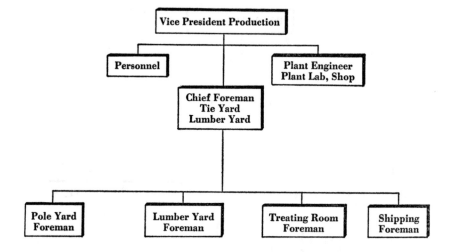

EXHIBIT 2

Termite Control, Inc.

Payroll Employees

Rowe Plant	184
Stramburg Plant	102
Office	99
	385

Office		*Plant*	
Janitors	2	Pole Yard	57
Truck Dept.	10	Tie Yard	25
Accounting	12	Lumber Yard	32
Purchasing	4	Shop and Construction	24
Inspectors	7	Treating	15
Sales	8	Shipping	30
Executives	4	Laboratory	1
Administration	3	Total Plant	184
Traffic	3		
Plant Offices	6		
Plant Supervisor	10		
Stramburg Plant	15		
Other*	15		
Total Office	99		

* Includes Washington, New York, New Jersey, and Virginia employees.

26

Citizens Telephone Company

THE CITIZENS TELEPHONE COMPANY, a small independent utility, provides telephone service for about 6,500 subscribers. It employs about fifty-five people and is locally owned. In 1956, Mr. A. M. Yeakel became general manager of the company. Yeakel is a graduate of the University of Michigan and a certified public accountant.

Aware of the importance of good public relations in a company of this type, Yeakel believes that good personnel relations are a prerequisite to any successful public relations program. In support of this belief the company has provided liberal employee benefits in comparison with the other organizations, even those of national scope, in that area. They include paid sick leave, group insurance, an annual bonus equal to one week's pay, two weeks' paid vacation, and a funded pension plan. These benefits, says Yeakel proudly, compare favorably with the benefits of any industrial company in the area. Wages in the company are in line with wages paid by other telephone companies in the state.

The superintendent of construction and maintenance for the company is Bob Pender. Pender has 12 men working under him. All wage increases in this department have to be approved first by Pender and then by Yeakel. Each man is considered for a rate increase periodically, generally once a year, on his service anniversary. When a man's record is being reviewed Pender evaluates the quantity and quality of his work and makes a recommendation to Yeakel. After a final decision, Pender informs the employee that he either has or has not been granted a raise.

"In my department," comments Pender, "there is always some gripe about wages. Just the other day, I was walking out of my office and overheard the tail end of a bull session among the boys. Jim Farnes, our cable splicer, was saying, " 'Hell, I haven't received a raise in two years now!' " The truth of the matter is that Jim was overpaid when he was hired. Jim came to us in 1956 from a contractor who was doing some work for us. We were in the middle of an expansion program and needed a cable-splicer bad. Jim can do the work but we had to pay him $2.25

an hour to get him. Then, Mr. Yeakel, when he came with the company, tried to even out wage inequities. Allowing for Jim's experience before he came with us, he was still two years ahead of the wages paid for splicers in the bigger companies. I explained the situation to Jim as best I could and told him that Mr. Yeakel would be glad to talk to him about the matter. Jim made no comment to me—didn't go to see Mr. Yeakel. Still, he puts in his two cents worth every time wages are mentioned."

"I've only turned down two other men when their wage increase came due. One of the men had missed several days' work to go hunting. He even went hunting one Saturday when he was supposed to work. We only work two men on Saturdays. Each man catches weekend work about every six weeks. I had a helluva time finding a man to take his place that Saturday morning. When his raise became due, I told him his work and attitude did not indicate that he deserved a raise. He took the matter to Mr. Yeakel. Mr. Yeakel backed me up 100 percent. About six months later the guy quit."

"The other man I had to turn down had been having wife troubles. He *really* had troubles with that woman. Between chasing after her in the day time and fighting with her all night, he wasn't able to offer much to the company. I think he had expected to lose his raise. Just said he agreed that he hadn't been doing the job but would try to improve."

Mr. Yeakel was aware that there were complaints regarding wages in the company. In order to alleviate the situation he devised a wage scale for the various job classifications in the construction and maintenance department. The following notice was presented to Bob Pender, who was to present it to his men at their weekly meetings:

NOTICE TO EMPLOYEES

The following job classifications with maximum rates of pay are hereby established for Outside-Plant Employees of the Citizens Telephone Company.

1. GROUND MEN—Starting rate of pay is $1.25 per hour, with increases each six months, until two years of service are completed. Annual increases thereafter until six years of service are completed. Maximum weekly salary for forty (40) hours is $64.00

2. ASSISTANT INSTALLER and CABLE-HELPER—Starting rate of pay is $1.25 per hour with increases each six months until two years of service are completed. Maximum weekly salary for forty (40) hours is $76.00.

3. LINEMAN—INSTALLER REPAIRMAN—Starting salary after two years of service or previous service experience is $64.00 per week, with annual increases to a maximum of $94.00 per week after ten years' service.

4. CABLE-SPLICER, TEST DESK, SUPPLY CLERK—Starting salary with three years of experience or equivalent is $74.00 per week, with annual increases to a maximum of $100.00 for ten years service.

5. CENTRAL OFFICE EQUIPMENT INSTALLER—REPAIRMAN and LINE FORE-MAN—Starting salary with three years' experience or equivalent is $80.20 per week, with annual increases to a maximum of $110.00 per week for ten years of service.

All salary increases will be based on quality of work. Each employee will be periodically considered for the salary increases. If the salary increase is not given at the scheduled time, the employee will be informed by his immediate supervisor and the salary increase will be granted as soon as the quality of work meets the required standards.

Exhibit 1 is a copy of Mr. Yeakel's wage scale. The wages for the various categories are based on the rates paid by a larger company for similar jobs. "The size of our company," says Mr. Yeakel, "makes advancement from one job category to another much slower than would be the case in the larger companies. To compensate for this slower promotion from job to job, I have used the same maximum and minimum wages for each category as we have had in the past, but extended the period necessary to reach the maximum by reducing the amount of each pay increase. Thus a man continues to make progress wage-wise within a job for a longer period of time." This detailed wage schedule was not to be seen by the employees.

QUESTIONS

1. What is your opinion of Yeakel's public relations philosophy?
2. Aanalyze each of the following examples cited by Pender:
   a. Jim Farnes, cable-splicer
   b. The man who went hunting
3. Analyze the wage scale.
   a. that was presented to the men
   b. the detailed breakdown
4. How do you evaluate the decision to extend time required to reach maximum of a classification, thus granting more wage increases.
5. Why does the word "quality" as an apparent synonym for "merit" present difficulties in administration?
6. If you were Pender how would you present this wage scale at your weekly meeting?

EXHIBIT 1

Citizens Telephone Company

Schedule of Wages by Job Classification

	Ground-man	Asst. Installer Cable Helper	Lineman Installer Repairman	Cable Splicer Asst. Supply Clerk Test Desk	Central Office Equipment Installer Line Foreman
Start	$1.25	$1.25			
6 Months	1.29	1.31			
12 "	1.33	1.37			
18 "	1.37	1.43			
24 "	1.41	1.49	$1.60		
36 "	1.45	1.55	1.70	$1.85	$2.05
48 "	1.50	1.64	1.80	1.95	2.15
60 "	1.55	1.73	1.90	2.05	2.25
72 "	1.60	1.82	2.00	2.15	2.35
84 "		1.90	2.10	2.25	2.45
96 "			2.20	2.35	2.55
108 "			2.27	2.45	2.65
120 "			2.35	2.50	2.75

27

Luminite Company

AFTER BUYING THE CHICAGO PLANT in December, 1960 from another manufacturing concern, Luminite modified the plant so as to serve as its headquarters for the company's newly established Commercial Control Division. The modern, 95,000-square foot building, occupying a thirty-five-acre site, was originally built there on the outskirts of Chicago in 1953. The newly acquired plant began successful operations in the spring of 1961. The Commercial Control Division which manufactures and markets pressure, float, and vacuum switches for a variety of industrial applications was placed under the supervision of Peter DeVoe.

During the past sixty years, the Luminite Company has grown from a small, two-man operation to an organization which manufactures its products in seventeen plants in the United States, Canada, Mexico, and Great Britain. It sells and services those products through more than one hundred Luminite offices, backed by an international network of over eight hundred authorized electrical distributors. Luminite makes a complete line of the kind of equipment which is needed to distribute and control electricity. Within the electrical industry, Luminite ranks eighth in size.

Peter DeVoe, manager of the Commercial Control Division, was quite pleased with overall operations at the Chicago plant. Since the plant first began production, several new products had been added until now the plant manufactured a line of products that had to do with electrical control of the following media: air, temperature, pressure, vacuum, liquid levels, and liquid flow. The plant employed roughly three hundred skilled and semiskilled workers. An organization chart for this division of Luminite is appended (See Charts 1, 2, 3).

In April, 1963, the home office of Luminite, located in Ohio, notified DeVoe that a general wage increase of $.05 an hour per employee would become effective on January 1, 1964. Furthermore, the company was establishing a pension program for its workers which would cost the company an additional $.03 an hour per employee. This pension plan, paid for entirely by the company, would also go into effect on January 1, 1964.

Since the Chicago plant was a self-contained unit, as can be seen from its organization charts, DeVoe became worried over the prospect of a decline in plant earnings for the next year. He calculated the total increase in cost for the two proposals as follows:

$$.05 = \text{wage increase}$$
$$\underline{.03 = \text{pension plan}}$$
$$.08 = \text{total increase per hour per employee}$$

$$2,000 = \text{total hours worked a year by each employee}$$
$$\underline{.08}$$
$$\$160.00 = \text{total yearly increase in cost to plant per employee}$$

$$\$160.00$$
$$\underline{300 = \text{total number of workers employed}}$$
$$\$48,000.00 = \text{total increase in cost}$$

It became apparent to DeVoe that he must find some way within his division to recapture the $48,000 being put out in next year's production cost in order to operate at the same profit level as before. In the event that he did not come up with a solution to this problem, the stockholders might become dissatisfied due to a decline in company earnings and possibly dividends, and all of this could conceivably come back to him as the manager. With the latter thought in mind, he set out to find a solution.

Two alternatives seemed feasible. The division could either increase productivity or raise prices. During a careful analysis of the two alternatives, it was decided that the competitive situation within the electrical industry would not allow the division to raise the prices of its products. Therefore, some method of increasing productivity had to be found.

The method DeVoe finally reached to increase productivity and to decrease labor costs was to automate certain functions within the plant. He sent for Robert Post, the personnel manager, to find out his views concerning the workers' morale and their attitude toward possible automation. Post told him that worker morale within the plant was good and pointed to the failure of a union drive to organize the workers at the plant, just last year. Furthermore, he said that the company paid wages comparable with any in the area and that the level of employment had increased steadily over the past two years with no layoffs. Workers at the plant were covered by liberal group health and insurance plans. They received seven paid holidays a year. Post also noted that two coffee breaks, one in the morning and the other in the afternoon, cost the plant $20,000 annually.

With these thoughts in mind, DeVoe held a conference with George Watts the works manager and with Frank Stover the industrial engineer supervisor. After explaining the situation concerning the necessity for reducing production costs, he asked the two men which function or functions in the factory could be automated most rapidly and most effectively. Stover stated that he could develop an automated machine which would reduce the assembly group of pressure control workers by ten employees. This saving alone would amount to about $50,000 a year, and the cost of machinery and controls would be taken care of through increased productivity in assembly.

After being given the go-ahead by DeVoe, Stover had the automated machine built. When completed, the machine was taken to the pressure control department for a trial run which proved successful.

For several days, the automated machine lay idle in the pressure control department. The sixty workers in this department became worried that the new machine would soon be followed by others, and that all of their jobs were in jeopardy. News of the automated machine spread rapidly by the grapevine throughout the factory. All of the workers had been told when hired that they had no guarantee of a job. They knew that their jobs depended on the profitability of the plant. They also knew that qualifications or merit were given top consideration over seniority in regard to job changes.

Stanley Wojehowicz, foreman of the assembly group of pressure control workers, realized that strong feelings of insecurity had developed among his employees. "Who would be laid off?" was the number one topic of conversation. Both production and quality of work declined within his department. More than once he reported this condition to Brice Wallinsky, the factory superintendent who finally became so concerned that he asked Watts what could be done. Watts immediately consulted with DeVoe. This was early in February. The next day, a Thursday, DeVoe called a meeting with Post, Stover, and Watts to plan strategy for alleviating anxiety and for working out final details of policy on worker changes that would take place when the new machine went into production. It so happened that the semiannual meeting of all plant employees was scheduled for Monday of the following week.

QUESTIONS

1. What do you think of Post's appraisal of morale and of factors that contribute thereto?

2. How do you feel about DeVoe's decision to reduce production costs by means of installing automated machinery? What other means of reducing production cost could he have considered?

3. What role should the personnel manager play in helping the workers to overcome their fears of automation?

4. When and under what conditions do you feel that automated machinery should be installed in a plant?

5. Do you think that displaced employees in this plant should be laid off? If so, on what basis, with how much notice, and should there be any severance pay? If there is no layoff, how can the machinery be placed in operation without a reduction in the work force?

6. If you were Mr. DeVoe, what would you say at the semiannual meeting of plant employees the following Monday?

7. What else can be done and by whom to reduce employee fears and anxieties?

CHART 1

Luminite Company

General Organization Chart

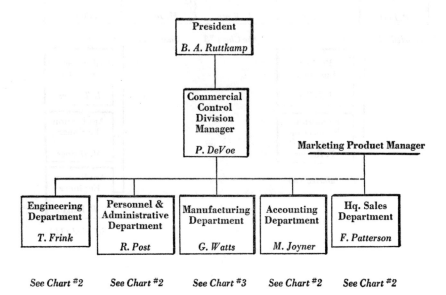

CHART 2

Luminite Company

Commercial Control Division

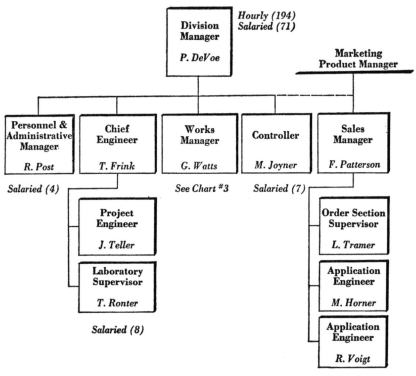

CHART 3

Luminite Company

Manufacturing Department, Commercial Control Division

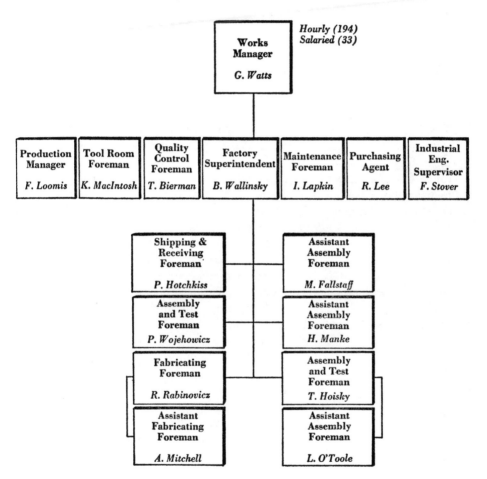

28

Department of Radio and Television

THE DEPARTMENT OF RADIO AND TELEVISION is a small department at a state university in the Far West. The department gives courses leading to professional degrees—BA and MA in Communications. These courses range from performance through staging and production to writing and management. Some of these courses are all or part laboratory where the students put on closed circuit radio and television productions. Several years ago, it was determined that the department required additional room and facilities. Money was allotted for an addition to the existing building which the "R and T" department occupied.

Dr. Robert Bandeis was chairman of the department when the idea for this expansion began. In June, 1963, Bandeis left for a similar position with a larger university. Dr. Benjamin Thurmond was named acting chairman, and in September, 1964 was made chairman.

Dave Gattey, director of operations for the department, was to handle all of the technical details for building and equipment installation. Gattey had been with the department for ten years. When he started, his position was mainly one of keeping the radio equipment operating. Several years later, he added a recording laboratory to the department's facilities. This recording studio did commercial recording of high quality. Profits from this operation were turned over to the department to augment its operating budget.

After several years of planning and building, the annex was finally completed. It was accepted by the university in March, 1964. After some delay in deciding, new equipment for the new building was ordered in the middle of April. According to the contracts, all items were to be delivered by July 1, 1964.

Gattey decided that the first work to be done in the old building was that the FM station's studios would be completely remodeled, including tearing down a dividing wall to enlarge the control room area. (The FM

186

studios were to remain in the basement of the old part of the building.) Also, the FM transmitter was in dire need of repair and tuning. When all of this was completed, the next project would be the installation of new television equipment. Then, the student master control for radio productions would have to be designed and constructed, and a large classroom fitted out for both radio and television. Finally, the old television facilities would need to be torn down and rebuilt, their control area integrated with the new studio. Gattey's estimates showed that there would be enough work to keep three or four full-time people busy until at least Christmas. These people would cost the department $7,000 in wages alone.

Two graduate students in the department expressed interest in installing the equipment. They were close friends, having graduated in electrical engineering from the same college. One of them, Roy Niles, had seven years' experience in radio and two years in television. The other, Larry Ames, had four years' radio and two years' television experience. Both held FCC (First Class Radio-telephone Operator's) Licenses. Nick Davis, also an electrical engineer, applied for installation work. He held a FCC also and had done work for Gattey before. Charles Adams, an undergraduate in the department, applied for general installation work with emphasis on lighting in the television studios. And Henry Stevens, who had worked with Gattey for several years in the Recording Lab, also applied for installation work.

Gattey arranged for Nick Davis to do the transmitter overhaul at $2.50 per hour. Funds available for this job were to be expended by the end of June. Davis started work during the middle of May on the transmitter which was located on a high hill in the northern part of the city. Gattey was not able to go to the transmitter building often because he could not spare the time.

Dr. Thurmond called Ames and Niles for an interview. Dr. Thurmond started by saying, "Dave Gattey tells me that you both are qualified to do equipment installation. Will you work for us at the rate of $2.00 per hour?" Both Ames and Niles said that they would not. They indicated that they both had offers that would allow them to make more during the summer. Dr. Thurmond then asked, "What will you work for?" Niles replied that he would work for $2.50 per hour. Ames concurred, saying that he would need at least $1,700 for his summer work. Dr. Thurmond then said, "Well, O.K." He proceeded to tell the men that he would expect them to work as much as they were physically able—that the entire installation had to be finished by the time classes started in September. With these remarks, the interview was terminated.

Charles Adams was hired at the rate of $1.25 per hour to assist Niles and Ames. Henry Stevens had worked for the department in the past, and so Gattey did not feel that his application could be refused. Although Dr. Thurmond was not pleased with Stevens' previous work, Gattey intervened in his behalf, and Dr. Thurmond allowed Stevens to install the New Recording Lab. Stevens would get 15 percent of gross when the lab was operational again. Dr. Thurmond felt that since he had only received $3,000 for installation wages, he could use Recording Lab profits to augment the wages account.

All of these interviews took place during the last week in April. During the first week in May, Dr. Thurmond approached Ames, Niles, and Adams. He explained that if he did not use all of the money in one of the wage accounts by the last day of June, the account would revert back to the university and he could no longer use it. That date was the end of a fiscal year. He asked if he could begin paying the three as of that day, even though none of them had yet begun work. The condition would be that each of the men repay the hours to the department at his own convenience. All three accepted the terms of the offer and agreed to it.

Classes in the university ended in late May and Niles and Ames began working on the FM studios. Actual work went slowly. Most of the hours for the first several weeks went into planning the new installation and dismantling the old setup. Tearing out the dividing wall was a larger task than anyone had expected. Because of it, all of the electrical wiring had to be redone. Ames and Niles were left on their own to do as they saw fit. The only contact with Gattey came when they needed parts that were not planned on. Gattey would do the paperwork to get the parts for them. But as time progressed, Gattey asked them to do the ordering themselves.

The university had a semimonthly payroll. In light of the unusual pay agreements, Ames and Niles requested that they be paid for only sixty-five hours each pay period. This would allow them to work off the hours they owed the department without building up too much time. Ames took off almost two weeks to get married, but he was still paid for sixty-five hours. In fact, neither Ames nor Niles gained much ground on the number of hours owed.

About the first of August, Adams was offered a full-time job with a television station. He accepted the job and left the department still owing them for a number of hours.

In the middle of August, Gattey turned in his resignation to Dr. Thurmond, effective the first of September. Dr. Thurmond immediately asked to talk with both Niles and Ames. He explained to them about Gattey's resignation and offered the job to whichever one of them wanted it. Both said that they would like to think it over for a day or so, since it would mean postponement of their degrees. They were told that the job would pay $7,500 per year, and that Dr. Thurmond was seeking permanence. Immediately after Niles and Ames left Dr. Thurmond's office, Frank

Perkins, another graduate student, was called in. He was filling in for the director of radio who was on sabbatical leave. He too was offered the job. He immediately accepted and indicated that he would like it as permanent employment. Later that day, Dr. Thurmond saw Ames and told him to forget about the job, that Perkins had asked for it on a permanent basis. Ames was to pass the word on to Niles. Frank Perkins held a FCC License likewise. His undergraduate major was Business.

Remodeling of the FM studios had not yet been finished. Unexpected complications slowed progress early in the project. One day Niles and Ames went to Perkins with a list of parts that they needed to finish the project. Perkins asked for complete written information as to manufacturer, cost, use and reason needed. When he got this list, he kept it for several days and then returned it saying, "O.K., go get them." This action was highly resented by both Niles and Ames. They claimed that Perkins had insulted their intelligence and their professional integrity.

When the FM studios were finished, Ames and Niles started to plan the television installation. Before he left, Gattey had told them that Perkins knew nothing about television and that the TV setup would be their "baby" to design and install. Both Ames and Niles had given a sigh of relief. They felt sure that Perkins would then leave them alone. Instead of leaving them alone, he asked even more questions. And instead of holding equipment lists up for several days, he held them up sometimes for weeks with no explanation other than "I should have done something about them, but I have been very busy."

In the area of wages, Perkins placed both Ames and Niles on straight one hour of pay for one hour of work. Dr. Thurmond upheld Perkins' decision. Perkins said that the time still owed could be made up after the wages ran out. The explanation given was that it would be easier to plan on when the money would run out if it were done his way, and that the books were too hard to keep under the present system.

Due to delays in shipment of the television equipment, Ames and Niles started on Radio Master Control, since all of its new equipment had arrived. During the week before classes were to begin numerous small items had to be installed in the building. Bulletin boards, book cases, and curtains had to be hung; boxes had to be moved to storage; and the front door did not open properly. Perkins told Niles and Ames that these jobs had to be done to get the department going for its fall schedule of teaching, and that they were expected to do them. Several days of painting and carrying boxes passed. One morning Perkins told Ames that he had some boxes to be moved that afternoon. Ames retorted that he did not intend to carry any more boxes. He was being paid to be an engineer and not a janitor. Perkins then said that *he* had been in on enough installation jobs to know that there was some "physical work" involved, and that Ames was expected to do it. Perkins said that they would talk later since he was busy right then. To this date, the two have never discussed this incident.

When classes started, Henry Stevens stopped his work in the Recording Lab. It was temporarily installed but had not yet started to make a profit. Thus, no additional funds were available for the wages account. Allocated wages ran out at the end of September. Ames and Niles had only received $1,450 of the $1,700 that they felt was promised to them. Moreover, both men still owed the department about one hundred hours each. They kept working on the installation of the Master Control area. Four weeks later, Perkins called Niles and Ames in and told them that he was "hiring" again. The department had obtained some more wage money— enough to last until the end of January. He asked if they would work sixteen hours a week excluding school vacation times for $2.50 per hour. Both men agreed, since they had finished paying back the hours owed.

This was the situation then in mid-January when preparations were underway for the start of the spring semester in early February. Perkins was again confronted with the problem of considerable moving in order to ready additional facilities for class use. A compounding factor was the space made available by Niles' and Ames' recently completed installations.

Recalling how Ames had resisted "chore" work in the fall, regreting that he had not finally disposed of the issue at that time, and yet having no budget for "moving," Perkins decided to see whether there was anything that Dr. Thurmond could do to help. Thurmond's reactions were that there was no money in the budget for this work and that Perkins should handle it in any way he saw fit—within the budget. Perkins left the interview somewhat "at a loss" but turned at once to the task of pondering over the strategy he should employ for approaching the two men.

QUESTIONS

1. Comment on the process of selection of personnel.

2. What do you think of the methods of determining wages?

3. If you were Dr. Thurmond, how would you have handled the interview with Ames and Niles?

4. How would you have handled the situation of having to use money for wages by a deadline or else lose the use of the money altogether?

5. Assuming that Perkins knew Ames and Niles were offered his job, how might this have affected his subsequent actions in relation to them?

6. What do you think about Perkins trying to have Ames and Niles perform unskilled work in preparation for the opening of school?

7. For the January "carrying" work, should Perkins approach both of the men at the same time, see one before the other, or just assume that this was part of their work since installation was completed?

8. If Perkins anticipated resistance, what means were at his disposal to motivate the men?

9. What other phases of salary administration are suggested by this case?

29

Worlichs and Company

WORLICHS AND COMPANY, in the small city of Nordelphia, Illinois, was one of a large national chain of department stores. The store handled such items as men's, women's, and children's wearing apparal; home furnishings; hardware; household appliances; and automobile accessories. Located in the heart of the central shopping district, it catered to a broad clientele consisting largely of low- to medium-income groups.

Worlichs and Company was founded in 1910 in a small building in Philadelphia. For the first thirty-five years of its existence, the business gradually mushroomed out of Philadelphia, extending branch stores westward through Ohio, Indiana, and Illinois. The phenomenal growth of the company over this period was such that by 1927 the firm had reached a gross sales volume of nearly $70 million. When chain store competition began to multiply in the late 1920's, Worlichs entered into a frantic race for retail store locations. During the two years, 1928-1929, more than fifty (50) Worlich Stores were opened with hasty planning and site arrangements undertaken by men with limited experience or skill, some without any background in department store retailing.

Consequently, with the added impact of the depression, 86 percent of the stores were being operated at a loss and at the close of 1931, thirty-six of them were in the process of being closed. Dividends on the common stock had been stopped in 1930. The corporation suffered a loss of over $6 million during 1931 and 1932.

From that time until the present, a major effort of the management has been to correct mistakes of unwise store locations, to eliminate the many uneconomical lease obligations which had been incurred, and to build the corporation's finances.

Worlichs had occupied its present quarters branch in Nordelphia since 1928. The company had made no major improvements on the building since that time. Consequently, working conditions and employee facilities were not as good as those in other department stores of comparable size in the area.

The Worlichs building was three-storied and in addition had a basement with space nearly equivalent to that of the main floor. Wearing apparel was located exclusively on the main floor. On the second floor were the credit department, the manager's office, and home furnishings. The top level was utilized for storage space and for the maintenance of a service department. Hardware, appliances, and automobile accessories were concentrated in the basement. The firm maintained a warehouse some three blocks distant from the store in which were stored the company trucks and the larger part of the inventory.

John Keen was the store's general manager. Keen was 56 years old and had held his present position for the past ten years. Raymond Bateman was assistant manager. Bateman had been at this location for only two years, having been an assistant manager at a Worlichs department store in a larger Midwestern city prior to his arrival at Nordelphia. At thirty-seven, he was an extremely energetic young man. Subordinate to the assistant manager were the various department managers, some of whom had assistant managers while others did not.

Total employment at Worlichs' Nordelphia store at present is 37 men and women, of whom 19 are direct salespersons. Seven of these salespersons work in the household appliance department, where about 50 percent of the store's annual sales of nearly $1,000,000 takes place. In this department are refrigerators, home freezers, electric and gas ranges, air-conditioners, vacuum cleaners, washing machines, sewing machines, oil heaters, television sets, radios, record-players, and tape-recorders.

The most recent addition to the staff of appliance salesmen is Frank R. Crone, a young man of twenty-five. In May, Crone applied to the Worlichs Company for a job as an appliance salesman in answer to an advertisement which appeared in a Nordelphia newspaper. The general manager, to whom Crone went first, told him that employment for appliance salesmen was handled exclusively by Durwood Jones, the appliance manager. Jones had served in his present capacity as department manager for one year, having previously worked for five years as a salesman since his graduation from high school, and at 25 was the youngest department manager in the store.

Crone's interview by Jones was informal and lasted only about ten minutes. Jones learned that Crone had just been released from the Army after having served four years as an officer in the Quartermaster Corps. Crone said that he received his commission from Officers Candidate School after having attended a small college for three years. He also told Jones that he was married and that his wife was expecting their first child in about two months. When asked if he had ever worked as a salesman, he replied that he had not.

Jones then explained that the company was seeking a salesman to bring the sales force to the level necessary to handle increased demand for appliances during the summer and fall seasons, but that since the department had been understaffed for the past three months, the job would be permanent. Jones then gave Crone an application to fill out and told Crone that he would be notified in a day or two. (The application blank asked for no further information other than what Crone had divulged in the interview except for a listing of personal and credit references.) After John Keen, Worlichs' general manager at Nordelphia reviewed the application and approved, Jones notified Crone of his selection. Keen commented to Jones that Crone was the only salesman in the store who had attended college.

As was customary, Crone was placed on a "draw" of $60 per week for the first two weeks of his employment. During this time, his main task was to orient himself to the store, familiarize himself with the appliances and their prices, observe the various selling techniques of the other salesmen, and make what sales he could with the understanding that commissions from such sales would be distributed among the other salesmen. At the end of the first two weeks, he would be given the choice of remaining on a salary of $60 per week or receiving only the commissions on the products he sold without a guarantee of salary. Jones told him that his decision would be irrevocable and that no salesman in the department ever elected to be paid on a salaried basis. He also told Crone that in view of the liberal commission policy, commissions of less than $100 per week would be considered by the company to indicate lack of selling effort.

Salesmen worked on the salesfloor in the store only on alternate days. Every other day they canvassed private homes and businesses in the surrounding area. For this, salesmen received an automobile expense allowance equal to 1 percent of their weekly sales made outside the store. As far as Crone was concerned, however, Jones instructed him to work entirely in the store during his two-week training period.

In addition to selling duties, the salesmen were responsible for deliveries and installing all appliances except gas ranges and air-conditioners. Installation of these two items was the responsibility of the customers. Although company trucks offered general delivery service to customers, the more fragile appliances, such as television sets, were not only installed by salesmen, but were delivered by them in their personal automobiles. Salesmen were also responsible for receiving appliances delivered to the store from the warehouse; for uncrating, assembling, and displaying merchandise; and for cleaning and polishing appliances traded in to be resold.

At the end of the two-week training period, Crone elected to be paid on a straight commission basis. He expressed doubt, however, respecting his ability to conduct a good sales presentation in a prospective customer's home and even as to using the pamphlets and folders provided him for this purpose. Consequently, he asked Jones if he could accompany him on a private call and observe the sales manager's technique.

Jones replied that his duties as department manager left him little time to make personal sales calls but that any of the other salesmen would be glad to take him along on a personal call. Jones said also: "Glad to see you taking such an interest in your work, boy. You should do all right this summer, especially now that air-conditioners and freezers are moving so well. I wish I were back on a commission basis instead of drawing a straight salary."

Crone accompanied one of the other salesmen on a canvass of an apartment house the following morning. Although no orders were received, Crone thought that he had benefitted from his observations of the other salesman.

It was customary for each salesman to distribute his personal calling card to every customer he assisted in the store. The salesman would then ask the name and address of the shopper. If a sale was not made, the name would then be filed in the salesman's personal file, dated, and noted as to the particular type of appliance discussed. Should that customer return within 90 days from the date his name was filed and purchase the particular type of appliance noted in the salesman's file, credit for the sale was given to the man who could produce the prospect's data card, regardless of which salesman actually consummated the sale.

Responsibility for claiming credit in the event of such a sale made by another salesman rested with the individual who had recorded the data on the customer in question. The procedure for so doing was merely to confront the salesman who had written the sales ticket with that customer's data card and request that your name be substituted on the sales ticket in place of his. If this was not done before the weekly commissions were paid, further claim to the sale became invalid.

In view of the fact that on any given work day, half of the sales force was in the store while the other half was soliciting outside sales, it was often difficult for a salesman on canvass to determine whether, in fact, sales were being made to customers for whom he held prospect cards. Although this policy frequently caused confusion and ill-feeling among the salesmen, Jones explained that he felt this control necessary to prevent an employee from losing a sale from a prospect due merely to his being out of the store on the particular day that the customer chose to buy.

One afternoon, after he had been employed for nearly six weeks, Crone was demonstrating a refrigerator to an elderly couple who were obviously very much interested in the appliance. Keith Appleton, one of the other salesmen, rushed up to the trio saying: "Well, how do you do, sir? It's good to see you again." Then turning to Crone, he said: "It's all right, Frank, these are my customers." Crone, noting the bewildered expression on the old man's face, said: "Look here, Appleton, if you will excuse us for a few minutes, I'll talk with you later."

"What are you trying to do, steal my sale?" said Appleton, loudly. "Didn't I talk with you the other day about a refrigerator, sir? Did you ask to speak to me when you came in the store?"

The woman flushed and began to fidget with her gloves. It was obvious that she was embarrassed. The old man said that he was sorry but that he had been in and out of a number of appliance stores recently and did not remember seeing either of the two salesmen previously.

Appleton then said: "What's your name, sir? I'll see if I have it in my file."

The man replied that it was not that important. He said that he and his wife were only shopping, anyway. He then took his wife's arm and began steering her toward the exit.

QUESTIONS

1. What would you consider to be important attributes for this type of salesman?

2. What do you think of the company's policy of distributing a new salesman's commissions for the first two weeks among the other salesmen?

3. Discuss the company's monetary compensation policy for salesmen, considering all phases of the salesman's responsibilities.

4. What do you think of the policy of having equipment installations handled by the salesmen?

5. Evaluate the company's program of training for salesmen.

6. What method of compensation for a sales manager such as Jones might increase his motivation? In what respects does a straight salary basis provide a superior method of compensation for a sales manager?

7. Evaluate Jones' policy of allowing the salesmen to compile individual prospect files. What might improve on this policy?

8. How could management prevent a recurrence of the type of incident involving the elderly couple?

30

National Power Tools Company, Inc.

NATIONAL POWER TOOLS COMPANY, INCORPORATED, is a leading manufacturer and distributor of small power tools for carpenters and mechanics. In addition to the production of items for established markets,
the company also does considerable research in the field of new metal
alloys, refined machinery designs, and improved products for the general
line.

The production and research departments of the company are operated
completely independently of each other except for joint staff services.
Each department maintains its own seniority rosters, although continuous
service dates count in either department.

National Power Tools prides itself on its excellent company-worker
relationships, and the way in which it has always treated each worker
with respect and dignity. It is the purpose of the company to maintain
an atmosphere in which each worker can feel that he is not only a worker,
but an important member of the company "family."

In early March, 1963, the company was preparing to announce a retirement plan for nonsalaried workers. This plan carried the following eligibility requirement:

> Those wage employees who completed three or more years of continuous
> service prior to January 1, 1963, will become members of the plan immedi-
> ately. Other employees may join the plan on the 1st day of January of the
> year following their completion of three years of continuous service.

In keeping with the policy of strong management-worker relations, it
was decided to announce the plan to the employees by means of a mime-
ographed letter from Mr. Robert Pearce, president of the company (see
Exhibit 1). Copies of this letter were to be placed in envelopes addressed
to each worker, and delivered to them personally by their immediate
supervisor. Each envelope was to have in the upper left hand corner
either "I" or "E." "I" would indicate that the particular worker was not

yet eligible for membership in the plan, while "E" would signify that the worker could join immediately. The plan had been discussed with the supervisors, and they had been instructed to explain the meaning of the symbols and to answer any questions which the workers might have.

Shortly after reporting to work one morning, Stan Jackson, a worker in the production department, received his letter from his shift supervisor, Dick Sims. When he inquired as to the meaning of the "I" on his envelope, Sims explained the eligibility requirement, telling Jackson that since he had not had three years' continuous employment as of January 1, 1963, he could not yet join the plan, but that he would be eligible later on.

"Later on?" Jackson yelled. "Why, I've been with this company over ten years. Don't tell me we're going to go through all this again. This is the third time that this thing about my length of employment has come up. It's high time the thing was settled once and for all."

To avoid creating a scene on the spot, Sims told Jackson to continue his work, and that he would see the personnel director immediately to determine whether an error had been made.

"Maybe Mr. Green can straighten this thing out," Jackson said. "I sure didn't get anywhere with that other fellow."

Sims left and went directly to the office of Bryan Green, personnel director of National Power Tools since February, 1961, at which time he had succeeded Ted Landreth, who had left to assume a position with another company. After hearing Sims' account of the situation which had prompted his visit, Green stated that, while he had not had any personal dealings with Jackson since coming to National, he would certainly look into the problem immediately.

Green's first step was to check Jackson's service record. He found it marked as follows:

> October 10, 1952 — Hired.
> August   4, 1960 — Voluntary termination, other employment.
> August 15, 1960 — Rehired.

A red line had been drawn under the August 4, 1960 entry, which was the standard procedure for indicating broken service or termination. Green next called Jackson to his office and questioned him about his earlier remarks to Sims. He pointed out that, according to his service record, Jackson's continuous service date was clearly August 15, 1960.

"But I've read the company manual," stated Jackson emphatically, "and I know where it says that any worker who has been here more than five years, and is laid off, can come back to work within nine months and keep his original service date. (See Exhibit 2.) I've been over all this before. I don't see why it keeps coming up."

"The policy to which you refer applies only to cases of termination for lack of work," said Green. "Your record states that you left voluntarily to take another job."

"I left when they did away with my job," stated Jackson, rather sarcastically.

"What do you mean?" asked Green.

"Well, back in 1960, they decided to do away with the job that I was working on. They told us to be looking around for another job, because they wouldn't be able to use us after that. Couple weeks later they called me and wanted me to come back, and I've been here ever since."

Green recognized the conflict between Jackson's story and the information on the service record. He decided that a thorough investigation was necessary. He thanked Jackson and told him to return to work, stating that he would check the matter more closely and get in touch with him in a few days.

After consulting supervision, and having a conference with all parties who had any knowledge of the case, Green was able to put together the following facts surrounding Jackson's situation.

In July, 1960, it had been decided by the company's management that the production department had capacity in excess of peak needs, and that certain operations could be integrated at an overall saving of 35 percent over the combined total cost of operations. Therefore, the decision had been made to discontinue these separate functions by such integration with August 15, 1960 as the target date. An analysis of personnel needs for the integrated operation indicated that ten employees would have to be terminated for lack of work. These men were called into a meeting by their supervisor on August 1, 1960, and were told that as of August 15 they would have no jobs, and that he would advise them to be looking around elsewhere for employment.

On August 4, 1960, Jackson, who was one of the ten men to be terminated on the 15th for lack of work, visited the personnel director, Mr. Landreth, and told him that he was quitting on that date because he had a job with another company. The personnel record of Jackson indicated that his continuous service date with the company was October 10, 1952. Landreth marked Jackson's record as follows:

8-4-60—voluntary termination—other employment

On August 13, 1960, a vacancy developed in the production department. The supervisor had told Landreth that he would like to have Jackson for the job if he were willing to take it. Accordingly, Jackson was notified to return to work if he would like to have the job. He accepted, and returned to work on August 15. Landreth marked Jackson's record as follows:

8-15-60—rehired

In December, 1960, when the semiannual vacation bonuses were paid, Jackson got none. He asked his supervisor to check with Personnel and find out why he did not get a bonus. The supervisor and the personnel director examined Jackson's file and determined that he had quit voluntarily on August 4, 1960 for other employment and had been rehired with a new continuous service date of August 15. The personnel director pointed out to the supervisor that the eligibility date for the bonus was May 31, 1960. The supervisor explained this to Jackson, who let the matter of the bonus drop.

In December, 1961, Jackson told his supervisor that he had never been quite satisfied with his treatment on bonuses, and asked that the matter be restudied. Once again he was given the same answer about broken service.

After considering the facts as thus presented, Green realized that he was faced with a real problem. Did the termination of August 4, 1960, although announced by Jackson himself as "quitting," actually have a voluntary aspect? Jackson had been told previously that he would have no job in two weeks, and was advised to look for employment elsewhere, which he did. Could the fact that he had chosen the date of his leaving by terminating his employment a matter of eleven days before being forced to do so be considered "voluntary termination"? Green further noted that Jackson had immediately accepted re-employment and reported back to the company at the earliest possible date after having been notified of a vacancy.

Not only was Jackson's immediate eligibility for membership in the retirement plan at stake, but other adjustments would be necessary should Green decide to reverse the initial ruling of Mr. Landreth. These involved: (1) awarding Jackson a 4 percent vacation bonus for the six months' period ending 11-30-60; (2) a 2 percent adjustment in bonus payments for the six months' periods ending 5-31-61, 11-30-61, 5-31-62, and 11-30-62.

EXHIBIT 1

National Power Tools Company

Letter from Company President to Workers, announcing new retirement plan

TO OUR EMPLOYEES:

This letter relates to a matter of utmost importance to you and your family. We hope that you will read it carefully.

For the past year, the management of National Power Tools Company has been studying the question of how to provide for your future security, in addition to and beyond the benefits which you have already had as an employee of this Company. We wanted a program which would also provide for your further participation in the Company's progress and success.

It is with genuine pleasure, therefore, that I am able to announce that National Power Tools Company has established a *Profit Sharing Retirement Plan* for you.

The new plan is being put into effect right away. Its major provisions are listed in the attached outline. Within the next few weeks, you will be given full details of the plan, and you will receive a handbook which covers all aspects of this new and very valuable benefit.

The Profit Sharing Retirement Plan involves no cost to you. The amount of money credited to your account will depend upon the profits of the company. We believe that the plan will thus be an added incentive for all employees to help increase profits. Each of you, by reason of this new program, will now have a greater personal stake in the profits earned by the Company each year.

I am gratified, of course, that National Power Tools Company is maintaining its leadership by the establishment of such a program. It will continue to be National's policy, as it has always been, to pay wages that are at the top level of the industry, and also to maintain all benefits at the highest possible level, consistent with the economic conditions of our business.

The success of the new Profit Sharing Retirement Plan will depend upon our Company's ability to continue profit improvement in each and every operation, despite the very competitive conditions which we face. Your own efforts —doing the best possible job you can—will mean much to the success of this plan and your own security and benefits under it.

I want to thank you for your past cooperation. "Working together" has been the theme all through the years in National, and I am confident that, by continuing to work together, all of us can look forward to an even better future.

Sincerely,

(Signed)   ROBERT PEARCE
President

EXHIBIT 2

National Power Tools Company

Extracts from Company Policy

TERMINATION FOR LACK OF WORK

Reinstatement
". . . Employees with more than sixty days but less than five years' continuous service terminated for lack of work and recalled within ninety days will reclaim their original continuous company service date.

Employees with five years or more continuous service terminated for lack of work and recalled within 270 days will reclaim their original continuous company service date . . ."

VACATION BONUS

Eligibility

". . . Employees with more than six months but less than five years continuous service as of November 30 and May 31 shall receive 2% of their gross earnings for the six months periods.

Employees with five years or more continuous service as of November 30 and May 31 shall receive 4% of their gross earnings for the six months period . . ."

RETIREMENT PLAN

Eligibility

". . . Membership in the Retirement Plan is based on three years' continuous service . . ."

Definition

". . . The date on which an employee was first employed and since when he has worked without a break in service by voluntary termination, or involuntary termination for unsatisfactory work or misconduct.

Recall from termination for lack of work within the periods(s) specified by policy shall not constitute a break. Authorized leaves of absence shall not cause breaks in service. Employment elsewhere during a period between termination for lack of work and recall within the period(s) specified by policy shall not cause a break in service . . ."

QUESTIONS

1. What, in your opinion, should Green's decision be? Why?
2. Do you feel that Landreth was, or should have been, aware that Jackson was one of the men who was to be terminated for lack of work?
3. What do you make of the fact that Jackson returned to the company as soon as he learned of a vacancy, despite the fact that he reportedly had found employment elsewhere?
4. Can you detect any ambiguities in company policy which might allow situations such as this one to develop?
5. Do you feel that a situation such as this one calls for specific policy?
6. Why do you feel that Jackson had been willing to "let the matter drop" on previous occasions, although he obviously was not satisfied with the decision of the personnel director?
7. Why do you think that this situation developed in the first place? What steps should the company take, if any, to prevent a recurrence?
8. What do you think is a fair policy on "continuous service" for matters such as lay-off, shift preference, vacation pay, consideration for promotion, and retirement?

The Management
of Labor Relations

As DISTINCT FROM OTHER FACETS of personnel management, *labor relations* has to do with groups rather than with individuals. A broad view of labor relations, such as that taken here, includes within its scope administration relative to minority groups, collective bargaining, and the general quality of management-employee relations. Any group poses special problems in personnel management. Accordingly, it behooves everyone in management to become familiar with research findings in group dynamics and to understand supervisory and policy problems that occur in working with groups.

The first cases in this section center around two minority groups, the handicapped and the Negro. Both handicapped persons and Negroes have in common their being victims of prejudice. For this reason, the administrator has to overcome problems of resistance to the employment and upward mobility of minority groups. The next two cases are in the realm of collective bargaining, one being considered in a grievance stage, the other in arbitration. Basically, both cases involve the administration of grievances, which are a salient part of the day-in, day-out functioning of collective bargaining. This is much more meaningful to labor relations in action than is the negotiating of an agreement. The final two cases concern (1) a union-organizing case which also has undertones of minority group relations (Negroes) and (2) a case of deteriorating relations within one department of a steel mill. While it is true that a high percentage of industry in this country is organized, it is also true that a high percentage is not organized, and so attention still needs to be paid to the organizing process. The last case, on relations within a department, bears testimony to the fact that problems so often exist in clusters, that a number of difficulties mushroom when a group of employees becomes disequilibriated.

31

Nancy Williams and Her Dog

RICHARD SMITH, age forty-five, was office manager of Interstate Farmers' Cooperative Association. After receiving his A.B. degree in business administration from the University of Kentucky at Lexington, he joined the association as assistant manager in 1950 and in January, 1961 succeeded the manager who retired from the post. The home office was in Louisville, Kentucky, where the association had, in 1961, an office force of seventy-four clerks and supervisors. Smith with the approval of his board of directors increased the number of office employees to ninety shortly after he became manager.

At the recommendation of the Kentucky Commission for the Blind, Smith agreed to hire Miss Nancy Williams in April, 1961 with the understanding that there would be a three-months' probationary period. This arrangement was made with the Blind Commission by whom Miss Williams had been trained in typing and transcribing. As for Miss Williams, she was under the impression that she was to complete her training in the Farmers' Cooperative office, and she was taken to the Louisville office by a representative of the Blind Commission.

Smith was well pleased with the accuracy of Miss Williams' typing work. On the first day of the second month of her employment he went to her desk and praised her before the other employees. He declared that she was a regular employee from that date on and said, "Miss Williams, we are glad to have you with us and we hope that you will enjoy working here. Your associates are fine people; please feel free to ask me for help, if you ever need any."

Miss Williams soon became friendly with the employees. They liked her because of her good nature and were ready to help her in every possible way. Three typists worked beside her. Any one of them gladly took her to the women's room at her request. They customarily asked her if she wanted any drink or candy whenever they went outside to get such things for themselves. Miss Williams made few typing mistakes and whenever she made a mistake she felt it at once. Any one of the three girls typing close to her corrected such mistakes at her request.

Miss Williams was a stranger to the town and she lived in a two-room apartment ten blocks away from the office. Smith thought it necessary that the company messenger escort her from home to the office every morning until she became familiar with the streets. Nearly every evening she was offered a ride by one worker or the other. Any evening she did not get one, she asked the messenger to escort her back home. After a month or so she told the messenger that she was able to come to the office by herself and that she needed help no longer. However, the employees continued offering her rides home almost every evening.

In July, 1961, a civic organization wished to present her with a seeing-eye dog. The organization wanted her to undergo a four-week dog keeping and training program before she got a dog. Smith granted her four weeks' leave on full pay, although this was an unprecedented favor. After she came back with the dog, the employees offered her rides only if it was raining.

The other typists soon noticed that Miss Williams became restless if they did not correct her typing mistakes immediately upon request. Often in the past, they would not help immediately, because of completing a sentence or paragraph first. For some time the girls did not object to her changing behavior; but it became irritating to them after four months' time. By then she had developed the habit of making demands rather than requests of the girls with whom she worked; it was quite common for her to order the girls: "Bring me a coke." or "Correct my letter" or even "Give me a ride home." Sometimes the girls acceded to her wishes and sometimes not, depending on their mood and also on the girl to whom she made her request. However, they all tried not to be harsh with her, although some girls were extremely annoyed. At the same time, most of them felt genuinely sorry for her.

One day Miss Williams told Smith that she needed somebody to take her back home every evening, because the evening traffic was too heavy. Smith asked the messenger to accompany Miss Williams. However, after a week he realized that the orderly would have to be paid five hours overtime a week for this extra service and so he refused Miss Williams the messenger's services. He contended that her dog was competent enough and that she needed no other help.

On top of these various complications and annoyances, Miss Williams' dog soon became spoiled. He growled if any employee went near his mistress. He was not kept neat nor was he washed so that his smell grew offensive. On more than one occasion he vomited on the office floor. When he turned out to be a nuisance, the employees brought the matter of the dog and of Miss Williams' changed attitude to Smith's attention.

It was the first time that he had heard about Miss Williams' demands. He talked to her and hinted that she should take care of her dog properly. However, he never mentioned that her associates did not like her manner of dealing with them. Her behavior toward the executives, incidentally, had remained as pleasant as ever.

After four more years, having found that Miss Williams was not trying to correct her behavior and that she was not taking care of the dog properly, Smith informed the Blind Commission that he was unable to keep Miss Williams on the payroll. After making inquiries, the Blind Commission agreed with Smith. They informed Miss Williams' mother about the situation and asked her to live with her daughter. On the advice of her mother Miss Williams resigned. In all, she worked with the association for almost five years, during which period she was given four wage increases. Until the very last day her work was excellent. Smith looked on her resignation as his own failure. His motto was, "The firing or resigning of an employee is a failure of the executive." And he admitted that he had not dealt with Miss Williams as he would have dealt with a nonhandicapped worker.

QUESTIONS

1. Do you agree with Mr. Smith that "the firing or resigning of an employee is a failure of the executive."

2. In your opinion, at which points did Smith prove himself to be weak or to make a faulty decision?

3. What in your opinion should an executive do to keep himself well informed about employees' mutual relationships and their attitudes toward the management? Should an executive necessarily know all about that sort of thing?

4. Why did Miss Williams become discourteous to her associates?

5. What could Smith have done to salvage Miss Williams?
    a. In relation to girls with whom she worked?
    b. In counseling with Miss Williams?

6. Was Smith justified in seeking a separation for Miss Williams?

7. What is the responsibility of business in such situations?

32

Trans-Appalachian Power Company

THE TRANS-APPALACHIAN POWER COMPANY has actively worked with integration of Negroes into the work force since World War II. For a number of reasons, however, a number of occupations have remained segregated—unavailability of qualified applicants, resistance (largely covert) of some craft unions and some supervisors, and consideration to customs in particular rural localities—especially the problem of housing. Despite various difficulties, T.A.P. management, operating under a strong policy of equal job opportunity has worked diligently to recruit and introduce qualified Negroes into the work force whenever the opportunity has arisen.

In Kentucky an oddly-segregated situation had developed over the years with a "hot-line" maintenance crew (working with "energized" equipment). They had operated in eastern Kentucky and West Virginia, on into Virginia since 1946, the crew composed entirely of Negroes working under the supervision of a white foreman. This was an efficient crew and a high-morale group that operated under an autocrat, a foreman who supervised with an iron hand.

In late 1962, the foreman retired and a decision about the crew was necessary since its makeup had changed over the years. As the original crew had grown older, replacements were largely by less skilled men unable to perform the full range of lineman functions. In fact, much of their work came to be devoted to painting. It became largely a crew of men whose experience was limited since they were introduced as apprentices and remained upon graduation despite their right to transfer to other crews under terms of the union-management agreement.

The decision was to break up the crew and place its members with hitherto exclusively white crews. Transfers were discussed with the I.B.E.W. which agreed to the move, the international representative saying, "These men are members and will be treated no better, no worse than anyone else."

One of the transfers, Harry Turnbow, was a young apprentice (age twenty-two) who had completed about one-fourth of his training for operations and maintenance work.

Before the transfer the personnel officer for the division, Bruce Mostan, arranged a meeting involving a colored personnel administrator with long service in T.A.P., Frank Dawse; the division director, A. F. Chipperman; and Harry Turnbow. Mr. Chipperman explained that the only place where there was an opening was with the crews at Lorain, Kentucky, at the foot of Tar Mountain. The construction men had said that trouble would ensue if a Negro worked in that vicinity. The reasons were that he could not obtain housing nor would local whites permit him on their property. Turnbow obviously apprehensive asked, "Isn't there some other place you can put me?" At this point the division director, Mr. Chipperman said, "We think it best for you and the cause of integration to go where the need is regardless of the local situation. We will do our part in attempting to relieve any complications that arise." That ended the conference.

In order to avert any potential "trouble" attendant on Turnbow's transfer, the director of power construction, A. F. Chipperman, the personnel officer, Bruce Mostan, and the international Representative of the I.B.E.W., Stu Robey, talked with the entire force of 100 men who worked in that area. As Mostan put it, "a few loudmouths" spoke up at the meeting, but there was no serious opposition voiced by the group as a whole. It was known that the general foreman Tampscott, a construction supervisor with twenty-six years' service who was originally from Jackson, Mississippi, was somewhat opposed to the idea, but as Mostan put it, "He was smart enough not to raise any questions in view of Mr. Chipperman's and Stu Robey's positive stand on the matter."

The meeting took place on a Friday afternoon in December, 1962, and the next Monday Turnbow went to work in Lorain. He commuted from Ramey, Kentucky, some twenty-odd miles away. Turnbow's work had been confined largely to painting so that he lacked skill in many important dimensions of lineman work. As the general foreman put it, Turnbow "grabbed a-holt of 'most everything" in order to improve.

From January 1, 1963, to May 8, Turnbow had three injuries. Twice he struck his knee against steel and suffered nasty abrasions: once his "spud wrench" slipped, cutting his face under the right eye. As a consequence of these injuries, the personnel officer conducted an inquiry, disturbed about possible causes stemming from ineptness, carelessness, or preoccupation. The reply of the top supervisor in the area, who had in turn investigated the situation, was: "Supervisors are in agreement that those accidents stem solely from Turnbow's excessive desire to help and to learn." On the basis of this information, Mostan called in Turnbow to reassure him, telling him that there was no cause for worry and that his work performance was good. As it turned out, Turnbow never had any recurrence of accidents nor did he have any trouble with the people of Tar Mountain.

The construction crew was shifted in the summer of 1963. Part went to West Virginia along with groups that had not attended the meeting prior to Turnbow's transfer. One thirteen-man crew with its five linemen began to fall behind with work because one man had quit and another was absent due to sickness. In this crew, linemen had never worked with Negroes.

The general foreman, one Friday afternoon in August, told Turnbow to move back and help the three linemen who were falling far behind in their work. When Turnbow walked back to the crew all three were "up in the steel." Of the three, one was an ex-apprentice, Albert Fremoyle, with about ten years' service, whose home was in Lenoir City, near Morgantown, West Virginia. The second was an "in-and-outer" from the extreme western part of Virginia who fitted the industry designation "boomer"—he worked wherever the greatest amount of overtime was. He was Nathaniel Hix and had worked in Florida, Arizona, and Illinois, as well as with T.A.P. from time to time. The third crew member and leader was Bradford Jones, a man with fifteen years' service who came originally from western North Carolina near Murphy. Jones had helped train Fremoyle and was definitely the leader of the linemen.

When Turnbow appeared, the three men came down. Jones went to general foreman Tampscott and said, "I've climbed for twenty-five years and I've never climbed with a Negro. What's more, I'm not going to now. And neither will Fremoyle or Hix."

QUESTIONS

1. If you were Tampscott how would you talk with the three men?
2. If you decided (as Tampscott) to see your superintendent, what would you recommend to him?
3. If you were the superintendent, what would you decide?
4. In case the situation reached the personnel officer, Bruce Mostan, what would you recommend as to his action?
5. What dangers do you see in each of the following alternatives:
    a. Remove Turnbow
    b. Terminate the three men
    c. Suspend (lay-off) the three men
    d. Transfer the three men
    e. Tell them if they do not return to work with Turnbow on Monday they are terminated

    Which (or what other solution) would you elect?

33

Langenderfer Manufacturing Company

THE LANGENDERFER MANUFACTURING COMPANY is engaged in light sheet-metal fabrication, and has an outstanding reputation for high quality and dependability of product. It is located in a city of approximately 30,000, primarily in an agricultural area, and is the largest industry in the community. The company employs approximately 4,000 hourly workers who are represented by a strong union affiliated with the international union which was certified as representing the production and maintenance employees in 1942.

Relations between the company and the union have been largely stable over the years. Management attributes this to several important factors:

1. Policies and practices over the years, both before and after the advent of the union, have been designed to assure fair and just treatment of its employees.
2. Management has consistently recognized that its responsibility to manage the business included the responsibility of maintaining discipline and of securing a fair day's work for a fair day's pay. It has recognized that these responsibilities must be discharged with due consideration for the rights of its employees and with fairness and equity, but also with consistent firmness.
3. Relations with the union have been established and maintained on a businesslike basis. This has resulted in mutual respect and an understanding of their respective responsibilities by both Management and the Union.
4. The union has been represented by capable officers and committeemen who have accepted their share of responsibility for maintaining stable relations while at the same time effectively and energetically representing their members.
5. Both management and the union have a high respect for their contractual commitments. Neither is given to making or seeking outlandish concessions in agreement administration.

While there have been two major strikes arising out of contract negotiations which have effectively closed the plant, it has never been closed as a result of a strike in violation of contract. There have been four instances, since 1942, where small groups of employees have engaged in minor work stoppages in violation of contract for a part of one shift. Only one of these occurred in recent years. The union was not considered to be in any way responsible. A group of twenty-odd employees was involved; the action appeared to be spontaneous; no leadership was identified. All employees were given the same penalty—a disciplinary layoff of five working days, only two days of this penalty to be applied ". . . unless within a period of six months from the date of this decision the employee is guilty of a violation of any shop rule or commits any act which is properly subject to discipline, in which event there shall be added to the suspended portion of this penalty the appropriate penalty for the additional violation, and the total resulting penalty shall then apply."

The agreements between the company and the union contain certain provisions pertinent to the situations hereafter presented:

1. There is express recognition of management's right and responsibility to "maintain discipline and efficiency of employees."

2. A grievance procedure is established for the settlement of all disputes arising under the contract, including those arising out of management's exercise of its responsibility to maintain discipline and efficiency. In brief, this is a five-step procedure:

    A. Grievances are first handled by the foreman. An employee may take up a problem with his foreman, with or without his committmen, but if he asks for the committeeman it is the foreman's obligation to call the committeeman before any further discussion of the matter at issue.
    B. If the matter is not settled at the First Step, it is reduced to writing on standard grievance forms, the foreman's answer is shown and may then be appealed by the union to higher supervision, where it is discussed by one or two members of the committee with a designated member of higher supervision, usually a superintendent. The answer given at this step is also recorded on the grievance form.
    C. Failing of settlement at the Second Step, the grievance may be appealed by the union to the Third Step, which is the regular weekly meeting of the shop committee with management. The procedure at this step is more formal, the union presenting a Statement of Grievance in writing which, after discussion, is answered by management in writing.
    D. Failing of settlement at the Third Step, the grievance may be appealed to a review committee, consisting of a member of upper management which has not previously handled the case with the union, usually the director of industrial relations, the personnel manager who has previously handled the case, an international representative of the

union who has not previously handled the case for the union and the chairman of the shop committee who has previously handled the case. Other members of management and of the union organization may also be involved at this step, but essentially this is a four-man Review Committee. Grievances appealed to this step are in the form of written briefs exchanged by the parties setting forth the case and their respective arguments in considerable detail. Generally any evidence or argument not advanced at this step may not later be introduced.

E. If the case fails of settlement at the Fourth Step, it may then be appealed in writing to an arbitrator whose decision is final and binding upon both parties. Briefs are presented by each party to the arbitrator and the case is also verbally argued before him, but argument must be confined substantially to the issues set forth and evidence submitted in the briefs.

3. The Agreement between the company and the union contains a No Strike–No Lockout clause with respect to any issues which the Agreement provides may be taken to arbitration. In the event of such a lockout, the union has the option of cancelling the Agreement, and in the event of illegal work stoppage the company has the same right. Further, and directly pertinent to this case, the right to take disciplinary action in the event of an illegal work stoppage is explicitly reserved by the company.

There is also a practice of long standing, although not explicitly covered by Agreement language, that after a case is appealed to arbitration, representatives of the international union and of the company, who in fact have not previously had anything to do with the case, will review it for their respective sides to determine whether the case may appropriately be submitted to arbitration. At this level, both parties have been pretty consistent in reviewing each appealed case on its merits and if either side finds that its position is untenable under the Agreement it initiates either a compromise settlement or withdrawal. Where the case is withdrawn by either side without compromise settlement, it is usually without prejudice to the withdrawing party's position in any future case, but otherwise it constitutes acceptance of the position taken by the other party with respect to the case at issue.

CASE

On Saturday, March 7, 1960, Superintendent Rossall Armstrong, sitting in an office in a comparatively remote area of the plant, observed an employee, Hiram Joshua, roaming apparently aimlessly in the adjacent plant area which was not then being used for other than storage. Under the circumstances, Armstrong suspected that the man was loitering.

Armstrong, who was dressed in sports clothing, without identifying himself approached Joshua. The following is an account of the conversation that ensued as reported by Armstrong:

A. What the hell are you doing out here, and why aren't you working?
J. None of your ——— ——— business!
A. What do you mean it is none of my business? Who is your foreman?
J. Foreman Botsford.
A. Let's go! You come with me and we'll see about this.

Then they proceeded to contact the foreman, James Botsford. After discussion between Armstrong, Botsford, and Joshua, during which Joshua denied having used profane language in replying to Armstrong and further contended that he did not recognize Armstrong as a supervisor, Joshua was given a disciplinary layoff for the balance of the shift and one additional shift for insubordination.

Joshua's request to see his union representative, Committeeman Rambon, was granted and the two men went to a nearby office to discuss the case. Subsequently a grievance was filed protesting management's action.

Within a few minutes, and while Rambon was in discussion with Joshua, one of Joshua's fellow workers, together with nine other employees, approached Foreman Botsford and demanded to know what management intended to do about Joshua. During the ensuing discussion, employee Hammond stated, "If Joshua is disciplined by a layoff, we're all going to walk out," thereby threatening a violation of the No Strike provisions of the Agreement between the parties.

Botsford told the employees that if they "walked out" they would be committing a very grave offense and would be disciplined accordingly. He told the employees to immediately return to work and take up any complaints which they wished to make through the established Grievance Procedure. In response to the request of one of the employees, Botsford stated that he would make the committeeman available on his return to the department, as he was then talking with Joshua.

Shortly afterward, Committeeman Rambon became available and, together with Shop Committeeman Dushane, requested and was granted permission to talk to the group of employees who had approached Botsford at his desk. During the discussion that followed, both men pointed out to the group that their threatened action would be in violation of the Agreement, and advised them to permit Joshua's case to be handled through the established Grievance Procedure.

During the discussion between the group and their union representative, Hammond was observed to leave the group. Hammond approached Foreman Botsford and requested permission to leave the plant on the grounds that he was ill. Botsford told Hammond that if he were sick he should report to the Medical Department. Botsford, disbelieving Hammond's story, called the Medical Department advising them of the situation and requesting that they not issue a Medical Pass unless they were satisfied that Hammond was in fact ill.

When Hammond arrived at the Medical Department, the nurse could find no evidence of illness, but accepting his statement that he was suffering from a severe headache, offered medication. She suggested that he lie down and wait in the Medical Department until she could call the doctor in to examine him. Hammond refused by stating, "I'll see my own doctor" and then left the Medical Department apparently in ill humor and proceeded to leave the plant.

When Hammond signed out "sick" at the Plant Police Station, the patrolman on duty asked for his Medical Pass. Hammond said that he did not have one and repeated that he would see his own doctor. In view of Hammond's contention that he was ill and his having twice stated that he would see his own doctor, he was called at home by Botsford who told him that it would be necessary for him to clear through the Medical Department before returning to work, that he would have to submit medical evidence that he was able to return, and that the question of his behavior that morning would be held open pending an opportunity to discuss the matter with him upon his return to work.

Hammond cleared through the Medical Department on the following Monday morning, stating he did not see his own physician because he felt much better shortly after he got home.

During the discussion with respect to Hammond's behavior the previous Saturday, Hammond stated that he did not remember saying, "If Joshua is disciplined by a layoff, we're all going to walk out." However, he did state that he had been designated as spokesman for the group that had approached Botsford demanding to know what management was going to do about Joshua. In answer to the question as to whether he was a self-appointed spokesman, he stated that "the fellows asked me to be spokesman."

Hammond was given a disciplinary layoff for the balance of his shift and two full shifts for acting as spokesman or leader in threatening the violation of the Agreement, and an additional layoff for one full shift for leaving the plant the previous Saturday without permission in violation of a plant rule which states that no employee is permitted to leave the plant during working hours without permission.

The other members of the group were each issued a written reprimand which stated that there should be no repetition of their misconduct and advised that any violation or threatened violation of the No Strike clause of the Agreement is grounds for serious disciplinary action.

Hammond promptly filed a written grievance protesting the disciplinary layoff and demanded that his "record be cleared" and that he be reimbursed for all wages lost. Each of the other members of the group also filed a grievance protesting the written reprimands and warnings they received and demanded that the memo be removed from their respective personnel records.

In the meantime, the case between Joshua and Superintendent Armstrong was resolved. Joshua, who had a spotless record for eighteen years prior to the subject incident, apologized to Armstrong and the disciplinary penalty was then rescinded.

None of these grievances were settled at either the First or Second Steps of the Grievance Procedure and all were consequently appealed to the Third Step.

At the regular meeting between Management and the Union, held on March 16, 1960, Hammond's grievance and the grievances filed by the other members of the group were taken up as two separate cases, the latter grievances having been combined into one case because of the common issue involved.

The union's verbal arguments in discussing the grievances at this step were consistent with the arguments advanced at Steps One and Two:

1. They argued that there had been no violation of the No Strike clause of the Agreement inasmuch as no unauthorized work stoppage had been charged, that management exceeded its rights in undertaking to discipline any employee or group for the threat of a violation, although it might properly warn those involved that the violation should not occur.

2. They further contended that Hammond and the other employees were understandably concerned with respect to what they felt to be unjustified disciplinary action involving a fellow employee, particularly as he was a working member of their group. They further contended that acting as spokesman for the group in discussing this matter, Hammond was conforming to the established Grievance Procedure which recognized that an employee might file a grievance in his own behalf or, as a designated member of a group, pointing out that the mere fact that a grievance had not been reduced to writing did not alter the basic fact that a grievance was in existence as normally grievances were not reduced to writing until after failure of settlement at the first Step.

3. The union stood by its demand that the disciplinary penalty assessed against Hammond be rescinded with back pay and that the disciplinary employee memos involving Hammond and the other members of the group be stricken from the record.

4. The union further argued that Hammond was in fact sick, that the foreman's call to the Medical Department was not justified, and that it had caused the Medical Department to refuse a pass which otherwise would have been issued. They contended that Hammond leaving the plant under the circumstances was understandable and should be excused.

Management refused to modify the penalty assessed against Hammond for threatening an illegal walkout, and refused to modify the disciplinary employee memos issued to the other employees. It did, however, state that in the interest of settling the grievances, and without prejudice to its position that Hammond had improperly left the plant as this position might apply to any future case, it would withdraw that specific charge and rescind the one-day penalty with back pay.

The union presented a Statement of Grievance confirming its position, and management gave its answer in writing as required at the Third Step of the Grievance Procedure, both under date of March 17, 1960. The Union rejected management's answer and appealed both cases to the Fourth Step of the Grievance Procedure.

The parties exchanged written briefs as required at this Step of the Grievance Procedure and a Fourth Step meeting to consider these cases was held by mutual agreement on March 23, 1960.

QUESTIONS

1. How do you evaluate the situation involving Joshua and Armstrong?

2. What do you think of the medical policies of the company?

3. Why do you think Botsford did not believe that Hammond was sick?

4. How worthwhile are disciplinary layoffs? Warnings?

5. What is your opinion of the solution of the Joshua-Armstrong controversy?

6. Do you think that the review team for management, or that for the union, would alter the respective positions and, if so, to what extent and why? In considering this, remember that the review team for the union has the final decision as to whether the case will be placed before the arbitrator. Management can only withdraw the case from arbitration by effecting a settlement acceptable to the union.

7. Assuming that the case goes before the arbitrator, and also assuming that each party remains consistent in its position and arguments before the arbitrator, what decision do you think the arbitrator would make and why?

8. How do the events in this case fit in with "factors" outlined in the introduction to the "case"?

34

The Maynard Company

In December, 1963, both the Garment Workers Union of America and the Maynard Company were anxiously awaiting the arbitrator's decision in a recent dispute. Although the dispute involved only two workers and was considered to be minor, the arbitrator's decision would probably establish a policy with regard to interpreting a section of the contract between the union and the company. Relations between GWUA and Maynard were considered to be good. Maynard had excellent worker relationships, and payroll deductions for dues showed that about 40 per cent of the workers belonged to the union.

The Maynard Company was an established high quality men's garment manufacturer, serving a national market. Maynard was by far the largest employer in a small town. There were three similar but entirely separate Maynard plants in the town.

Maynard officials felt that their company had an obligation to the town, and Maynard attempted to provide work for high school graduates whenever possible. In June, 1960, Maynard officials decided to build an experimental sewing machine in the maintenance shop of the Kenly plant. They felt that this might prove to be less expensive than to purcase a new machine, since a large supply of serviceable spare parts was on hand. Since this was to be a temporary job, John May, the sewing-room foreman, decided to hire two recent high school graduates on a temporary basis to help an old, experienced millwright in the job. Neither of the two new workers, Melvin Fisk and David Hamer, had ever worked in any industrial company before. In fact, they had only worked in short, part-time jobs until their graduation from high school that June. Dewitt May, considered by the company to be a capable foreman, cautioned Fisk and Hamer that this job would only last about two months, and that they were hired as temporary employees.

The Maynard Company had all jobs in the company classified, with a pay rate established for each classification. When an employee started to work with Maynard, however, he was first paid a beginner's rate, which was less than the established rate for the job. The exact beginner's rate depended on the man's experience, age, and education. After a trial period of three months, the employee had to be either discharged or paid the established rate for his particular classification. He was then considered to be a permanent employee.

When Fisk and Hamer were hired by the Maynard Company, they received a rate of $1.40 per hour. It was then Mr. May's job to classify the two men, since the union contract compelled the company to classify all workers. May decided that the most accurate classification which then existed was a millwright (A). Millwright (A)'s were workers highly skilled in overhauling and repairing the sewing machines used in the manufacture of garments. Normally a worker had to be with the company for two or three years as a maintenance worker before he could become a Millwright (A) trainee. Since Fisk and Hamer were to work only two months, however, May knew that the men would not finish the three-month trial period and become permanent Millwright (A)'s, a job which carried a pay rate of $2.00 per hour.

About one month after Fisk and Hamer started work, May was promoted to another plant. Jack North, who had been working as assistant foreman in another department, then became sewing-room foreman. North was a capable young man, age thirty, who had little trouble assuming the duties of sewing-room foreman. As foreman, North had about 65 employees in his department. Although he delegated authority to his assistant foremen well, he was kept especially busy learning his duties as foreman. Consequently, North did not have time to analyze in detail his employee records and classifications.

Meanwhile, the project on which Fisk and Hamer were working was completed and was judged to be a highly successful experiment. The plant manager, upon recommendation of North, decided to build all new sewing machines in the local shop. Fisk and Hamer gladly accepted the Maynard Company's offer of continued work. Therefore, Fisk and Hamer continued working at the same job and rate of $1.40 per hour for approximately three years, until 1963.

The Maynard Company had three separate but similar plants. Although there was a central personnel department, each plant was responsible for maintaining its own personnel department. The central personnel officer interviewed, screened, and recommended potential employees to each of the three plants. Once the plant accepted the employee, it was responsible for maintaining the personnel records of the employee. Eugene Jones was the personnel director at the Kenly plant, where Fisk and Hamer were employed.

On February 20, 1963, Jones discovered that Fisk and Hamer were classified at Millwright (A), which had a pay rate of $2.00 per hour, and yet both men were receiving only $1.40 per hour. Jones immediately contacted North. As North then knew his department well, he understood what had taken place when Fisk and Hamer were initially hired. North stated that Fisk and Hamer were definitely not qualified to receive the pay of a Millwright (A), and that the $1.40 which they were earning was fair. He further stated that if they had to be paid any more, the rebuilding of the sewing machines would be unprofitable; consequently, Fisk and Hamer would be laid off. After discussing the situation, Jones and North decided to establish a new classification for the two men. Effective the next day, Fisk and Hamer were classified as Millwright (B), a classification which had not previously existed. The pay rate for a millwright (B) was set at $1.40 per hour. As required by the union contract, notification of the reclassification was forwarded to the union.

Fisk and Hamer had not joined the union. However, when Charles Ashley, the local union representative, received notice of the reclassification of Fisk and Hamer he immediately contacted those men. When he heard their employment history, he pointed out that they were underpaid for their classification for almost three years. Ashley further stated that the union would be interested in obtaining a settlement from the Maynard Company for the men. Fisk and Hamer joined the union and signed an official grievance against the Maynard Company, demanding that they be paid $.60 for every hour they had worked from three months after they joined the firm to the date on which they were classified as Millwright (B).

The grievance was received by the company from the union on April 5, 1963. Rone Ling, from the Maynard Company central personnel office, met with Ashley in an attempt to reach an agreement. The Maynard Company, realizing their mistake, offered to pay Fisk and Hamer $100 each in order to prevent arbitration, since arbitration was time-consuming and costly. However, this offer was refused, and an impartial arbitrator was called in to hand down a decision, which both parties were bound to accept under the union agreement.

The union, in the arbitration sessions, maintained that the men were underpaid from the day on which they became permanent employees (three months after their first day of work) to the day on which they were reclassified to Millwright (B).

The company, on the other hand, argued that Fisk and Hamer were not and never were qualified to be Millwright (A), although they were ecconeously classified as such. However, the company's main argument, and what finally became the central issue in the dispute, arose from the following clause in the company-union contract:

> Any retroactive adjustment made as a result of a grievance arising from changed rates or working conditions will be to the date of the change provided the grievance is filed within sixty (60) days. After sixty (60) days, any retroactive adjustment will be to the date of the grievance.

The company argued that the grievance was filed some three years after erroneous classification, the date Maynard failed to change the men from temporary to permanent employees, and therefore the request for back wages was void. Since the union was always notified of all classifications, the company representative argued, it was not Maynard's fault that the grievance was not filed when it should have been. Further, since the grievance was not filed within sixty days of the change, any retroactive adjustment should be to the date of the grievance. In this case, the men were classified properly from the date of the grievance to the present. In answer to this, the union argued that the erroneous classification had existed until February 20, 1963, and that the grievance was filed on April 5, 1963, and therefore the grievance was filed within sixty days of the erroneous classification. The union claimed that since the grievance was filed within sixty days of the period in which the improper classification existed, that the grievance legally covered the entire three years period.

The company closed its argument by stating that the clause in the contract was obviously intended to impose a statute of limitations in the case of wage-rate disputes, and that the union had agreed to this time limit by signing the contract. The arbitration board, which consisted of an independent arbitrator, a company representative, and a union representative, then retired in order to reach a decision.

QUESTIONS

1. What do you think was the basic reason this arbitration case arose?
2. With regard to job classification,
    a. Who do you think should have the authority to establish classifications in the Maynard Company?
    b. Who should have the authority to assign workers to a classification?
    c. Who should be responsible for reviewing existing classifications?
    d. How often should they be reviewed?
3. How would the company's having made an offer to the union jeopardize its case?
4. What would happen if both the company representative and the union representative disagreed with the arbitrator's decision?
5. How could this case have been prevented from arising?
6. If you had been the arbitrator in this case, what would have been your decision?

35

The Lee Plant of the Delta Corporation

THE DELTA CORPORATION has several plants in the southeast, including a plant in Louisiana. The Delta plant in Lee, Louisiana, makes electrical capacitors for use in television sets, radios and radar, and ignition capacitors for use in automobiles. Delta began operations in Lee in December, 1952, with seven machines and 7 employees. In July, 1953, Delta expanded at Lee by building a million-dollar plant. The Lee plant employs between 1,200 and 1,400 workers, depending on the demand for capacitors. Ninety percent of the workers are women who sit at long tables assembling capacitors. Seventy-five percent of these women are from farms, and most of them have never worked anywhere else in their lives. Beginning wage rates are $1.40 an hour and increase to $1.50 an hour after six months. The work force consists of white people except for Negro maintenance and custodial employees.

James Reed, plant manager of the Delta plant in Lee, was a harassed and worried man. For over a year now he had been fighting the efforts of the International Brotherhood of Electrical Workers to unionize his workers. Twice it had seemed that the company had won, but each time the victory had gone sour. The results of the first election in July, 1962, showed that the company had won by a margin of only nine votes. However, the IBEW filed objections to the election with the regional NLRB office, charging that the voting list (prepared by Delta's personnel manager) was inaccurate and that unqualified persons had been allowed to vote. The union also charged that Delta had refused repeatedly to make the voting list available for checking by the union. Because of these violations the NLRB regional director ruled that the results of the election could not be said to reflect the wishes of the Delta employees. For the next several months the case was "lost" in the Washington office of the NLRB. In the meantime, the union kept up its organization efforts while Delta lawyers worked to have the election ruled legal. Reed's efforts during this time were spent in writing denial after denial that he was using illegal tactics to stall, delay, and confuse the issue. Several months later the Washington office of the NLRB ruled that questionable practices had been used in the election and ordered a new one to be held within three months.

As soon as the NLRB decision was announced, the union organizers stepped up their pace and strove to win public sentiment by using hand-bills, the newspapers and the radio to tell the people of Lee about the "underhanded tactics" Delta had used in the election. As a result of this, public sentiment was turning against the Delta plant, and this troubled Reed greatly.

Not only were the townspeople turning against Delta, but the employees were showing signs of dissatisfaction. Before the election the company had promised a substantial wage increase and additional company benefits. A few weeks after the NLRB ruling the company announced a three-point program of worker benefits which included a wage increase of 3 cents an hour to all employees, an increase in group insurance so as to provide $8 hospitalization instead of $5 a day and an increase in life insurance from $500 to $1,000 per worker, and a two weeks' vacation pay to those eligible for vacation pay upon completion of five years of continuous service.

Reed had felt sure that these increased wages and benefits would satisfy the workers and convince them that they could get what they wanted without a union. However, this was not the case. Some of the workers seemed to feel cheated when the union pointed out that the workers in Delta's union plants had won a raise of 5 cents an hour and a concession of 50 percent of a year's vacation pay for new employees if they had worked as much as 1,000 hours with the company at vacation time; whereas, the Delta workers in Lee got no vacation pay at all until they had worked at least 1,500 hours. At this same time the union pointed out that in Lee, where there was little organized labor, the average weekly earnings were $65.91; whereas, in a more highly unionized city like Atlanta, Georgia, the average weekly earnings were $76.72, or $10.81 above the Lee average. The union's argument that "organization doesn't cost—it pays" was convincing, and, as a result, the supervisors heard more and more talk from employees of having been cheated and "bought off cheap."

With the second election approaching, Reed set to work in a final attempt at convincing the workers not to join the union. He took workers off their jobs department by department, and spoke to them in the cafeteria. He had the vice-president in charge of personnel come down from the central office in Baltimore to talk with the workers. The personnel manager at the Lee plant talked to the workers at their jobs practically every day for two weeks in an effort to convince them that the union would do no more good for them than the company would.

Cole, the personnel manager at the Lee plant, had not worked in collaboration with Reed to fight the union but went about it in his own way. Reed had not expected very much help from Cole since he regarded the personnel manager as a man who interviewed applicants, handled the safety program, resolved arguments among the workers, and handled the arrangements for the Christmas party every year. Reed thought that Cole had neither the education nor the background to handle the labor relations. Cole had obtained a B.S. degree in chemistry in 1929 and had worked as a salesman in the Lee area for over twenty years. When Delta began operations in Lee, December, 1952, Cole was hired as manager over the small shop. When the new plant was built, Cole was retained as personnel manager because "he knew all the people around Lee." Despite the general feeling that the union would win by a landslide in the second election, Cole continued to tell Reed that the union would not win and that he would even bet $50 on it.

The results of the second election were shocking to Reed, the union, and the people of Lee; the union was defeated by the wide margin of 275 to 1021. At first Reed was elated and thought that his troubles were over. Then the blow came. The union had positive proof that Cole had personally told every worker in the plant that if the union were voted in, the union would within a month's time have Negroes working side by side with the white workers. This had apparently persuaded most of the pro-union workers to vote against the union. The union was charging Delta with underhanded, threatening, and undemocratic tactics and was asking for a new election as soon as possible. The people of Lee, much as they favored segregation, were highly critical of Delta's methods of "union busting." They were beginning to make statements to the effect that Delta was run by a group of "unscrupulous Yankees" who would continue to exploit the Delta workers unless the union won the next election.

James Reed knew that things looked bad for his plant. The NLRB would grant another election, and the union would win hands down. Furthermore, it would take a lot of time and effort to restore good relations with the employees and the people of the community.

QUESTIONS

1. What could Reed have done after the first election to prevent trouble later?
2. What questions are raised by Cole's claiming the union would put Negroes to work in the plant?
3. What should Reed do about Cole?
4. How could Reed have used Cole to better advantage during the union campaign?
5. What should Reed do now?
6. How can Reed restore good relations within the community?

36

Thor Steel Company

THE THOR STEEL COMPANY is a medium-sized steel fabricator with a strong local union. The shipping department of the Metal Joist Division had long been a trouble spot in labor relations and had caused the division to fall behind its production schedule during the past six months. Complaints from both customers and salesmen were increasing.

This division, headed by division superintendent, Phil Stanley, produced steel joists for use in building and bridge construction. All work was on a job-order basis though the production process was fairly standardized. The division paid significantly higher wages than its competitors and was able to compete successfully only by offering earlier delivery dates to its customers. Production was seasonal to a degree, with large numbers of men laid off each winter. The layoffs usually lasted for one to three months.

The two main operating departments in Stanley's division were the Shipping Department and the Production Department. The shippers unloaded the steel bars and rods from flatcars, stockpiled them, and delivered stock to the first machines in the production line as it was called for. In the Production Department the stock was sheared, bent, welded into finished joists, and dip-painted. The completed joists were set on a ramp at the end of the production line where the shippers picked them up and loaded them onto waiting trucks and railroad cars.

All movement of materials was done with overhead cranes. Three men formed a crane team, one operator and two hookers. The hooking job required no training other than learning the location in the stockpiles of the various sizes of rods and bars. Although no lost time accidents had occurred recently, there was some danger involved in the hooking job. The plant safety engineers stated that the two most important causes of shipping accidents were carelessness and lack of coordination between the crane operator and his hookers.

The total stock tonnage that the shippers delivered to the production line varied markedly from time to time because of the different sizes produced. All stock was 60 feet long. Thus if the orders called for 15-foot joist as opposed to 45-foot joist, a smaller amount of stock was used while production time was not reduced proportionately. Also, the hourly stock requirements were irregular.

All shippers were paid on an hourly wage basis. Shipping crane operators received the standard wage for the area. The hookers, however, received approximately $20 a day which was considerably greater than the general area wage for unskilled labor and also greater than neighboring companies paid for the same work. The hookers had achieved this high rate through prolonged agitation involving protracted negotiation, several strikes, and wildcat walkouts.

The last walkout had occurred a year ago as a result of the shippers' demands for an incentive system similar to the one used in the production department. They had long desired an incentive system; but the company refused, stating that the work was not suitable for such a system and that the men were already receiving higher wages than the work warranted. Since the walkout was unauthorized, the company issued an ultimatum through the local press and radio stating that any of the shippers who did not report for work the next day would be fired immediately. All of the men returned the next day.

The Production Department was on an incentive system which consisted of a flat hourly wage plus a bonus for production above a given rate. The majority of the machine operators averaged $28-$30 daily and their helpers $23-$25. Most of the helper jobs required little or no skill. The crane operators in the Production Department received a base wage equal to that of the shipping crane operators plus a bonus based on an average for the production line over which they worked. Hookers in the Production Department were paid under a similar system. Management was certain that the production crane teams had to work faster than the shipping teams.

Seven months previously, the Shipping Department foreman, Tony Cuccinello, retired. Cuccinello had come to the United States from Italy as a young man and had been with the company since his arrival in this country. He knew most of his men well since the majority were of Italian descent and lived in the same neighborhood as Tony. With a few exceptions, the men liked Tony and said that he was a "right guy" and "wasn't always on your back." The few that did not like Tony claimed privately that Italians got all the best assignments.

Though he was fond of Tony personally and had once worked under him for a summer, Stanley had not been completely satisfied with Tony's work. He knew that none of the foremen "went by the book" on such matters as coffee breaks, absenteeism, and drinking on the job, but Tony was more lax than most. However, the shipping foreman's job was not a complicated one and Stanley had his hands full with production problems, so he did not bother the old man much.

As a replacement for Cuccinello, Stanley had recommended Raymond Jabonski. The recommendation had, as usual, been approved by the plant superintendent who held the final authority on all promotions above the assistant foreman level. Stanley thought that Jabonski would be good for the Shipping Department. He was a big man physically, in his early thirties, loyal to the company, and a driver.

For two weeks prior to Cuccinello's retirement, Jabonski worked as Tony's assistant foreman. There was some disgruntlement among the men apparently because no one from the department had been picked as Tony's replacement. Jabonski, of course, sensed the coolness and noticed that whenever he approached a group of men the group would break up.

The day after Cuccinello had left the plant for good, Jabonski spoke to the men after the weekly safety meeting which was held throughout the plant each Tuesday. He told the men that the Shipping Department had a bad reputation in the plant and that this was going to be changed. Further, he told them that in his last department "the men did a —— of a lot more work and got paid a —— of a sight less." The group took the information silently, but later there was considerable cursing and uncomplimentary references to "that —— Pollack."

Three days later Jabonski found one of the hookers asleep in the stockpile. He sent the man home immediately, which was all his authority permitted. He then reported the incident to Stanley with the recommendation that the man be dismissed. Workers outside the Shipping Department described the man, Gino Angelina, as "no good" and stated that he was one of the more vocal agitators in the past labor troubles of the department.

Stanley called the man into his office the next morning and the following conversation ensued:

"Were you sleeping in the stocks last night, Angelina?"

"Yes sir, but the work was caught up and Tony said our time was our own as long as the work was done."

"Jabonski is your foreman now. Do you know the regulations against sleeping on the job?"

"Yes, but hell, nobody. . . ."

"You're fired Angelina. You can pick your check up at the main office this afternoon. That's all."

The hookers were sullen and resentful over the dismissal. Some stated that management had been "out to get" Angelina. The union representative told them that the union could do nothing about it since the contract specified that sleeping on the job was ample justification for dismissal. Thereafter, the work seemed to slow down gradually. When stock deliveries were late, the production superintendent would call Jabonski and ask him why. Then Jabonski would try to find out why and correct it. No one ever refused one of his orders. There was no open disobedience. When he asked the cranemen why the stock was late, they just shrugged and said that they could only go as fast as the hookers. The hookers said that they were doing the best that they could. At the same time, the hookers began to agitate for an incentive system similar to that used in the production department. This condition had lasted for the past six months and showed no signs of abating. The union emphatically denied any connection with the slowdown and, indeed, would not admit that there was one. Even when asked by a worker from another department, the shippers themselves would deny that they were deliberately slowing down.

Relations between the shippers and the Production Department had gone from bad to worse. The production men had been idled by the shippers' walkouts and strikes previously and friction between the two groups was increasing. When the shippers were slow in getting the necessary stock to the production line, the production men lost money and were not at all reluctant to express their opinions to the shippers. The shippers returned the comments in kind, and there was a good deal of time lost in heated arguments. Since the shippers earned considerably less than the production men, they had little sympathy for the complaints.

The Production Department foreman was Tom Dillon, an aggressive little Irishman in his early forties. Dillon was well liked by his men and by Stanley, too. At first, when his men complained that stock deliveries were lagging, Dillon would call Jabonski on the office phone. Soon, however, it became apparent to Dillon that this procedure was not getting the desired results. To complain to Stanley would have been a slap at a fellow foreman; therefore Dillon began going out into the stocks and thoroughly "chewing-out" the particular crane team responsible for the holdup.

Many times after Dillon had done this, the stock was delivered in a position that made it extremely hard for the production men to get the individual pieces out. When questioned about this, the hookers would say that they were sorry and were just doing the best they could. However, they would not pick the load back up and reset it unless ordered to do so by the foreman.

Another source of friction lay in the ordering of stock by the production men on the first machine. This was supposed to be done far enough in advance of actual need that the shippers would have a reasonable time in which to deliver it. Quite often, however, the men would be producing at a rate which would put their earnings over the $30 maximum which the machine operators had tacitly agreed would be their limit. Rather than slow down their working speed to a point where it would be evident they were loafing, the men would just not order the stock they knew they would need. Then when the present stock ran out, they would order new stock, report a "stock delay," and sit down until the stock was delivered.

When Dillon asked if they ordered the stock ahead of time, they would reply "sure, but you know those —— shippers."

Dillon's private opinion was that the company ought to fire the whole bunch of shippers, but he realized this was impossible. The union contract would not permit wholesale transfer of the shippers to another department unless this transfer was voluntary. Since job assignment was based on departmental seniority, none of the shippers wanted to transfer. Dillon did not blame Jabonski for the situation at all. To Dillon, the shippers were just a bunch of lazy "dagoes"; they were already overpaid and still would not work.

QUESTIONS

1. Why was Jabonski rejected as a leader?
2. Are there any ethnic considerations in the case and if so, what causal importance can be attached to them?
3. Why would a group of workers deliberately hold down their own earnings?
4. Why should the shippers be dissatisfied with their wages?
5. How does group interaction affect this situation?
6. Why would an incentive not help this situation?
7. What actions would you recommend and what would the probable reactions be? Why?